D0670569

1918

OSPREY
PUBLISHING

WINNIPEG PUBLIC LIBRARY

1918

1918

WINNING THE WAR, LOSING THE WAR

EDITED BY
MATTHIAS STROHN

OSPREY PUBLISHING
Bloomsbury Publishing Plc
PO Box 883, Oxford, OX1 9PL, UK
1385 Broadway, 5th Floor, New York, NY 10018, USA
E-mail: info@ospreypublishing.com
www.ospreypublishing.com

OSPREY is a trademark of Osprey Publishing Ltd

First published in Great Britain in 2018

© Osprey Publishing Ltd, 2018

Nicholas Carter, Matthias Strohn, David T. Zabecki, David Murphy, Jonathan Boff, Mitch Yokelson, Lothar Höbelt, Robert Johnson, Michael Epkenhans, James S. Corum and Mungo Melvin have asserted their right under the Copyright, Designs and Patents Act, 1988, to be identified as Authors of this work.

All rights reserved. No part of this publication may be reproduced or transmitted in any form or by any means, electronic or mechanical, including photocopying, recording, or any information storage or retrieval system, without prior permission in writing from the publishers.

A catalogue record for this book is available from the British Library.

ISBN: HB 978 1 4728 2933 7; eBook 978 1 4728 2934 4; ePDF 978 1 4728 2935 1; XML 978 1 4728 2936 8

18 19 20 21 22   10 9 8 7 6 5 4 3 2 1

Maps by Bounford.com
Index by Sandra Shotter
Originated by PDQ Digital Media Solutions, Bungay, UK
Printed and bound in Great Britain by CPI (Group) UK Ltd, Croydon CR0 4YY

Front cover: (top) SE 5s over St Omer, France. (Spencer Arnold/Stringer/Getty);
               (bottom) German troops attack through a burning village. (IWM, Q88075)

Osprey Publishing supports the Woodland Trust, the UK's leading woodland conservation charity. Between 2014 and 2018 our donations are being spent on their Centenary Woods project in the UK.

To find out more about our authors and books visit **www.ospreypublishing.com**. Here you will find extracts, author interviews, details of forthcoming events and the option to sign up for our newsletter.

ACKNOWLEDGEMENTS

I cannot claim to have written or produced this book all by myself. It is the result of work carried out by many people.

First and foremost, I would like to thank the authors for their contributions. Their professionalism and ability to work towards deadlines made my role as editor an easy and enjoyable task. This book provides an overview of the last year of World War I and it does so from different angles. In addition to providing a general narrative, it also encourages the reader to engage with some of the debates that still surround the year 1918. As a consequence, the chapters sometimes differ in the analysis of certain events, actions, and personalities. This did not just happen, it was an intended outcome. All these different views combined have produced this book on the last year of the cataclysmic conflict that we call World War I.

I would like to thank Osprey Publishing and the team that has worked with me on this book, in particular Gemma Gardner and Marcus Cowper. Their professionalism is second to none and, as always, working with the team was a real pleasure. Also, my sincere thanks to the design team Stewart Larking and Beth Cole and the cartographers from Bounford.com.

The idea for the book was born when I was working at the Royal Military Academy Sandhurst and it gained real traction after my secondment to the British Army's think tank, the Centre for Historical Analysis and Conflict Research. One of my main tasks there is to support the British Army's commemoration of World War I, the so-called 'Operation Reflect'. This book is one of the fruits of this task. I would like to thank both the RMAS and the CHACR for creating such research-friendly atmospheres in which academic output is valued more highly than physical presence behind an office desk.

My parents have not had a direct influence on this book, but without all their love and support I would not be where I am today. It is only when one becomes a parent oneself that one is able to realise this fully. The simple truth is also that parents hardly ever receive the recognition they deserve. Vielen Dank für Alles!

Every time I start a new book, I promise my family that this time there will be no more night shifts and long hours in which I disappear into my study. Every time I fail. I cannot thank my family, especially my wife Rocio, enough for supporting me during the writing and editing period. This book – and I – owe you a great deal more than you imagine.

I dedicate this book to Jacob and Wilhelm. Wilhelm's great-great-grandfather fought in World War I and his great-grandfather in World War II. They have all carried the same name. Members of his family fought and died all over Europe in these dark days. Wilhelm's father saw military action in a far-away land. I hope that Jacob and Wilhelm will be allowed to live in peaceful times.

Vor uns liegt ein glücklich Hoffen
liegt der Zukunft goldne Zeit
steht ein ganzer Himmel offen
blüht der Freiheit Seligkeit. (Theodor Körner, 1813)

CONTENTS

CONTRIBUTORS

General Sir Nicholas Carter KCB, CBE, DSO, ADC Gen commissioned into The Royal Green Jackets in 1978. At Regimental Duty he has served in Northern Ireland, Cyprus, Germany, Bosnia, and Kosovo and commanded 2nd Battalion, The Royal Green Jackets, from 1998 to 2000. He attended Army Staff College, the Higher Command and Staff Course and the Royal College of Defence Studies. He was Military Assistant to the Assistant Chief of the General Staff, Colonel Army Personnel Strategy, spent a year at HQ Land Command writing the Collective Training Study, and was Director of Army Resources and Plans. He also served as Director of Plans within the US-led Combined Joint Task Force 180 in Afghanistan and spent three months in the Cross Government Iraq Planning Unit prior to the invasion of Iraq in 2003. General Carter commanded 20th Armoured Brigade in Iraq in 2004 and 6th Division in Afghanistan in 2009/10. He was then the Director General Land Warfare before becoming the Army 2020 Team Leader. He served as DCOM ISAF from October 2012 to August 2013, became Commander Land Forces in November 2013, and was appointed Chief of the General Staff in September 2014.

Dr Matthias Strohn FRHistS was educated at the universities of Münster (Germany) and Oxford. He has lectured at Oxford University and the German Staff College (Führungsakademie der Bundeswehr). From 2006 until 2016 he worked as a Senior Lecturer in the Department of War Studies at the Royal Military Academy Sandhurst. He is currently on secondment to the British Army's think tank, the Centre for Historical Analysis and Conflict Research in Camberley. In addition, he is a Reader at the Humanities Research Centre at the University of Buckingham where he works in the areas of Military History and War Studies. He holds a commission in the German Army and is a member of the military attaché reserve, having served on the defence attaché staffs in London, Paris, and Madrid. He has published widely on 20th-century German and European military history and is an expert on the German Army in World War I and the inter-war period. He has advised British and German government bodies on the World War I centenary commemorations.

Major General (Ret'd) Dr David T. Zabecki retired from the US Army in 2007. He started his military career as an infantry rifleman in Vietnam in 1967 and 1968. In 2003, he was attached to the US State Department as the Senior Security Advisor on the US Coordinating and Monitoring Mission (Roadmap to Peace in the Middle East), where he negotiated between the Israeli Defense Force and the multiple Palestinian security organizations.In 2004, he was the commander of US forces supporting the 60th anniversary commemorations of the D-Day Landings, Operation *Market-Garden*, and the Battle of the Bulge. In 2005–06 he was the senior US Army commander in Europe south of the Alps, based in Vicenza, Italy. He holds a PhD in Military History from the Royal Military College of Science, Cranfield University, where his supervisor was the late Professor Richard Holmes. In 2012 he served as the Dr Leo A. Shifirn Distinguished Professor of Military History at the US Naval Academy, Annapolis. He is an Honorary Senior Research Fellow in the War Studies Programme at the University of Birmingham (UK). He is the author or editor of numerous military history books. In 2016 his encyclopaedia, *Germany at War: 400 Years of Military History*, won a Society for Military History Distinguished Book Award.

Dr David Murphy is a lecturer at the Department of History, Maynooth University, Ireland. Since 2006 he has taught defence studies programmes at the Irish Military College and he has also given guest lectures at various international military colleges, including the Royal

Netherlands Military Academy in Breda and the US Army Command and General Staff College at Fort Leavenworth. He is a member of the Royal United Services Institute and is an external examiner for the Department of Defence Studies, King's College, London. His research currently focuses on WW1 and his publications include *Breaking Point of the French Army: the Nivelle Offensive of 1917* (Pen & Sword, 2015), *Lawrence of Arabia* (Osprey, 2011) and *The Arab Revolt, 1916–18* (Osprey, 2008), among others.

Dr Jonathan Boff FRHistS is a Senior Lecturer in the Department of History at the University of Birmingham, where he teaches courses relating to war from Homer to Helmand. He specializes in particular in World War I. His publications include *Winning and Losing on the Western Front: The British Third Army and the Defeat of Germany in 1918* (Cambridge University Press, 2012) and *Haig's Enemy: Crown Prince Rupprecht and Germany's War on the Western Front* (Oxford University Press, 2018). He has undertaken consultancy projects for the British Army and the BBC and serves on the Councils of the National Army Museum and the Army Records Society.

Professor Mitch Yockelson is a Professor of military history at Norwich University and the author of four books: *Forty-Seven Days: How Pershing's Warriors Came of Age to Defeat the German Army in World War I*; *Borrowed Soldiers: Americans under British Command, 1918,* named one of the best military history books by *The Independent* (UK); *MacArthur: America's General*; and *Grant: Savior of the Union.* He directs the National Archives and Records Administration-Archival Recovery Program where he leads investigations of thefts of historical documents and museum artefacts. His work has been featured in the *New York Times, Washington Post,* and *Los Angeles Times,* and he has appeared on 60 Minutes, Fox News, PBS, and the History Channel. The chief historical adviser to the US World War One Centennial Commission, Mitch regularly leads tours of World War I battlefields for the *New York Times* Journeys and frequently lectures on military history. He lives in Annapolis, Maryland.

Professor Lothar Höbelt was born in Vienna 1956 and graduated with honours from the University of Vienna in 1982. He was Assistant Visiting Professor at the University of Chicago in 1992, and has been Associate Professor of Modern History at the University of Vienna since 1997, and Lecturer at the Military Academy Wiener Neustadt since 2001. The main focus of his research is the history of Austria(-Hungary) in the 19th and 20th centuries. His publications include *Franz Joseph I: Der Kaiser und sein Reich: Eine politische Geschichte* (2009), and *Die Habsburger: Aufstieg und Glanz einer europäischen Dynastie* (2009). His latest work is '*Stehen oder Fallen?' Österreichische Politik im Ersten Weltkrieg* (2015).

Dr Rob Johnson is the Director of the Changing Character of War (CCW) Research Centre at Oxford University and a Senior Research Fellow of Pembroke College. His primary research interests are in the history of strategy and war, and their contemporary applications. A former British army officer, he is the author of *The Great War and the Middle East* (Oxford University Press, 2016) as well as several other works on conflicts in the Middle East, Asia, and Europe. He is also the author of *True to Their Salt* (2017), a history of partnering local forces, and its part in indirect strategies used by Western powers.

Professor Dr Michael Epkenhans is the Director of Historical Research at the Centre for Military History and Social Sciences of the German Armed Forces (ZMSBw) at Potsdam. He is an expert in German and European History of the 19th and 20th centuries with a special emphasis on military history. His main field of research is German military history before, during and after the First World War. In addition to his role at the ZMSBw he is Professor at Potsdam University and editor of Germany's leading journal on military history, the *Militärgeschichtliche Zeitschrift*. Professor Epkenhans holds a commission in the German Navy with the rank of Commander (Naval Reserve).

Dr James Corum teaches military history at Salford University UK, having been Dean of the Baltic Defence College 2009–2014. From 1991 to 2004 he was a professor at the US Air Force School of Advanced Air and Space Studies at Maxwell Air Force Base, Alabama. In 2005 he was a Visiting Fellow at All Souls College, Oxford, where he held a Leverhulme Fellowship, and then an Associate Professor at the US Army Command and General Staff College, Fort Leavenworth, Kansas. Dr Corum is the author of several books on military history, including *The Roots of Blitzkrieg: Hans von Seeckt and German Military Reform* (1992); *The Luftwaffe: Creating the Operational Air War, 1918–1940* (1997); *The Luftwaffe's Way of War: German Air Doctrine, 1911–1945*, with Richard Muller (1998); *Airpower in Small Wars: Fighting Insurgents and Terrorists*, with Wray Johnson (2003); and *Fighting the War on Terror: A Counterinsurgency Strategy* (2007). His eighth book on Cold War history is *Rearming Germany* (2011). He is the editor-in-chief of the translation (from German) of the *Encyclopedia of the First World War* (two volumes) (2012). He has also authored more than 60 major book chapters and journal articles on a variety of subjects related to air power and military history. Dr Corum served in Iraq in 2004 as a lieutenant colonel in the US Army Reserve. He holds a master's degree from Brown University, a Master of Letters from Oxford University, and a PhD from Queen's University, Canada.

Major General (Ret'd) Mungo Melvin CB OBE is the author of *Manstein: Hitler's Greatest General*, first published to critical acclaim in 2010. In 2011 it was runner-up in the prestigious Westminster Prize; in 2012, it won a distinguished book award as best biography of the year from the US Society for Military History. Now retired from the British Army, General Melvin was commissioned into the Royal Engineers in 1975, and saw operational service in Northern Ireland, the Middle East, and the Balkans. During the latter part of his 37-year career as a member of the General Staff he specialized in strategic analysis, professional military education, and doctrine. A former President of the British Commission for Military History, he is currently advising the British Army on the World War I centenary commemorations, and has edited the Army's battlefield guide to the Western Front (2014). He is author of *Sevastopol's Wars: Crimea from Potemkin to Putin* (2017), also published by Osprey. He is a Senior Associate Fellow of the Royal

United Services Institute and a Senior Visiting Research Fellow of the Department of War Studies of King's College London. He is a Fellow of the Institution of Royal Engineers, Chairman of the Royal Engineers Historical Society, and Vice President of the Western Front Association. He lectures widely on strategy and military history in both the public and commercial sectors.

FOREWORD

General Sir Nicholas Carter KCB, CBE, DSO, ADC Gen
Chief of the General Staff

Even after a century, World War I still exerts a strong hold on the consciousness of many nations. For all engaged, it was a transformational experience and its legacy on states, institutions, communities, and individuals was profound. While it was predominantly destructive, it was also constructive, forging new national identities and the establishment of a global 'league of nations' intended to prevent future conflict. This legacy and the scale of human loss help to explain the war's enduring place in popular sentiment and why, in the UK, the centenaries of Jutland, the Somme, and Third Ypres have provoked renewed public interest. Understandably, this has focused largely on human experiences; but for politicians, academics and the military there is much to be gained by understanding how wars start, are fought, and, looking to 1918 as this volume does, how they are brought to an end. For, as each chapter reveals, World War I did not peter out through mutual exhaustion, but continued to the Armistice with growing intensity and extended range: across the Western Front, Russia, Italy, Greece, the Middle East, and Africa; as well as on land, at sea, and in the air.

In recognition of the war's importance across so many fields of human endeavour, since 2014 the British Army has run an extended programme of reflective study, as part of a national commitment to mark its centenary.

Appropriately, our work has been known as 'Operation Reflect', with two of its aims being to honour all those who served and to remember all those who suffered and died. However, this reflection has also had a strong instructive element, with its other two aims being to educate modern soldiers about the actions and achievements of their forebears and, perhaps most importantly, to learn lessons that may help to guide our development for an uncertain future.

The importance that I attach to learning from the past is worth expanding upon. It is not in many fields that actions a century old can retain the ability to inform and instruct a modern professional cohort, but in the military sphere I am clear they do. For a start, mercifully, wars are not frequent events, so armies must prepare for them, in part, by studying how conflict is and has been conducted. Such study reveals, as Carl von Clausewitz observed, that war has a 'nature' (violent, contested, and determined by human will) that is constant, and a character (the ways and means of its conduct) that continuously changes. Therefore, in training for war, the military must understand, and be ready to deal with, both constant and changing elements. It is to help modern soldiers meet these intellectual challenges that I established the Army's Centre for Historical Analysis and Conflict Research (CHACR), under whose auspices this volume has been published. Its role is to conduct and sponsor research into the nature and character of conflict, and act as a hub for military scholarship, to sustain and develop the conceptual (i.e. the thinking) component of fighting power (the others being physical and moral). Hence, it has been instrumental in shaping and supporting Operation Reflect and in encouraging modern soldiers to study the history of the war and their profession in general. The CHACR is just part of a raft of initiatives that have been implemented to re-emphasize the conceptual component of fighting power within the British Army.

I find World War I a particularly rich source of instruction as it came at a time when the British Army was neither designed for, nor recently experienced in, a major conflict against a peer competitor and when technology was driving a rapid evolution in the character of conflict. Thus it had to adapt rapidly to a war for which it was unprepared, most notably by creating a mass citizen army that endured a brutal induction to the character of modern warfare. While its failings and losses cannot be ignored, the British Army was by 1918 a victorious force that combined mass with professional sophistication. This argues that its ability to adapt and innovate, while fighting every step for over four years, was genuine and greater than has sometimes been acknowledged.

I think this resonates with today's challenges. As in 1914, the British Army exists within an uncertain strategic environment in which the threat of miscalculation could lead to direct conflict – a conflict we would not choose, but in which we might be compelled to fight. And this could well be further afield than Europe. This conundrum of coordinating coherent strategy and precious military resources across multiple theatres echoes that faced by Britain's government throughout the war. Another parallel is the rapid evolution of the means of warfare and the ways in which they are employed. World War I saw industrial capacity and technical innovation transform warfare, a highly interactive and gradual process that all armies struggled to master. In our own time it is pervasive information that is driving a rapid evolution in the character of conflict; a challenge that demands a similar commitment to innovation and adaptation. Hence, understanding how a small army can adjust its structure rapidly, expand, exploit emergent technology, adapt its doctrine and innovate tactically is close to the heart of our modern conceptual challenge. Studying past conflicts will not offer us a ready template for how to fight the 'war we might have to fight', but it will reveal many enduring truths about how armies prevail amidst the violent, contested, and frictional nature of war.

In pursuit of such insights, Operation Reflect has addressed its core themes through a series of major 'staff rides'[1] to the battlefields of the Western Front. These have been significant endeavours, each engaging over 100 participants, including representatives from many of the combatant nations: Britain, France, Germany, Canada, Australia, New Zealand, Ireland, South Africa, and, in 2018, the United States. The first of these, in 2014, took an overview of the war on the Western Front, while the second, in 2016, focused on the battle of the Somme in 1916 that so marked the British Empire's experience of the war. The third and final Army Staff Ride in 2018 will focus on the decisive events on the Western Front in 1918, which brought the war against Germany to an end.

In preparation for the 2016 staff ride, Dr Matthias Strohn assembled a selection of thematic essays by leading historians, providing a companion volume for those participating, which set the strategic and military contexts for the Somme in 1916. This new volume has been born of similar intent to provide a strategic context for those participating in the Army Staff Ride in 2018. This staff ride is the most ambitious yet, reflecting the full span, scale, and significance of the ultimately decisive events on the Western Front in 1918. Most importantly, it is being conducted in partnership with our French, German, and American allies, whose chiefs share my emphasis on learning from our shared past. Accordingly, the staff ride programme has been constructed around the central theme of 'four armies in four days': focusing by turn on the German spring offensives; the French counter-attack in the Second Battle of the Marne; the British Expeditionary Force's counter-offensives from Amiens to the breaking of the Hindenburg Line; and the American Expeditionary Force's offensive through the Meuse–Argonne region to the Meuse River.

This volume does much more than reflect the primacy of these four armies and the Western Front as the decisive theatre of operations. It captures vividly the global span and the strategic complexity of nations that had committed the full capacity of their dispersed imperial possessions to winning a war that anticipated what the generation which followed called a 'total war'. In so doing, its component chapters serve to illustrate the unifying themes that I have assigned to the Army Staff Ride in 2018.

The first of these is the importance of 'coalition warfare', then and now. In 1918 both sides were extensive coalitions and a great virtue of this book is that it offers such a range of perspectives from many of these combatant nations.[2] Each coalition experienced the many benefits of partnership, but also the inherent frictions of fighting without unified direction, and there is good reason to conclude that ultimate victory went to the coalition that best cohered its collective strength to strategic effect. As we have learned latterly in Iraq and Afghanistan, coalitions are no easier to manage today and there is much to learn from the way in which in 1918 France, Britain, and Italy managed the loss of one partner in

Russia, absorbed the arrival of another in the United States and, belatedly, achieved a more unified military command structure. By contrast, it is arguable that the Germans failed to exploit the full potential of their own coalition with Austria-Hungary, Bulgaria, and the Ottoman Empire to achieve strategic success.

The second theme is the 'restoration of manoeuvre' to achieve operationally decisive effect. In 1918 this was about breaking the physical stasis imposed by the advantages technology had bestowed upon the defending side in trench warfare. Both sides sought to achieve this by combining material might, technological innovation, and tactical adaptation. The last of these was focused on achieving closer coordination between the expanding capabilities of land and air forces to deliver an integrated 'all-Arms battle'. The Germans led the way with a series of great offensives in the spring of 1918, but for all their tactical gains, operational success and ultimately strategic victory eluded them. As these offensives culminated in early summer, the Allies wrested back the initiative, their newly unified command structure coordinating their attacks to roll the Germans back, first to their start lines of March, and ultimately further east, liberating much of occupied Belgium and northern France. Today we are embracing our own conceptual transformation as we appreciate that the ability to manoeuvre to gain advantage over an opponent lies not only in the physical, but also in the information domain. This has led the British Army to espouse a new unifying doctrine, that of Integrated Action. This places emphasis on analysing all audiences – friendly, enemy, and neutral – before applying actions across all domains to achieve the appropriate effects upon each audience.

The third theme is 'adaptation and innovation', which focuses on the abilities of the respective armies to learn and implement change (whether their structure, equipment, tactics, training, or leadership) in order to achieve success. The German, French, and British armies of 1918 had transformed out of all recognition from those that had first engaged in 1914. This was a product of constant striving for competitive advantage, with innovation, adaptation, and experimentation (across the technical and tactical domains) central to what we might see now as an institutional learning culture. Peacetime armies have an often-deserved reputation for conservatism, which contrasts starkly with the imperative to be aggressively radical in war. In an era of constant competition we cannot wait to adapt or innovate until war is upon us; we must ensure that we are changing constantly so we can maintain a competitive edge that will deter adversaries from attacking our interests or allies. We can only do this by emulating the armies of 1918 in embracing a learning culture, with the instinct and energy to question orthodoxy, experiment relentlessly, and learn by the experience.

The fourth theme combines the enduring military issues of 'command, leadership, and morale'. On the one hand, this highlights the technical challenges of communicating command direction to thousands of men across a dispersed and devastated battlefield, which reflects the modern challenge of assuring our ability to exploit the medium of a contested electro-magnetic spectrum. On the other, it focuses on the human experience of war: the leaders and the led. To modern minds the ability of citizen soldiers to function amidst the horrors of industrial warfare seems almost super-human, but it is certain that the strains that contemporary war will impose upon the human mind and body will be no less than those of a century ago. Hence, we will remain dependent upon the courage and stoicism that has characterized the British soldier down the ages, while ensuring that he or she is consistently provided with exemplary, inspiring, and enlightened leadership.[3]

The final unifying theme is 'conflict resolution', or, in simpler terms, how wars end. Today we see terms like 'defeat' and 'victory' as being harder to define given that success is often more about the triumph of a narrative as opposed to the facts on the ground. The experience of 1918 illustrates this conundrum neatly. While the Armistice of 11 November 1918 brought welcome relief to the exhausted armies, it was also met with dismay on both sides. For a German Army that considered itself to be unbeaten, it was not a defeat but a betrayal, a conviction that played its part in the rise of Nazism and the renewal of conflict in 1939. Meanwhile, some on the Allied side, noting that their opponents did not yet accept that they were beaten, felt that the war would not be won until the Germans had been driven back into their homeland and forced to accept defeat. While militarily this was both feasible and pragmatic, fighting on was a political impossibility for all nations.[4] As Clausewitz reminds us, the origins of all wars lie in politics and it is to politics they must return at their end.

Over the past four years, I have found it both intellectually and professionally rewarding to renew and revise my understanding of World War I. While it is ever-more remote in time and there has been a complete transformation in the political, social, technological, and military aspects of warfare, it remains highly instructive to study how our forebears addressed the many challenges with which the war confronted them. Thankfully, a generation of dedicated scholarship has freed us from a tendency to dismiss the war as pointless and wasteful, and therefore not deserving of study. This work has led us to a deeper and more nuanced understanding of this war and how it was fought, without diminishing in any way the honour and respectful remembrance that we bear towards its combatants. I believe this volume adds further to that scholarly work, perhaps most significantly in assembling a comprehensive set of international perspectives. Too often we seek to understand wars from a single perspective, which fails to reflect the essentially contested nature of warfare.

I commend this book to military and civilian audiences alike, as a penetrating and thought-provoking exploration of the final phase of, what was then dearly hoped to be, the 'war to end all wars'. That this proved a vain hope, is, perhaps, the most salutary lesson of all.

CHAPTER 1

INTRODUCTION

1918: the final year of World War I and its
long shadow in history

Dr Matthias Strohn

On 28 June 1919, a German delegation signed the Treaty of Versailles with
the Allies.[1] The treaty was signed in the Hall of Mirrors in the Versailles
Palace on the outskirts of Paris, the same place in which in 1871 the united
German Reich had been founded. Hostilities had ceased on 11 November
1918, when Germany had surrendered to the Allies, the last state of the
Central Powers to do so. And yet, only a few months earlier, it had seemed
as if the Central Powers were winning the war; on 23 March 1918, two
days after the beginning of Operation *Michael* in the West, the German
Emperor, Kaiser Wilhelm the Second, made the joyful statement that 'The
battle is won, the English have been utterly defeated'.[2] How did the
pendulum of victory swing so quickly from one coalition to the other and
leave the Central Powers, seemingly expecting to end the war victorious,
with the bitter aftertaste of defeat?

In order to understand the events of 1918, it is necessary to begin the
story in the previous year. Seemingly, 1917 had been a successful year for

the Central Powers and a less successful one for the Entente and its associated powers. On the Western Front, the offensives conducted by the Allies did not break the German lines. The main British offensive in Flanders resulted in a bloody stalemate and so did the French offensives against the German positions, in particular at the Chemin des Dames. There was one exception to this general trend. In November 1917, the British had broken through the German lines at Cambrai, not least because of the use of tanks. As a result, church bells in Britain rang for the first time since the start of the war. However, the British did not exploit their success, and German reserves were moved quickly to the front, where they launched a counter-attack. In the end, this battle ended as yet another draw.

In the Italian theatre of war, eleven battles had been fought on the Isonzo front between Austria-Hungary and Italy between 1915 and the summer of 1917. Although these battles had resulted in huge casualties on both sides, the front had hardly moved. This only changed with the twelfth battle, which lasted from 24 October to 7 November 1917. The Austro-Hungarians, reinforced and spearheaded by German troops, managed to break through the Italian front and routed the Italian forces in front of them. The front collapsed and the Italian Army withdrew to the Piave River, having lost over 3,000 artillery pieces and 334,000 men. Over 290,000 of these were soldiers captured by the Central Powers; a clear indication of the collapse of the moral component of the Italian Army's fighting power.[3]

In the Balkans, the front had also held. In June 1917, Greece entered the war on the side of the Entente, but the army's poor training and lack of equipment meant that the declaration of war did not result in an immediate increase of fighting power on the Entente side. By the summer of 1917, the Allies had 24 divisions on the Macedonian front. The so-called Allied Army of the Orient contained French, Serbian, British, Italian, Greek and Russian troops in what the Central Powers called 'Our biggest prisoner of war camp'; the French Premier Georges Clemenceau called them the 'gardeners of Salonika' due to their inactivity. [4]

In the greater scheme of these developments, certain set-backs for the Central Powers in the Near East did not seem overly worrying.

The Ottomans (with their German advisers and small troop contingents) had been pushed back by the Allied forces, and on 11 December 1917 General Allenby entered Jerusalem, effectively ending Muslim control over the holy city for the first time since the end of the Crusades.[5]

The developments described so far would have been enough to make 1917 a successful year for the Central Powers, but one front has not been mentioned yet. On the Eastern Front the Central Powers achieved their biggest victory of the year, indeed of the entire war. In March 1917 the so-called February Revolution (in accordance with the Julian calendar that was being used in Russia at the time) resulted in the Tsar's abdication and it was clear that Russia would not be able to continue the war for a long period, even though the new Russian Provisional Government tried to do exactly that. At the very latest the failed Kerensky-offensive[6] of July 1917 showed that Russia was no longer a reliable partner in the alliance against the Central Powers.

When the Bolsheviks seized power in the October Revolution – supported by the German government which had it made possible for Lenin to return to Russia from his exile in Switzerland – the situation changed rapidly. One of the most popular slogans of the Bolsheviks had been 'Peace, Land and Bread', and the new government acted quickly. On 8 November 1917 the 'Second Congress of the Soviets of Workers', Soldiers' and Peasants' Deputies' signed the Decree of Peace, which called upon all the belligerent nations and their governments to start immediate negotiations for peace and proposed the withdrawal of Russia from the war. On 15 December 1917, Soviet Russia signed an armistice with the Central Powers, and on 22 December peace negotiations began in Brest-Litovsk. The Russian delegation, in particular Leon Trotsky, tried to prolong the negotiations and, as a consequence, the Central Powers resumed their offensives. This action had the desired effect and on 3 March 1918, the Bolshevik government signed the Treaty of Brest-Litovsk. The Central Powers had won the war in the East and were the masters of central and Eastern Europe. This eliminated one major theatre of war and opened new strategic and operational opportunities. Yet the political situation in the East still demanded a troop's presence, in particular in the Ukraine, which was seen as the bread-basket of Europe and whose puppet-regime had agreed to send food and horses to the undernourished people of Germany and Austria-Hungary, who were suffering because of the British naval blockade.[7]

With the benefit of hindsight it is easy to say that the impressive victory in the East was levelled by the United States' entry into the war on 6 April 1917. Helmuth von Moltke the Elder, the chief of the Prussian and Great General Staff between 1857 and 1888, had allegedly described the US Civil War as 'two armed-mobs running around the countryside and beating each other up, from which very little of military utility could be learned'. This view of an unprofessional, ill-equipped US Army might have persisted in 1917, but the entry of the US into the war arguably changed the outcome of World War I and thus shaped the history of Europe and the world. The question of whether the US involvement was crucial or not for the outcome of the war is one that has been debated passionately ever since – and to a degree this is also visible in some of the chapters in this book. This is not the right place to enter into this debate; it suffices to say that the arrival of the US doughboys gave a huge moral boost to the Allies, while the Germans realized that their ever-dwindling resources would now have to be used not only against equally exhausted British and French troops, but also against the fresh (albeit inexperienced) Americans. Also, the US Army saw its fair share of fighting: during the war, the USA lost nearly 53,500 men. This figure is dwarfed by the losses of the other major belligerents, for example 1.3 million French soldiers and approximately 900,000 from Britain and the Empire. Over the entire war, France and Britain lost an average of 900 and 457 men a day, respectively. The overall American average for its participation stood at 195 deaths a day, but this includes the first year of US participation in the war, when the army was being built-up and trained. Once American troops started fighting in earnest, their losses mirrored those of their Allied counterparts. In the summer and autumn of 1918, deaths stood at an average of 820 a day, not far off the French figure and almost twice as many as the British.[8] These figures can be interpreted in different ways, and indeed they have been over time. They can be seen as proof of the ferocious fighting that the American encountered, or as their overall lack of preparation for the realities of war in 1918.

Economically, the US was in a different league compared to the other belligerent nations. In 1913 its gross domestic product was more than twice that of Russia or Germany.[9] Its pre-war steel production outclassed all the other nations; it exceeded that of France, Germany and Britain combined.[10] Interestingly, in this war, unlike in World War II, US armament production did not dominate the scene; its heavy weapons and aircraft largely came from French factories, even though the US provided much of the steel that was used in those factories and the petrol needed to fuel them. The most important contributions – in addition to manpower – were of food, raw materials, and finance. While it was at war, the US outspent all the other belligerents: $42.8 million per day from mid-1917 to mid-1919, compared with Britain's $32.6 million, France's $32.4 million, Germany's $32.2 million and Italy's $10.4 million.[11]

With these figures in mind, it seems clear that for the German *Oberste Heeresleitung* (OHL, the Supreme Headquarters of the Field Army) the only option was to bring the war to a successful conclusion in the West, before the US presence would decide the outcome of the war. Remaining on the defensive was not seen as an option, because in the long run the Central Powers would not be able to withstand the combined forces of the enemy.[12] A small window of opportunity presented itself to the Germans: the end of the war in the East made it possible to transport troops to the Western Front. The situation in the East still demanded a military presence there if the natural resources were to be utilized for the Central Powers. Nevertheless, troops were moved from the Eastern Front to the Western Front. Divisions in the East had to release their younger soldiers (men under 35) and had their ranks filled with older replacements from the home front or the Western Front. Also, materiel and horses were moved from the Eastern theatre of war to the West. In total, the Germans moved 33 divisions to the Western Front from other fronts, and they increased their manpower in this theatre of war by approximately one million men.[13] All this, they thought, would enable them to bring the war to a successful conclusion in the spring of 1918. In 1918, the main enemy in the West were the British. The OHL was convinced that once the British Army had been defeated and driven back into the sea, the French Army and the American contingent would not present major obstacles on the path to victory. The USArmy was still too small and inexperienced. It was supposed that France would not be able to mobilize more troops and that it was running out of manpower. To a degree, there was also the belief that 'Germanic virtues' would be superior to 'Gallic weakness'; a rather interesting idea considering that the French Army had been fighting the Germans very successfully since 1914.[14] In accordance with this general thinking, the German offensives would have to be directed, directly or indirectly, against the British forces on the continent.

The first offensive, code-named *Michael*, was supposed to focus on the area of St Quentin. The reason for this was obvious: it was the junction of the British and French armies. Three armies were prepared for this offensive on the German side, and it was unleashed on 21 March 1918. Initially, the offensive predominately hit the British Fifth Army, which crumbled under the onslaught. General Erich Ludendorff, *Erster Generalquartiermeister* (First Quartermaster General) and practically the head of the German Army in 1918, succumbed to temptation: rather than follow the original operational design, he reinforced the German Eighteenth Army in the southern sector of the offensive, which had made the most progress in the early phase of Operation *Michael*. Ludendorff thus traded operational and possible strategic victory for tactical glory. As a consequence, when the offensive was called off on 5 April, it had achieved impressive tactical gains, but had not won the war – and it had cost both sides dearly. But whereas the Allies could replenish their reserves, the Germans could not.

Subsequent operations followed this general pattern; on 9 April 1918 the German launched Operation *Georgette* with 36 divisions against the British in Flanders towards the direction of the channel ports. On 11 April, the situation had become desperate for the British forces, and the commander-in-chief, Field Marshal Sir Douglas Haig, issued his famous order of the day, stating that 'With our backs to the wall and believing in the justice of our cause each one of us must fight on to the end'. Logistical problems – a common issue for the German Army in 1918 – and exposed flanks created issues for Ludendorff, as did counter-attacks by the British Second Army and a five-division detachment of the French Armée du Nord. As a consequence, Ludendorff ended the offensive on 29 April.

The German offensives, 1918

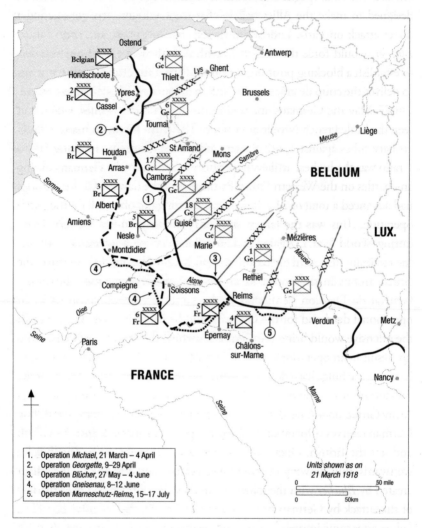

1. Operation *Michael*, 21 March – 4 April
2. Operation *Georgette*, 9–29 April
3. Operation *Blücher*, 27 May – 4 June
4. Operation *Gneisenau*, 8–12 June
5. Operation *Marneschutz-Reims*, 15–17 July

*Units shown as on
21 March 1918*

German chances of ending the war successfully were dwindling, but they were not yet willing to give up. The main objective remained the British Expeditionary Force (BEF) in Flanders. After reinforcements had arrived in the northern sector of the front, the Allies were now too strong there for a direct assault. Consequently, Ludendorff conceived a large-scale diversionary attack in the Champagne area, south of south St Quentin and west of Reims, designed to make the Allies believe that the Germans were conducting a direct attack on Paris. Ludendorff hoped that this operation, code-named *Blücher*, would force the French to withdraw their reserves from Flanders to establish a blocking position in front of Paris, thus enabling the Germans to deliver the coup de grâce to the BEF in an operation code-named *Hagen*. On 27 May the Germans attacked at the Chemin des Dames, which had seen the futile French Nivelle offensive in 1917. The Germans massed 5,263 artillery tubes against 1,422 French and British guns. The resulting 3.7 to 1 ratio was the highest artillery superiority achieved by the Germans during any battles on the Western Front. By the end of the day, the German troops had advanced a total of 21 kilometres, exceeding the objective for the entire operation. This was the largest single-day advance on the Western Front during World War I. Again, Ludendorff now faced a dilemma: continue the tactically successful operation, or shift back to the original objective, the British troops in the north. Again he succumbed to tactical temptation. Général de Division Ferdinand Foch realized that the offensive was an operational dead end for the Germans and he kept his nerve. Even though the offensive would bring the Germans within 70 kilometres of Paris, it did not result in an operational success. Actually, quite the contrary was true, as it created a bulge that left the Germans in a vulnerable and logistically difficult positon. The operation was finally halted by Kronprinz Wilhelm's Army Group on 4 June 1918. The subsequent deployment of the dwindling German reserves (Operation *Gneisenau*) again took place against the French and not the British. Operation *Gneisenau* was indented to extend *Blücher* westwards, thus drawing in more Allied reserves and also linking the salient created by *Blücher* with the salient at Amiens. The French had been warned of this attack by German prisoners, and as a result, the offensive became a failure after some impressive gains on the first day. On 12 June, the offensive was called off, because it was obvious that it would not achieve its objectives, but would be very costly and result in casualties that the Germans were no longer able to absorb.

Operation *Hagen* was now postponed and Ludendorff concentrated his forces for a final offensive against the French forces. Logistics played an important role here. Ludendorff hoped to improve the logistical situation of the German troops in the salient created by Operation *Blücher*, in particular by seizing the logistical hub of Reims. The offensive began on 15 July, but did not achieve any of its objectives. Operation *Marneschutz-Reims*, as the offensive was called, was a failure. Now the Germans were exhausted and the tide had turned.

On 18 July, French forces, supported by American, British and Italian troops, counter-attacked in the second phase of this battle, which has also become known as the Second Battle of the Marne.[15] For their attack, the Allies had over 3,000 guns available (although no prior artillery preparation took place in order to keep the element of surprise). As a consequence of this attack, the German Kronprinz suggested a general withdrawal from the Marne salient on 24 July, against considerable initial opposition from Ludendorff, who finally agreed to this withdrawal on the night of 25 to 26 July. In retrospect, it might be fair to consider this Allied operation as the clear and obvious turning point of the war. This is not necessarily a view shared amongst more Anglo-centric historians who identify 8 August as the turning point and the beginning of the final episode of the war, also called the 'Hundred Days'. On 8 August, Allied forces, including British, Canadian, Australian, US and French units, attacked German troops east of Amiens. For the first time, German troops collapsed before the enemy and a high number of Germans were captured on this day – approximately 13,000 by the British Fourth Army and a further 3,000 by the French forces. It was this collapse of morale which caused Ludendorff to call 8 August 'the black day of the German Army in the history of this war' and 'the worst experience I had to go through…'[16]

There then followed Allied offensive after offensive, the idea being to keep up operational momentum in order to wear down the dwindling German reserves that had to be moved from one field of battle to another. The French under Général de Division Charles Mangin attacked between the Aisne and Oise on 20 August, followed by attacks by British and French forces on the northern end of the *Siegfriedstellung* (the Siegfried Position – the Allies called it the Hindenburg Line) between 23 and 26 August. On 12 September, the Americans began their offensive in the St Mihiel sector. This limited offensive was regarded as a success, although the Americans under Pershing were not content with the limited scope of the operation. The reason why Maréchal Foch had restricted this offensive was because he wanted to deliver a decisive blow in the Argonne Forest. This offensive was unleashed on 26 September with 31 French and 15 American divisions, 4,000 guns and 700 tanks. Despite this huge concentration of force, the Allied offensive soon encountered severe problems in determined German resistance, logistical problems and the unsophisticated US way of fighting. The Germans were not able to trade space for time, because they had to protect a vital railway link in their rear. As a consequence, the fighting in this sector continued until the end of the war, even though in the last phase, lasting from 1 to 11 November, the US forces broke through the German lines and were now able to exploit and fight in open warfare. Further north, the BEF fought the battles for the Siegfried Position between 27 September and 8 October. The breaching of this formidable defensive line resulted in a German withdrawal and was – if this was still needed – the clear sign that Germany would not even be able to fight a defensive war successfully.

Even though the German Army still put up fierce resistance, it was obvious that it was exhausted. In six months, the strength of the German Army had fallen from approximately 5.1 million men to 4.2 million.[17] To make matters worse, the casualties were particularly high among the best-trained troops, the storm troopers. The OHL predicted that it would need 200,000 men per month to replace casualties. Convalescents returning to the front could make up 70,000–80,000 per month, but the next annual class of 18-year-olds would only provide an overall figure of 300,000 men, resulting in a further weakening of German combat power.[18] On top of this, the Germans were no longer in well-prepared defensive positions. Morale was low: they had expected a victorious outcome of the war at the end of their offensives, but now the war dragged on with no sign of victory. The influenza epidemic had further weakened the German troops. Major Ludwig Beck, the later Chief of the General Staff, wrote in his diary that 'the front is held by a mere spider-web of fighters'.[19] On 4 September 1918 Ludendorff ordered the field army in the west to abandon the sophisticated defence in depth for a more traditional and linear way of fighting.[20] Moral, manpower and training were no longer available to the necessary degree in order to fight the defence in depth. However, saying that the initial collapse of the German Army was fully caused by problems on the German side would be unfair to the Allies. All Allied armies, in particular the British and the French, had made steady and sometimes astonishing improvements in their fighting techniques. Some historians have argued that the Allies had overtaken the Germans on what they regarded as their area of expertise: the tactical and operational conduct of war on the battlefield.[21] On 30 September the OHL told the army group commander that it would no longer be able to provide any reserves and that the units and formations had to make do with what they had.[22] It only took a few more days to realize that all last battle-worthy reserves had been thrown into the fight and had been consumed. As a consequence, Generalfeldmarschall Paul von Hindenburg and General Ludendorff agreed that Germany had to ask the Allies for an armistice. On 4 October 1918, the Reichskanzler (Chancellor), Prinz Max von Baden, sent a message to that effect to the American President Wilson, whom the German saw as the most honest broker.

With the arrival of autumn, the reports from the other fronts began to paint a positive picture for the Allies, too; the Allied armies in the Balkans finally defeated Bulgaria, which signed an armistice on 29 September, and those in Palestine routed the Ottoman forces. The Ottoman Empire surrendered on 31 October, followed by Austria-Hungary on 3 November. The Central Powers had lost the war. As a consequence, German sailors mutinied in Kiel harbour in early November – they were not willing to sacrifice themselves in a glorious but deadly final assault on the Royal Navy. The German naval command had planned this in order to preserve the honour of the German Navy, which would make it possible to rebuild a great fleet in the future. By 6 November all of north-western Germany was under the control of the so-called workers' and soldiers' councils. On 8 November the revolution reached Saxony, Hesse, Franconia, and Württemberg in central and southern Germany, respectively. Faced with increasing pressure, Chancellor Prinz Max von Baden unilaterally declared the abdication of Kaiser Wilhelm II on 9 November, and Germany officially surrendered two days later. Signed at 0500hrs (French time) on 11 November, the Armistice came into effect at 1100hrs.

Interestingly, the returning German troops were often greeted enthusiastically by their garrisons' population. The troops seemingly offered some protection against marauding revolutionaries – but this hope would prove short-lived, not least because many units were dissolved quickly after their return home. But the troops had also achieved what many Germans saw as their war aims, regardless of the real war aims of the military and political elite: Germany had stood 'against a world of enemies' and the army had defended the fatherland; Germany was intact and had not been invaded as it had been in many wars before. For instance, the regimental history of the 13 Infantry Regiment from Münster states that 'on 8 December the city saw the festive return of the undefeated regiment to its old garrison'. The regiment reached its old barracks in the centre of the city 'covered in flowers'. [23]

But this joyous view was not shared by everybody. On 10 November 1918, a German soldier was recuperating in a military hospital in Pasewalk, a small town in Pomerania. In his memoirs, that have to be taken with more than a pinch of salt, he remembers how a priest came to the convalescents and told them that the war was lost and that Germany was now a republic. 'All had been in vain,' the soldier wrote, 'in vain the sacrifices and the hardships, in vain the hunger and thirst of sometimes endless months, in vain the hours, in which we, embraced by fear of death, did our duty and in vain the death of the two million who had died.' The consequence of this event, so the writer stated, was that 'I decided to become a politician'.[24] This particular phrase stands at the end of chapter seven of one of the most infamous books ever written by one of the most infamous people in history. The book was *Mein Kampf* and the writer was Adolf Hitler. This is not the place to analyse Hitler's role in World War I.[25] It suffices to say that without World War I, there would have been no World War II. At the beginning of World War I, Hitler was a nobody and at the very bottom of the class-based Wilhelmine society. In this system, he would never have risen to power. Only the political upheaval of 1918 and the subsequent political challenges made his rise possible – ironically as a consequence of the democratic structure that Germany adopted with the Weimar Republic.

The Treaty of Versailles, signed on 28 June 1919, was generally regarded in Germany as a harsh and unjust peace. One major point of discontent was the infamous clause 231, the 'war-guilt clause', which stated that Germany had to accept all responsibility for the outbreak of the war. It was almost universally rejected in Germany.[26] Even the head of government, the Social Democratic Reichsministerpräsident Philipp Scheidemann, who on 9 November 1918 had publicly proclaimed the end of the monarchy and the new era of democracy, made clear in in a speech given to the national assembly on 12 May 1919 that he was against the treaty: 'What hand should not wither that puts itself and us in such chains.'[27] Retrospectively, one might argue that the problem was that the treaty lacked a clear direction. Paul von Hindenburg allegedly once said that 'An operation without a point of main effort is like a man without character'. If this is true, then this was a treaty without character; it was not harsh enough to keep Germany down permanently, but too harsh to appease Germany and to incorporate it into the club of Western democracies. On the Right, the culprit was identified quickly: socialists and democratic parties had willingly accepted the defeat of Germany and had stabbed in the back the army that had been undefeated in the field.[28]

In addition, there was a widespread fear of Bolshevism and Left extremism in Europe. The fact that this ideology could eventually be contained did not mean that the threat had not been real. The expansion of Bolshevism was stopped in the Polish–Soviet War (1919–21). This war, largely forgotten in the West now, showed that the idea of Bolshevik expansion was not only an intellectual idea, but a real threat. And another factor played a role in the general perception of Bolshevik and extreme left movements: Jewish intellectuals and politicians, including individuals such as Karl Radek and Leon Trotsky in Russia and Kurt Eisner in Bavaria, were proportionally over-represented in prominent positions. It was therefore relatively easy to coin the extreme Left as a 'Jewish threat'. Once these ingredients – stab-in-the-back, the 'Jewish factor', and war-guilt – are combined, one can begin to see the recipe for Hitler's ideology. When one adds to this the experience of the British blockade, the picture is even more revealing. The impact of the blockade on the German nation and also the German psyche is widely forgotten today, but it did play an important role in the inter-war period and World War II. The experience of this still lives on in the unofficial name in German for rickets: it is still called the 'English disease'. The exact number of deaths caused by the malnourishment during the blockade is hard to quantify. An official German publication from 1918 claimed that 763,000 civilians died from starvation and disease caused by the blockade up until the end of December 1918.[29] Other studies have found that the figure is more likely to be in the region of 424,000[30] – all excluding the deaths that were caused between January and June 1919 when the blockade was lifted after the signing of the Treaty of Versailles. These figures also exclude the number of people who perished due to the influenza epidemic which hit Europe in 1918. All countries were affected, but the German population more so than others, because the people did not have the strength to resist the virus, which, interestingly, targeted predominately the young and usually fitter members of society. The consequences that some drew from this were logical: in a future war against the United Kingdom, Germany would suffer the same fate as in World War I. Consequently, it was important to find agricultural land close to home that might be utilized to feed the German population and that could not be cut off by the enemy. Geo-strategically, this land was to be found in the East. The fact that 'racially inferior' people lived there only made this more appealing to the National Socialists.

This ideological package and its firm grounding in the events of the end of World War I explain some of the support that Hitler gained in Germany and Austria before, and also into World War II. In propaganda terms, it was fairly easy to argue that large parts of the Nazi actions and ideology were directed at the Treaty of Versailles and the *Novemberverbrecher*, the 'November criminals', who had signed the armistice in 1918. Hitler's stunning successes, both in political terms before the outbreak of World War II and then the military victories in the first half of the war, have to be seen in this context; and they seemed to prove him right. To put it provocatively: if Hitler had died in 1940 after the defeat of France, he might have gone down in history as a great statesman and military leader.

At the end of World War I, societies all over Europe felt that the old ruling establishments had driven their countries into an abyss, and drastic changes in the political regimes all over the continent occurred. The US withdrew, once again, politically from Europe, even though its monetary ties to Europe remained strong. In fact the US did not ratify the Treaty of Versailles, and it did not join the League of Nations, which had been founded on 10 January 1920 in order to resolve future international disputes peacefully.[31] Three empires disappeared – the German, Austrian-Hungarian and Russian monarchies were no more – altering the balance of power in Europe. New states were created in Central and Eastern Europe. In the direct aftermath of the war, many European states became democracies. However, when World War II broke out in 1939, true democratic states were a minority in Europe and most states had adopted some form of authoritarian rule, from Franco's Spain in the West to Stalin's Russia in the East.

Even the most important remaining democracies in Europe, France and Britain were still suffering from the war. In order to finance the war, Britain had borrowed heavily from the international financial market; in particular it had relied on US money. In 1914, the national debt stood at £650 million; by 1919 it had sky-rocketed to £7.4 billion. As a consequence, much of Britain's national financial power was spent after the war on repaying debt and paying interest on borrowed money. By the mid-1920s, interest on government debt was absorbing an astonishing 44 per cent of all government expenditure. The spending on defence would overtake the interest payments only in 1937, once the writing was on the wall that a war with Germany was a clear possibility.[32] Britain – and France, for that matter – had mobilized the empires to fight the war. An awakening belief in the self-determination of the colonies' indigenous people was the consequence. To say it with Goethe; 'Spirits that I have cited, my commands ignore'.

France had suffered enormously during World War I. Parts of its territory had been occupied by the enemy, and in order to liberate these territories, *la Grande Nation* paid a terrible price. Approximately 1.35 million soldiers died in this struggle; together with the civilian casualties, this resulted in a blood loss of approximately 1.7 million people, roughly 4.29 per cent of the French population (compared, for instance, to approximately two per cent for the United Kingdom and 0.13 per cent for the USA).[33] The result was a belief in the power of the defence, embodied in the concrete works of the Maginot line, behind which the French Army believed itself protected. A new war against Germany should not cause the same blood loss as *la Grande Guerre*. As a consequence, the army remained passive in 1939 and 1940, while the Wehrmacht carried out its first invasions of neighbouring countries. Had the French Army occupied the Ruhr area in 1939 (as they had done in 1923) when war was declared and the German Army was busy fighting in Poland, the German war machine would have run dry very quickly. But the shadows of World War I prevented this from happening.

Hand in glove with this development went a radicalization of the political process, not least driven by the experience of violence of wide parts of society during the war years. The consequence of this was that in many parts of Central and Eastern Europe, the end of World War I did not bring peace, but instead a constant political and military struggle that shaped people's experiences and made them accept violence as an everyday occurrence.[34] Maybe Ernst Jünger, arguably the most famous German writer of World War I, was right when he claimed that:

> It is the war that shaped people and their time. A generation such as ours has never walked before into the area of the earth in order to fight for the power over its age. Because never before did a generation return from a gate as dark and tremendous as this war back into the light of life. And yet, we cannot deny it, even though some of us would like to: The war, father of all things, is also our father; it has hammered, chiselled and hardened us to what we are… It has brought us up to fight and fighters we shall remain as long as we exist.[35]

CHAPTER 2

THE GERMAN ARMY IN 1918

Major General (Ret'd) Dr David T. Zabecki

In his Final Dispatch of 1 March 1919 Field Marshal Sir Douglas Haig wrote:

> The rapid collapse of Germany's military powers in the latter half of 1918 was the logical outcome of the fighting of the two previous years. It would not have taken place but for the period of ceaseless attrition which used up the reserves of the German armies, while the constant and growing pressure of the [maritime] blockade sapped with more deadly insistence from year to year the strength and resolution of the German people. It is in the great battles of 1916 and 1917 that we have to seek the secret of our victory in 1918.[1]

In essence, Haig was defending the strategic legitimacy of the horrendous and widely criticized attritional battles of the Somme in 1916 and Third Ypres in 1917. Collectively they constituted what Haig called 'the wearing-out battle'. To this day, the battles of 1916 and 1917 remain the primary indictment against Haig's generalship.

Unquestionably, the Germans were weaker at the start of 1918 than they had been at any point in the war so far. The British campaigns of 1916 and 1917 certainly had inflicted a high level of attrition on the Germans, and their own 1916 attritional campaign against the French at Verdun only made their manpower situation worse. Nonetheless, the German Army on the Western Front still had plenty of fight left, as they demonstrated so forcibly during the five Ludendorff Offensives, also known as the Spring Offensive, from March to July 1918.[2] As a tactical instrument of war, the *Kaiserheer* was the best army of the Great War, and was still so even in its weakened state at the start of 1918. But a little more than ten months later the German Army lay in ruins. How did that happen? How did the best army of the 1914–18 war lose, and why did it disintegrate so rapidly between July and November? There is more to it than Haig's dispatch would lead us to believe.

Command, organization, and armament of the *Kaiserheer* of 1918

In the strictest sense, there was no 'Imperial German Army'. The German Empire was a confederation of four kingdoms, and 22 lesser principalities and states. The King of Prussia was also the Kaiser of the Reich, and in time of war he was Germany's *Oberster Kriegsherr* (Supreme Warlord), the titular head of the combined German armies. The military units of the lesser states were mostly integrated into the Prussian Army, but the Kingdoms of Saxony, Bavaria, and Württemberg all maintained distinct armies. Each had a general staff, but only the Prussian *Großer Generalstab* (Great General Staff) prepared war plans for the combined German Army. The King of Bavaria retained peacetime command authority over his forces, although the Kaiser had the right to inspect in peacetime to ensure the standardization of training and equipment. Saxony maintained a separate officer corps and a war ministry to administer its army, but the Kaiser exercised peacetime command. Württemberg's officer corps was integrated with that of Prussia's, but the Württemberg *Kriegsministerium* (War Ministry) retained control over certain administrative functions. After more than three years of war many of these distinctions had started to blur by the start of 1918, but some peculiarities remained. Prussians and Bavarians especially continued to regard each other with their traditional degree of wariness.

Like the fragmented and Byzantine civil government of Wilhelmine Germany, the Prussian Army was commanded and administered by three separate and often competing power structures. The Kaiser's *Militärkabinett* (Military Cabinet) controlled the career management and personnel actions of all officers, with the exception of the General Staff officers. The Kriegsministerium was responsible for all administrative functions, including recruitment, training, supply, pay, and issuing military regulations. All four kingdoms had war ministries, but in wartime the Prussian Kriegsministerium exercised centralized control. The primary peacetime function of the Generalstab was war planning, and during wartime, the actual conduct of operations.[3] The Chief of the Militärkabinett, the *Kriegsminister* (War Minister), and the *Chef des Generalstabes* (Chief of the General Staff) all had direct access (*Immediatrecht*) to the Kaiser. Although all three organs were equal in theory, the Generalstab had by 1918 long since eclipsed the other two.

The Generalstab was both an organization, and an officers' career branch. Entry to the Generalstab was highly competitive, and required a long and arduous accession process that had a very high attrition rate. In the years before the start of the war only 140 to 160 officers each year were accepted to the three-year *Kriegsakademie* (War Academy). It was an academically rigorous course with a high level of drop-out. The successful graduates then underwent a two-year probationary posting, followed by a final screening board. Only between six and ten officers per year made the final cut. The Generalstab itself was organized into two major branches, the Großer Generalstab, headquartered in Berlin, and the *Truppengeneralstab* (Units' General Staff), which formed the central cadres of the divisional, corps, field army, and army group staffs. Typically, a division had only one single General Staff officer, the *Ia Generalstabsoffizier* (operations officer), who also functioned as the divisional *Chef des Stabes* (chief of staff). General Staff officers alternated assignments between the two branches, and also served for periods as commanders of line units. Most commanders of the line units were not qualified General Staff officers, nor was such a qualification necessary to become a general officer. The *Chef des Großen Generalstabes* (Chief of the Great General Staff) had no influence on the efficiency reports and career development of the field commanders, unless they also happened to be General Staff officers.[4]

In time of war the Chef des Großen Generalstabes directed the German *Feldheer* (Field Army) in the name of the Kaiser. In all but name, he was the German Commander-in-Chief. The first Kaiser, Wilhelm I, may have been a competent and experienced soldier, but his inept grandson, Wilhelm II, had little qualification for high command. The *Oberste Heeresleitung* (OHL) was the Supreme Headquarters of the Field Army. Throughout most of 1918 the OHL was based in Spa, Belgium. In August 1914, the Chef des Großen Generalstabes was General Helmuth von Moltke the Younger, the nephew of the great Generalfeldmarshall Helmuth von Moltke. Within the first few months of the war Moltke was replaced by General Erich von Falkenhayn, who in turn was relieved in mid-1916 over the catastrophic failure of his Verdun Offensive. He was replaced by Generalfeldmarshall Paul von Hindenburg, the German commander on the Eastern Front and the victor of the 1914 battle of Tannenburg. Hindenburg was accompanied to the Western Front by his chief of staff, General der Infanterie Erich Ludendorff.

There was no real equivalent in the Allied armies to Ludendorff's position. Since Hindenburg himself was the Chief of Staff of the German Army, Ludendorff was what we today would call the Vice Chief of Staff. When the Hindenburg–Ludendorff 'Duo' assumed control at OHL in 1916, Ludendorff was offered the title of 'Second Chief of the General Staff'. He instead opted for the title of Erster Generalquartiermeister. A quartermaster was not necessarily a logistics officer in the German Army. A German General Staff officer who was a senior quartermaster (*Oberquartiermeister*) was a deputy chief of staff. Ludendorff's position, however, was even more unique. He demanded from the Kaiser and received 'joint responsibility in all decisions and measures that might be taken'.[5] It was an unprecedented level of authority conferred upon a staff officer, even in the German Army.

At all echelons of command, a German chief of staff had far more actual authority than any of his Allied counterparts. Rather than a strictly defined superior/subordinate relationship, a German commander and his chief of staff operated on a more collegial basis. In most armies, the commander initiated the operational planning process; but in the German Army the initial impetus often came from the chief of staff. The chief of staff had the right and even the responsibility to argue with his commander – albeit behind closed doors – right up to the point of decision. But once the decision was made, the entire staff got behind it. A chief of staff who had been delegated *Vollmacht* (literally, mandate or proxy) by his commander had the authority to issue orders directly in the commander's name, without necessarily conferring with that commander first. A German chief of staff was effectively a deputy commander in all but name, and if he had Vollmacht he was almost a co-commander. Ludendorff's authority as Erster Generalquartiermeister even exceeded the normal bounds of Vollmacht.

Another peculiarity of the German command system was the concept that position assignment took precedence over rank.[6] The Germans routinely appointed officers to command and staff assignments far above the actual rank they held. Once in the position, however, the officer functioned with the full authority of that position, regardless of the nominal ranks and pay grades of his functional subordinates. Corps chiefs of staff, who may have been *Oberstleutnante* (lieutenant colonels), routinely issued orders unchallenged to general officers commanding subordinate divisions. As a General der Infantry, Ludendorff himself never wore more than three stars, yet in 1918 he issued orders to field marshals commanding army groups. Such would be unthinkable in the British, French, or American armies.

German organizational structure was broadly similar to that of the Allied armies. German *Heeresgruppen* (army groups) first appeared in 1916. In late 1918 there were four Heeresgruppen on the Western Front. From north to south they were Heeresgruppe Kronprinz Rupprecht von Bayern; Heeresgruppe Deutscher Kronprinz; Heeresgruppen Gallwitz; and Heeresgruppe Herzog Albrecht von Württemberg. General der Artillerie Max von Gallwitz was the only army group commander who was not a member of one of the ruling families. German Kronprinz Wilhelm was a dilettante figure-head commander; but Rupprecht von

Bayern was one of the most competent senior German commanders of the war. Prinz Leopold von Bayern commanded the German Forces on the Eastern Front (*Oberost*), which after Russia left the war consisted primarily of Heeresgruppe Mackensen, a combined German–Bulgarian force commanded by Generalfeldmarschall August von Mackensen.

Korps (corps) consisted of two or more divisions. A *Generalkommando*, or GK (corps headquarters), tended to remain in the front lines for long periods of time, while the attached divisions rotated in and out as the situation required. An *Armeeoberkommando*, or AOK (army command), usually controlled two or more corps, plus the various field-army-level supporting troops such as artillery and aviation. An *Armeeabteilung* (army detachment) was a lesser organization that might contain only a single corps, along with various field-army-level support units.

In 1918 a typical German division was organized into three infantry regiments of three battalions each; a three-battalion artillery command (*Arko*); and various engineer, signal, supply, and support troops. Standard divisional authorized strength was 11,643, although actual front-line strength was always somewhat less, and continued to decline as the final year of the war progressed. By the latter half of 1917 the Germans started distinguishing between two types of divisions with different tactical functions. Defensive positions in the line were held by *Stellungsdivisionen* (positional divisions), which had relatively low mobility. The *Angriffsdivisionen* (attack divisions) were manned by younger men and trained and equipped to advance rapidly and deeply.[7] During the war, the Germans fielded a total of 251 divisions.

Tactical virtuosity

From a tactical perspective, the Great War started in 1914 as a 19th-century war, and ended in 1918 as the first true 20th-century conflict. Since the last major war on the European continent, the Franco-Prussian War of 1870–71, warfighting technologies had advanced so far and so fast that no one really had any idea what modern war would look like or how it should be fought. At the tactical level, the two basic elements of combat power are firepower and manoeuvre. Throughout history the two have alternated with each other for temporary dominance, based on the emerging technologies of the given period. But during the last decades of the 19th century and the first decade of the 20th, firepower technology had advanced far ahead of mobility technology. The bolt-action repeating rifle, quick-firing artillery, and especially the machine gun made the battlefield a very lethal place. Tactical mobility, however, was still limited primarily to the speed of human and animal muscle power. By the end of the war the internal combustion engine was starting to change that, and by the start of World War II firepower and manoeuvre had pretty much come back into balance. But for most of World War I, the problem was one of how to overcome massive firepower with limited mobility. Throughout the war the Germans were the leaders in tactical innovation.

With the exception of the Verdun Offensive in 1916, the Germans spent most of 1915–17 standing on the defensive on the Western Front, while they concentrated on defeating the Russians in the East. Defending against the massive French offensive in Champagne in 1915, and the British offensives at the Somme in 1916 and Arras and Ypres in 1917, the Germans developed and perfected most of the concepts we to this day associate with modern defence warfare. When Hindenburg and Ludendorff assumed command at the OHL in 1916, Ludendorff immediately presided over an all-encompassing review and revision of German tactics based on the battlefield lessons to date. Defence was the first function addressed. On 1 December 1916, the OHL published the German Army's new defensive doctrine as *Grundsätze für die Führung in der Abwehrschlacht im Stellungskrieg* (*Principles for the Leadership in the Defensive Battle in Position Warfare*).[8]

The new doctrine can best be described as flexible defence, or flexible defence-in-depth. It rested on three key principles: Flexibility, Decentralized Control, and Counter-attack. As the war progressed, the Allies centralized the command and control of their offensive operations at ever-higher levels. The Germans responded by giving their commanders in the defence an impressive amount of autonomy. Typically, a German infantry regiment in the defence was deployed with its three battalions in echelon. The front-line battalion commander had the authority to withdraw from the forward positions under enemy pressure as he saw the tactical necessity. More importantly, he had the authority to order the regiment's other two battalions echeloned behind him into the counter-attack when he judged the timing right.

The Germans conducted two different types of counter-attack. The *Gegenstoß* (hasty counter-attack) was immediate and violent. Its purpose was to hit the attacking enemy force before they had a chance to consolidate the newly won position or to move up reinforcements and especially artillery. The Gegenstoß was planned, launched, and commanded by the front-line battalion commander on his own initiative. The deliberate *Gegenangriff* (counter-attack) was centrally planned, more methodically prepared, and commanded at a higher echelon. It was the alternative course of action whenever a Gegenstoß failed or was impractical.

The Germans organized their deep defensive positions into three zones. The *Vorfeldzone* (outpost zone) was usually 500 to 1,000 yards in depth (although German doctrine said that this could extend in extremis to up to 8,000 yards), and held with sparsely positioned early-warning listening and observation posts. The *Kampffeld* (battle zone), was up to 2,000 yards deep, consisting of three or more successive trench lines reinforced with strongpoints and machine-gun positions. The leading edge of the forward zone was the *Hauptwiderstandslinie* (main line of resistance). The reserves and the counter-attack units manned the *Hinterzone* (rearward zone), typically sheltered in deep, reinforced bunkers. An intermediate position of multiple trench lines between the battle zone and the rearward zone formed the protective line for the artillery. Through the latter half of 1917 the French typically put two-thirds of their combat strength into their forward-most lines, while the Germans held their leading lines with only 20 per cent. During an artillery bombardment prior to an Allied attack, the German forces in the rear positions typically moved into their deep, reinforced *Stollen* (dugouts) to ride out the storm. The troops in the thinly held outpost line slipped out of their trenches and took cover in nearby shell-holes – while the Allied artillery pounded the empty trenches.[9]

By 1918 the German defensive system on the Western Front consisted of three deeply echeloned belts, with each belt further organized into outpost, battle, and rearward zones. The Allies called the leading belt the

Hindenburg Line, but the Germans called it the *Siegfriedstellung* (Siegfried Position). The Siegfried Position was only the central sector of that first echelon belt. The various sectors of the belts were named after Wagnerian gods and heroes taken from the German national epos, the *Nibelungenlied*. The Siegfried Position, which ran from Arras to Laffaux, near Soissons on the Aisne, was the strongest. It was constructed well behind the German line during the winter of 1916–17. Then in March of 1917 the Germans pulled back to that strong position during Operation *Alberich*. The Siegfried Position subsequently was extended from Arras north to the coast, designated the Wotan Position. The Alberich Position extended the Siegfried to the Aisne River, south of Laon; and the Hagen Position extended it to the east and then south to Metz and Strasbourg.

The second echelon Hunding Position was some 15 miles behind the Siegfried. The Hunding made excellent use of the terrain, especially between the Aisne and Oise rivers, but overall it was not as strong as the Siegfried. The Hermann Position extended the Hunding north to Douai on the Scarpe River; and from there the Ghent Extension ran toward the coast north of Ghent. The Brunhilde Position extended the Hunding south-east to Grand Pre, on the northern end of the Argonne Forest; and from there the Kriemhilde Position ran east behind the Hagen. At that point, however, the first and second echelon belts were only about six miles apart.

The third belt was the Freya Position, which only ran primarily behind the Hunding, Brunhilde, and part of the Kriemhilde Positions. Starting from the vicinity of Le Cateau, it ran south-east to the Meuse River, just south of Stenay. The Freya, however, had not been completed by the time of the Armistice. Behind that third belt the notional Antwerp–Meuse Position was planned to run from the Scheldt Estuary to the Meuse, just north of Verdun. Had it been built and occupied, the much-shortened Antwerp–Meuse Position would have allowed the Germans to concentrate their forces for a much stronger defence. One of Allied Supreme Commander Général de Division Ferdinand Foch's constant worries during the latter half of 1918 was that the Germans would make just such a withdrawal in a timely and orderly manner, which most likely would have dragged the war out well into 1919. Fortunately for the

The attack on the Siegfried Position, 1918

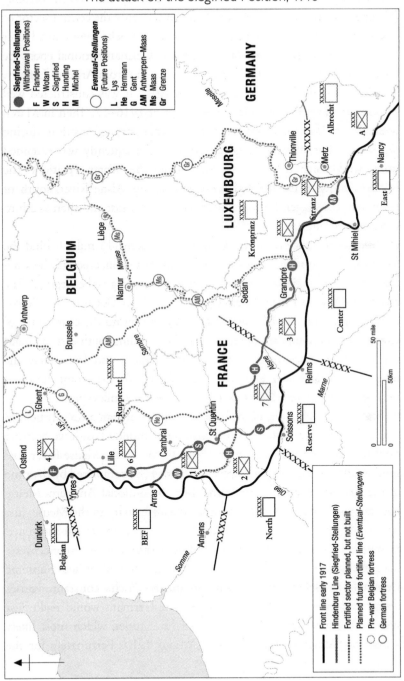

Allies, by the time the Germans started falling back to the Siegfried Position, they were woefully short of the necessary manpower required to establish that final fallback line on the Meuse.

Following a 13-month study of offensive doctrine, the OHL on 1 January 1918 issued *The Attack in Position Warfare* (*Der Angriff im Stellungskrieg*).[10]

The new doctrine issued in January 1918 organized the attack into two main phases. The first, a systematic assault against the enemy's leading fixed positions, required detailed preparation and centralized control. The second phase would be an aggressive extension of the attack to disrupt the enemy to the point where he could not reorganize and respond. The second phase relied upon decentralized execution and the individual initiative of the subordinate commanders on the spot. The second phase started from the enemy's intermediate zone, at which point the attackers would be beyond the range of most of their own supporting artillery. As opposed to defensive operations, the higher echelons of command maintained tighter control of the follow-on forces in the attack.[11]

The initial objective of any attack was to penetrate fast and deep enough to reach and overrun the defender's artillery positions on the first day. The intent was to disrupt the enemy's communications, and bypass and isolate his strongpoints, which later would be reduced by follow-on forces. The new doctrine marked a key conceptual shift from destruction to large-scale disruption – which is one of the basic principles of modern operational art. While the Allies attacked in successive waves, in order to relieve the pressure on their lead units, the Germans continued to press the attack with the lead units in order to maintain momentum. This, of course, burned out the lead units quickly, and within the framework of sequential operations it was counterproductive and had serious consequences for the Germans after March 1918.[12]

The new doctrine stressed infantry–artillery coordination and the need to move artillery forward to sustain the attack. Artillery was the biggest killer on the World War I battlefield, and once static trench warfare set in, artillery almost by default became the primary means of prosecuting the war. Destruction became the tactical mission of artillery – destroy the enemy's defences and defenders before one's own attacking infantry reached the objective; destroy the enemy's attacking infantry before they could reach your defensive positions. As the war progressed, the preparation and counter-preparation fires consumed hundreds of thousands and then millions of rounds of ammunition, and by 1917 lasted up to two weeks before the start of the infantry attack. But destruction proved impossible to achieve, no matter how many shells were fired. The long preparatory fires also compromised the element of surprise by telling the defender exactly where the attack would be coming. Worse still, the massive fires tore up the intervening ground over which the attacking infantry had to advance, reducing mobility and thereby increasing the attacker's vulnerability to the defender's fires.

By late 1917 some artillery commanders had begun to understand that properly planned and coordinated neutralization fires could be far more effective than destruction fires. One of those gunners was Oberst Georg Bruchmüller, arguably the most influential artillery tactician of the war, and perhaps of the 20th century. In 1914 Bruchmüller was an obscure, medically retired officer recalled to active duty for the war. General Max Hoffmann called Bruchmüller, 'an artillery genius';[13] and Ludendorff called him, 'one of the most prominent soldiers of the war'.[14] Starting on the Eastern Front as early as 1915 and culminating at the 1917 battle of Riga, Bruchmüller experimented with various fire support methods based on neutralization. At the battle of Lake Naroch in April 1916, Bruchmüller became the first artillery officer in the German Army to plan and coordinate fires above the divisional level.[15]

Bruchmüller recognized the counterproductive nature of the long, destruction-oriented preparations. Thus, while the artillery preparations in the West were lasting weeks, Bruchmüller planned and executed preparations in the East lasting only a few hours, yet achieving better effect. His preparation fires were not long, but they were incredibly violent – designed not to obliterate a defending enemy, but to stun him senseless. The British in 1918 came to call such preparations 'Hurricane Bombardments'. In Bruchmüller's own words, 'We desired only to break the morale of the enemy, pin him to his position, and then overcome him with an overwhelming assault.'[16]

Shortly after arriving on the Western Front in November 1917, Bruchmüller quickly became the principal champion of a newly developed technique to 'predict' artillery registration corrections based on the careful measurement of local weather conditions and the muzzle velocity characteristics of each gun tube in a battery. The system developed by Hauptmann (Captain) Erich Pulkowski is essentially the same as that used by all the NATO armies today, although the calculations are now all done by computer. Bruchmüller was not the only artillery innovator of the war, of course, nor did he personally develop all of the techniques he used so effectively. He did, however, perfect many of them on the battlefield, and he was the first to make them all work in a comprehensive system, tightly integrated with the scheme of manoeuvre.[17]

Operational ineptitude

The force with the best tactical doctrine, organization, and leadership may win all or most of the battles, but that is no guarantee it will win the campaign or the war. The German Army in 1918 is an example of this conundrum. Although the Germans were the tactical masters of the World War I battlefields, they had some serious blind spots at the operational level. This is particularly ironic, considering that prior to 1914 the Germans devoted more time and effort to operational thinking than virtually any other army. Ludendorff, however, consistently discounted the operational art in favour of tactics.

The key distinction between the tactical and operational levels is depth, not only in space, but also in time. Extended depth in time almost always means sequential operations, where the results of one battle or campaign form the basis for the next, and the effects of each battle become cumulative. But the Germans misinterpreted sequential operations as being synonymous with attrition warfare, which was anathema to a country with limited resources and population, and with potential enemies on both its eastern and western borders. Rather than prolonged operations, German thinking focused on winning any war through a single, massive, and decisive battle – a rapid knock-out blow. German doctrine called it the Battle of Annihilation (*Vernichtungsschlacht*). This is precisely what they tried to achieve in 1914 with the Schlieffen Plan. But when it failed, they had no planned sequel ready to go, and they spent most of the next three years groping for a solution on the Western Front. The Germans again made the same basic mistake during the first half of 1918, except this time with significantly advanced tactics. The five great Ludendorff Offensives were not the components of a sequenced and coordinated campaign; they were five separate battles, each a reaction to the failure of the one previous.

During both world wars logistics was the German Army's Achilles heel. As operations extend into both space and time, the importance of logistical sustainment increases as the key operational enabler. But with German operational thinking focused on the conduct of quick and decisive battles conducted relatively close to the nation's borders, their logistics system was always a minimalist structure, and supply work was one of the lowest prestige assignments for a staff officer. Ironically, the Germans were the undisputed masters of using their rail networks for force deployments and troop movements – which came under the realm of operations rather than logistics. Nonetheless, they habitually underemphasized supply and sustainment.[18] They also made the same mistakes when looking at their enemies. The Germans in 1918 most likely did not have the manpower superiority to prevail against the Allies in a direct force-on-force clash – especially with thousands of fresh American troops pouring into the continent every month. But the Allies, especially the British, had a significant vulnerability that might have yielded better results if it, rather than the main British forces, had been the objective. The British logistics system was extremely vulnerable and very fragile. Almost all British supplies entered the continent through six ports, three in the north of their sector and three in the south. Almost everything from the ports moved by rail, and the rail network in the British sector was very shallow and overburdened. There were two key choke points in the rail network: the rail centre at Amiens in the south and the one at Hazebrouck in the north. Almost all British supplies had to travel through those two centres, and there were very few work-arounds. The British themselves were only too well aware of these vulnerabilities and had multiple contingency plans to withdraw from the continent in the event that either or both rail centres fell.[19]

The Germans apparently never seemed to grasp the significance of these two critical logistics nodes. Neither Amiens nor Hazebrouck were primary attack objectives in March and April 1918, although the Germans came within a few miles of taking both. In May and through to July 1918 German inattention to their own lines of communications led them into an operational trap of their own making north of the Marne. And finally, when the Allies went on the offensive from 18 July onwards, they focused not directly on the main forces of the German Army, but rather on its key rail lines and centres. In the end, the German Army in the field died from logistical strangulation more than anything else.

Once the German victory at Riga in September 1917 effectively knocked Russia out of the war, the Germans started transferring forces to the Western Front. By the beginning of 1918 they had transferred 35 divisions with their organic artillery, plus more than 1,000 heavy guns. That put 194 German divisions on the Western Front, giving them roughly an 18-division superiority over the Allies. But the window of slight superiority was closing rapidly. Time was running out for the Germans as more American forces, albeit ill-equipped and poorly trained, continued to arrive.

Senior German military leaders in the West were divided on the question as to how to continue the war in 1918. The two principal army group commanders, Kronprinzen Wilhelm and Rupprecht, were convinced that Germany could no longer win a military victory. They wanted to make peace at almost any cost. Ludendorff, however, was unwilling to make any concessions for a negotiated peace, especially if this meant giving up control of the Belgian coast. Belgian neutrality, however, was a non-negotiable strategic imperative for Britain. Others took the opposite approach. Rupprecht's own chief of staff, Generalleutnant Hermann von Kuhl; the chief of staff of the Fourth Army, defensive expert Colonel Fritz von Loßberg; and Generalmajor Max Hoffmann, who had succeeded Ludendorff as chief of staff on the Eastern Front, all saw no alternative but to attack. As Loßberg wrote to Ludendorff at the time, 'The war can be decided in our favour only through an offensive'.[20]

While the OHL continued to debate whether or not to attack, and if so where, none of Germany's political leaders had any say in the decision. On 19 September 1917 Ludendorff told the army group and army chiefs of staff that a major attack in the West was out of the question. But on October 23 the chief of the OHL Operations Section, Oberstleutnant Georg Wetzell, issued a strategic estimate of the situation which argued that the only viable strategy was 'to deliver an annihilating blow to the British before American aid can become effective'. Wetzell estimated that the offensive would require 30 divisions. (The plan eventually expanded to 67 divisions.) Ludendorff approved the concept almost immediately.[21]

On 25 October Rupprecht sent Ludendorff an estimate of the situation that argued against a major offensive and recommended only limited counter-attacks, possibly in the Armentières area. Ludendorff, however, had decided already that the Germans must attack in force, but he still had not decided where, how, or when. His key advisors were even more divided on those questions than on the primary question of whether to attack or not. On 11 November Ludendorff met at Rupprecht's headquarters in Mons with Wetzell, Kuhl, and Kronprinz Wilhelm's chief of staff, Generalmajor Friedrich von der Schulenberg. Typically, no commanders were present, only chiefs of staff and their operations officers. They failed to reach a decision on where and how to attack, and Ludendorff then ordered the respective army group planning staffs to develop a set of preliminary courses of action for later decision.[22]

Ludendorff held his second major planning conference with the army group chiefs of staff at Kreuznach on 27 December 1917. Again, no final decision was made, but Ludendorff said that the balance of forces in the West would be in Germany's favour by the end of February, making it possible to attack in March. At the conclusion of the conference, the OHL issued a directive to the army groups to plan in detail and start preparing a complete array of operations spanning almost the entire Western Front. The completed plans were due on 10 March 1918.[23]

As the planning progressed, two basic sets of options emerged as the most viable. An attack in the north directly against the British main strength was designated Operation *Georg*. An attack farther to the south, along the general line of the Somme River, was designated Operation *Michael*. The objective of *Michael* was to attack the southern wing of the British Army, separate the British and the French, and then pivot to the north and roll up the BEF from the right flank.

Ludendorff announced his final decision on 21 January 1918 during a conference at Avesnes. Summarizing the various options, Ludendorff ruled out Operation *Georg* as too dependent on the weather because of the condition of the ground in Flanders. A late spring in the area might delay the start of the attack until May, which was far too late for Ludendorff. Operation *Michael* on both sides of St Quentin was the decision.[24]

Ludendorff clearly intended to win the war with one decisive Vernichtungsschlacht. During the planning for Operation *Michael*, Ludendorff specifically rejected any notion of sequential operations and cumulative effects. On the tactical level, the Germans brought to bear the full weight of their new offensive doctrine. Entire divisions (designated *mobile Divisionen*) were trained as stormtroopers, and the artillery support was based on Bruchmüller's concepts. But Ludendorff continued to focus on tactical details to the point of micromanagement. When during one planning session Kronprinz Rupprecht prodded Ludendorff about the operational objective of a certain manoeuvre, the Erster Generalquartiermeister exploded: 'I can't abide the word operations! We'll just blow a hole in the middle and the rest will follow of its own accord.'[25]

Operation *Michael* was launched on 21 March 1918 and achieved the most spectacular tactical gains in World War I to that point; but it failed operationally. By 23 March the Second Army in the German centre, which was supposed to be the main effort, was making poor progress, and the Seventeenth Army on the right flank was lagging far behind. In the south, however, the Eighteenth Army was making unexpected progress. The original supporting mission of the Eighteenth Army was to screen the German left flank against French intervention in support of the BEF. Deciding for opportunism over consistency of purpose, Ludendorff shifted the main effort to the Eighteenth Army.

Reinforcing success rather than failure is generally a wise course of action at the tactical level. At the operational level, it is an extremely difficult thing to do because of the massive troop and logistical shifts required in a short span of time. More often than not, the result is self-inflicted disruption. Thus, Ludendorff completely changed the operational scheme

Operation *Michael*, March–April 1918

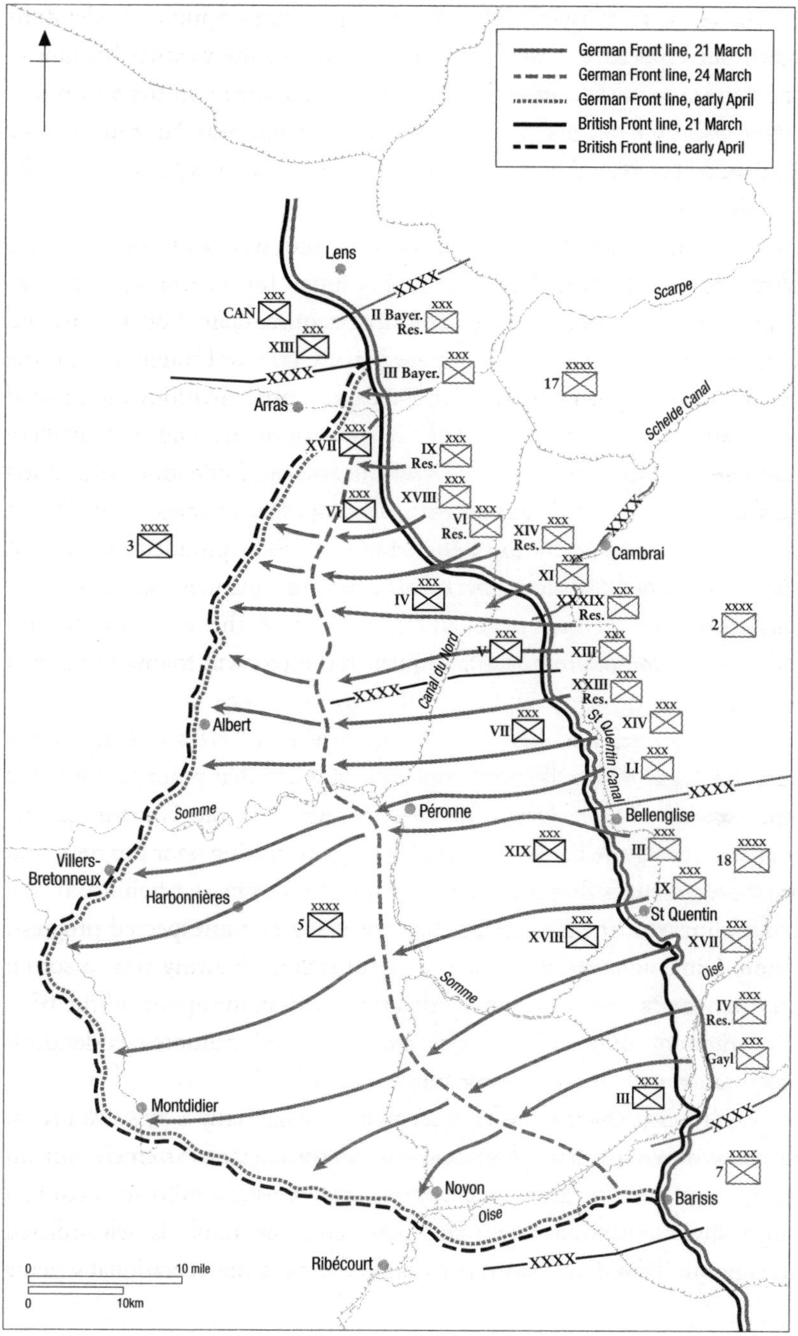
German Front line, 21 March
German Front line, 24 March
German Front line, early April
British Front line, 21 March
British Front line, early April
Lens
Scarpe
CAN
II Bayer. Res.
XIII
III Bayer.
17
Arras
Schelde Canal
XVII
IX Res.
XVIII
VI
VI Res.
XIV Res.
3
Cambrai
XI
IV
XXXIX Res.
2
Canal du Nord
V
XIII
XXIII Res.
XIV
Albert
VII
St Quentin Canal
LI
Somme
Péronne
Bellenglise
XIX
III
18
Villers-Bretonneux
IX
Harbonnières
St Quentin
5
XVIII
XVII
Oise
Somme
IV Res.
Gayl
III
Montdidier
7
Noyon
Barisis
Oise
Ribécourt
0
10 mile
0
10km

of manoeuvre in the middle of the battle. But the Allies had far more territorial depth to the Eighteenth Army's front, and there was no clear operational objective in that sector. In the end, the Eighteenth Army made the deepest advance, but all the Germans had to show for it was a much larger front line to hold. The Germans got to within ten miles of the vital British rail centre at Amiens, but they never took it.

When *Michael* failed, Ludendorff decided that the BEF was on the edge of collapse and he only had to hit them again, immediately and hard. He wanted to execute Operation *Georg*, but that proved impossible, because much of the force required for *Georg* had been committed for *Michael*. The OHL quickly cobbled together a much scaled-down version of *Georg*, and then launched Operation *Georgette* on 9 April 1918. As with *Michael* it initially made impressive tactical gains, but *Georgette* was too weak and culminated before it accomplished anything operationally significant. Although the vital Hazebrouck rail centre was not a specifically designated objective, it was in the path of the main attack, which got to within five miles of the city. But Ludendorff on 12 April again altered the entire scheme of manoeuvre, shifting the main effort north toward the line of the Flanders Hills.[26] By the time *Georgette* ended on 1 May the Germans had captured Mount Kemmel and had forced the British to pull back from the Passchendaele Ridge. But both operationally and strategically, *Georgette* was another failure. After almost six weeks of intensive fighting, the Germans had little to show for their two great offensives other than two very large salients that required far more manpower to defend than did the original starting lines. Moreover, the French had shifted a significant number of reserve divisions north to support the British, making another major assault in the north all but impossible.

Although *Michael* and *Georgette* had been complete failures, Ludendorff saw no alternative but to retain the initiative by attacking again. The British remained the primary strategic target, but because an attack in the north was now out of the question, Ludendorff decided to launch a major attack in the French sector with the specific objective of appearing to threaten Paris. That, he hoped, would draw the French reserves back down to the south to cover their capital. Once the northern sector was sufficiently weakened, the Germans would shift rapidly back to the north and deliver the final knock-out blow to the British. That final offensive would be called Operation *Hagen*.[27]

On 27 May 1918, the Germans launched their third massive offensive, advancing south from the Chemin des Dames. Long-standing popular opinion to the contrary, Paris was never the objective of this operation called *Blücher*. It was a feint. Its sole purpose was to draw the French reserves out of Flanders. But *Blücher* was a spectacular tactical success – too successful. The original objective line was the high ground south of the Vesle River. The Germans exceeded that objective on the first day. Rather than following the original plan, Ludendorff again fell victim to his own purely tactical success and ordered his forces to keep driving south toward the Marne River, but with no specifically designated objective. For the third time, he abandoned the scheme of manoeuvre in the middle of the battle, and it was a fatal mistake. It was another attack into the Allies' depth, with no strategically or operationally significant objective within operational reach. By the time *Blücher* culminated on the Marne River in early June, the Germans had yet another huge salient of ground to defend and hold. Furthermore, the anticipated number of Allied reserves had not been drawn off from the north, and the German forces were now hopelessly out of position to execute Operation *Hagen*.

The *Blücher* salient was an operational death trap. From west of Soissons to just west of Reims it was 35 miles wide. From the original line of departure behind the Chemins des Dames south to the Marne it was 27 miles deep. Most of the ridges, rivers, and roads in the salient ran east–west, but the German lines of communications primarily ran north–south. Only a single major rail line ran through the salient, along its northern base from Reims, to Soissons, to Compiègne. Major branch lines from each of those three cities ran north into German-held territory. But the Allies held both Reims and Compiègne, and the line from Soissons was blocked where it ran under the Chemin des Dames Ridge, because the Germans themselves had earlier blown up the tunnel at Vauxaillon. The Germans had 42 divisions inside the salient and no way to supply them except with horse-drawn wagons over small and winding roads.

Ludendorff had no other options at that point. He did not have the strength to attack anywhere else, and he could not afford to sit passively in the Marne salient while his forces slowly withered away logistically. On 7 June, the Germans launched Operation *Gneisenau* on the western shoulder of the salient, between Noyon and Montdidier. The objective was to shorten the line in that sector, and hopefully take Compiègne to open up the rail line.[28] Hastily prepared and under-resourced, *Gneisenau* was a complete failure even on the tactical level.

Still faced with the same strategic and operational problem, Ludendorff next ordered a huge two-pronged offensive to cut off Reims on the eastern shoulder of the salient. In addition to taking the rail centre and opening up the line, Ludendorff was certain that the threat to Reims would force the French to shift their reserves. A few days after cutting off Reims, the Germans would then rapidly shift back to the north and launch Operation *Hagen* against the BEF. The objective of this fifth offensive was Reims, not Paris. The main thrust line of the attack was away from the French capital, not toward it.[29]

Launched on 15 July 1918, Operation *Marneschutz-Reims* (the Second Battle of the Marne) was the last German offensive of the war. The attack got off to a bad start. Ludendorff nonetheless was determined to proceed with *Hagen*, and on 16 July much of the German heavy artillery in the Marne sector started moving north by rail. By 17 July Kronprinz Wilhelm's army group concluded that *Marneschutz-Reims* was a failure, but the heavy artillery kept moving north. The following day Ludendorff went to Kronprinz Rupprecht's headquarters for a final coordination meeting for *Hagen*. As he opened the meeting on the morning of 18 July, he dismissed all intelligence reports and rumours that the Allies were massing for a counter-attack in the Marne sector. Almost as soon as he finished making those comments, the reports of the Allies' attack started coming in.[30] From 18 July until the end of the war, the Germans were continually on the defensive.

Caught totally by surprise, the Germans were slowly and methodically pushed back into the salient created by Operation *Blücher*. By the end of the first week in August they had been pushed back to their starting point north of the Chemin des Dames. More significantly, by the third day of the Allied counter-offensive, Ludendorff had to face the fact that they would never be able to launch Operation *Hagen*. On 20 July Ludendorff summoned Loßberg, the German Army's defensive expert, to the OHL for consultations. Loßberg immediately recommended that the Germans conduct a phased and general withdrawal to the Siegfried Position, the starting line for the 1918 offensives. From there they could entrench to conduct a protracted defence, which in turn would buy time for a negotiated peace while the Germans were still in a position to bargain from some strength. Lossberg also recommended the immediate start of construction on the Antwerp–Meuse deep defensive position, which was still only a line on an OHL map. It was sound advice, but Ludendorff could not bring himself to abandon all the territorial gains the Germans had won since 21 March.[31] He continually dithered. The OHL only ordered the withdrawal to the Siegfried Position on 2 September, and the start of construction on the Antwerp–Meuse Position on 16 October. Both decisions came far too late.

The Allies now had the initiative. After pushing the Germans back north of the Chemin des Dames Ridge and eliminating the threats to their own rail centres at Reims and Compiègne, they followed up on 8 August with a successful surprise attack to the west of Amiens, eliminating the threat to that key rail centre. A shocked Ludendorff called 8 August 1918 'the black day of the German Army'. Loßberg did not agree with him. In his own memoirs Loßberg wrote: 'The exact turning point of the war did not come on 8 August 1918, but rather on 18 July 1918', the day that the French had launched their offensive against the German troops in the Marne sector.[32]

When Général de Division Ferdinand Foch was appointed Supreme Allied Commander in the spring of 1918, one of his most important priorities was the securing of the Allies' own vital rail lines.[33] The counter-attacks of 18 July and 8 August accomplished that. He now turned all his attention to his enemy's rail system. The Germans had six great trunk line railways running from Germany to the Western Front.

Behind the German lines facing the British in the north the two key rail junctions were Berlaimont and Roulers.[34] Running north–south between Metz and Liège, the main German rear-most lateral line had a capacity of

300 trains per day. A roughly parallel lateral line closer to the front ran from Metz through Mézières to Valenciennes. In the south, Mézières was the major choke-point closest to the French and American lines. Foch considered Mézières the jugular of the German forward logistical network.[35] If the Germans lost the four-tracked line south of Mézières, the entire German position in northern and north-eastern France would be threatened. That would leave the lines in the north running through Liège as the sole remaining withdrawal route for the German Army. It is precisely this concentration on the enemy's rail system that marks the key difference in the operational approaches of Ludendorff and Foch in 1918, and the main reason that Foch out-generaled Ludendorff.

The Allied General Offensive of 1918 consisted of a set of four converging attacks across the Western Front, with each vectoring toward a key rail objective.[36] Starting on 26 September, the US First Army and French Fourth Army in the Meuse–Argonne sector attacked in the direction of Mézières. The following day the British First and Third armies attacked in the general direction of Cambrai. On 28 September, the Flanders Army Group in the north attacked between the sea and the Lys River toward Liège. And on 29 September the British Fourth Army supported by the French First Army attacked in the direction of Busigny.

From that point on, the war was decided by the Allies' superior numbers. Under severe pressure all along the Western Front, and with their vital rail centres under constant threat, the Germans had very little flexibility in shifting their strategic reserve divisions, even though they had the nominal advantage of operating on interior lines. Ludendorff himself only made the situation worse. From 18 July until his final relief on 26 October, he was a psychological wreck, wildly swinging between the extreme poles of optimistic euphoria and defeatist depression. On 28 September, he suffered a nervous breakdown. Despite continuous prodding from Rupprecht, Kuhl, Loßberg and others, the Erster Generalquartiermeister procrastinated in taking the bold defensive measures necessary to stabilize the situation. By the time Generalleutnant Wilhelm Groener replaced Ludendorff on 26 October, there was little left for him to do but organize the withdrawal to Germany following the Armistice on 11 November.

Strategic bankruptcy

The Germans entered the war with a weak civil government that grew even weaker as the war progressed. In the process, the military leadership increasingly dominated the political leadership on all matters of strategy. One consequence of Germany's traditional fear of a protracted war of attrition was that its military thinking focused all too often on the short rather than on the long term. Consequently, strategic decisions often were made without adequate consideration of the second and third order effects. One such mistake was the decision to invade France through Belgium in 1914. There was little doubt that such an action would bring Great Britain into the war, but far too many military leaders disregarded the consequences. The Germans committed the same fundamental error once again in 1917, when the resumption of unrestricted submarine warfare, combined with the ham-fisted Zimmermann Telegram to Mexico, brought America into the war on the side of the Entente. Germany's military leaders assumed that any American army could not possibly be a significant force on the European battlefields until well into 1919. The German Navy's leadership assured Hindenburg and Ludendorff that Britain would be starved into submission long before that; and besides, not a single troopship carrying American soldiers would reach European waters without being sent to the bottom. Both assumptions proved erroneous, and German soldiers paid the price on the Western Front battlefields of 1918.

Despite the specific intention of the Schlieffen Plan, Germany from 1914 through 1917 had been fighting a two-front war, the fear of German military planners since at least the days of Frederick the Great. When Russia finally was knocked out of the war that September, the strategic problem eased somewhat, but only temporarily. American entry into the war brought the problem back in another dimension.

By the end of 1917 all of Germany's coalition partners were weak and growing weaker, requiring Germany to prop up especially Austria-Hungary. Three years of war had wrecked the German economy. The British maritime blockade brought the German civilian population to the verge of mass starvation during the infamous Turnip Winter (*Steckrübenwinter*) of

1916/17. Some historians have suggested that the Royal Navy played the decisive role in the war by completely breaking the morale of the German nation. Richard Holmes, however, has argued that although the blockade increased Germany's growing sense of desperation, it no more broke the country's morale than strategic bombing did during World War II.[37]

When Ludendorff and the army group chiefs of staff met at Mons on 11 November 1917, Germany's strategic situation was bleak at best. The combined populations of the four Central Powers (Germany, Austria-Hungary, Bulgaria, and Turkey) was 144 million. The combined population of Entente powers was 690 million, including colonies. The German Army was drawing on the country's last manpower reserves, and planning to call up the conscription class of 1919 a year early. The economic disparities were even greater than the population differential – even before America entered the war. In 1913 the American economy was larger than that of France, Britain, and Germany combined – minus their colonies. The United States produced more steel than all three combined. The Allies' total oil requirement in 1918 was 9.5 million tons, 6.6 million of which America supplied. The United States that year also supplied enough foodstuffs to feed 18 million Frenchmen for a year.[38]

Political chaos

The weak and insecure personality of Kaiser Wilhelm II was not the least of Germany's internal political problems. By 1918 Hindenburg had pretty much replaced the Kaiser in the minds of most Germans as the 'Father Figure of the Nation'. Initially, Wilhelm II liked to associate himself with Hindenburg, lending credence to the myth that the Kaiser was still Germany's Supreme Warlord. But by 1917 Wilhelm had come to view the Generalfeldmarschall's popularity with the people as a direct threat to his own position. The Kaiser also loathed Ludendorff as an upstart bourgeoisie. Ludendorff only rates one passing mention in the Kaiser's memoirs.[39] By 1918 the Kaiser had come to fear Hindenburg, who ironically remained loyal to the end to the office of the Kaiser and the idea of the monarchy, although he thought very little of Wilhelm personally.

Hindenburg and Ludendorff had a contentious and increasingly hostile relationship with Germany's wartime chancellors: Theobald von Bethmann Hollweg; Georg Michaelis; Georg Graf von Hertling; and finally, Prinz Max von Baden. As relations with Bethmann Hollweg continued to deteriorate, Ludendorff went so far as to order German commanders not to talk to the Chancellor during his visit to the front in June 1917.[40] The final straw came the following month when the Reichstag started debating the Peace Resolution. Hindenburg and Ludendorff forced Bethmann Hollweg to resign by threatening the Kaiser with their own resignations. Wilhelm completely gave in to The Duo because he feared the consequences. The Kaiser, with the backing of the OHL, appointed Michaelis as Chancellor, but the Reichstag nonetheless passed the Peace Resolution a couple of days later. Michaelis was forced out of office three months later and replaced by the ageing Hertling.

Supported by Hindenburg, Ludendorff increasingly meddled in political affairs, ultimately leading to what some historians have called the 'Silent Dictatorship'. Ludendorff, however, refused to consider the idea of an outright military dictatorship, despite at one point having the chancellorship almost thrust upon him.[41] Nonetheless, by the final months of the war Ludendorff held almost total political power in his hands, marginalizing the Kaiser, the Chancellor, and the Reichstag. Disingenuously, Ludendorff later quibbled in his memoirs: 'Unfortunately, the government did not state clearly and emphatically in public that it, and not General Ludendorff, was governing.'[42] In the attempt to exercise increasingly tighter control over all aspects of Germany's wartime economy and society, Ludendorff and his close circle at the OHL forced through three successive political measures that not only failed to achieve their stated intent, but actually caused greater damage and inefficiency, and lost effort at the time when Germany could afford it least. Throughout 1918 the combined effects of these three measures progressively corroded the German Army from within.

One of the first initiatives of the new Hindenburg–Ludendorff command team was to try to bring Germany's chaotic system of war production under control. The Hindenburg Programme, initiated on 31 August 1916, mandated a 100 per cent increase in ammunition and trench mortar production, a 300 per cent increase in artillery and machine guns, and substantial increases in aircraft and anti-aircraft artillery by the spring of 1917. Paradoxically, the programme also required the culling out of the labour force for military service. The Hindenburg Programme virtually ended civil government in Germany. Most industrial leaders enthusiastically supported the programme, but they also complained that there was not enough civilian manpower to carry it out. In response, Ludendorff ordered a phased release of skilled workers from active duty, which by the winter of 1916–17 reduced the front-line strength of the Field Army by some 125,000 troops. One of the second order effects was the reduction in the average strength of a front-line infantry battalion from 750 to 713.[43]

The Hindenburg Programme made worse almost every problem it was supposed to fix. The OHL itself had neither the control structures nor the expertise to manage it. The direction of the majority of the industrial resources towards conventional artillery and machine-gun production closed off any possibilities for developing the tank and anti-tank weapons. The programme even failed to rationalize the production of the focused weapons. In 1914 German factories were producing 14 different models of artillery. By April 1917 they were producing 77 models; and by January 1918, 100 different models.

The OHL quickly came to the conclusion that they needed a dedicated organization to manage the Hindenburg Programme, to include the control of all raw materials, labour, and munitions. On 1 November 1916, the *Allgemeines Kriegsamt* (General War Office) was established, headed by Generalleutnant Wilhelm Groener, who a little less than two years later would succeed Ludendorff as Erster Generalquartiermeister. Ludendorff originally intended that the Allgemeines Kriegsamt would be a direct subordinate of OHL. In one of the few bureaucratic battles he lost, the General War Office came under the Ministry of War. But Ludendorff retaliated by engineering the sacking of General Adolf Wild von Hohenborn, the Minister of War and a staunch critic of The Duo. Hohenborn was replaced by General Hermann von Stein, who was one of Ludendorff's allies.[44] The Allgemeines Kriegsamt, however, was nothing more than another layer on top of Germany's already ossified bureaucratic structure. As a strictly Prussian institution, it had no real authority over the war ministries of Bavaria, Saxony, and Württemberg, which all established their own independent General War Offices. The three kingdoms sent liaison missions to the Prussian General War Office, only adding more bureaucratic disorder.[45]

Ludendorff increasingly became obsessed with the problem of the 'cohesion of the people'. Under his muddled concept of Total War (*Totaler Krieg*) he believed that all of Germany's physical, economic, political, and psychological resources had to be directly subordinated to the war effort. In December 1916, he forced through the Reichstag the Auxiliary Service Law (*Hilfsdienstgesetz*), which made every German male between the ages of 17 and 60 liable for some form of involuntary wartime service. Ludendorff initially wanted to include females. Groener talked him out of it, but by June 1918 Ludendorff was again raising that issue. In October 1917 Ludendorff again tightened the screw of the Silent Dictatorship a notch, when he told Chancellor Bethmann Hollweg that the freedom of movement of civilian workers had to be restricted. The legal mechanism for that action was the Prussian State of Siege Law of 1851 (*Belagerungszustandsgesetz*).

The combined effects of all of these ill-fated socio-political-economic initiatives probably did as least as much to weaken the German Army of 1918 as did Haig's 'wearing-out battle'. The number of soldiers freed for duty at the front by the law never equalled the number released from the front to support the Hindenburg Programme. By the start of 1918 the war had strained Germany's archaic, rigid, and authoritarian political, social, and economic systems to the point where there was almost nothing left to support the army in the field. The virtual dictatorship of Germany was a function for which both Hindenburg and Ludendorff had absolutely no competence. In fact, German officers of the period generally prided themselves on their detachment from all things political and their contempt for politicians. Nor did The Duo have the time for something like that. Every hour they devoted to wrestling with Germany's intractable domestic and diplomatic problems detracted accordingly from their ability to plan and direct military operations.

Fed up with what they perceived as the lack of support from Chancellor Hertling, The Duo finally pushed him out of office. He was replaced on

3 October 1918 by Prinz Max von Baden, who right from the start had no intention of letting himself be bullied by Ludendorff. The friction between the two flared-up almost immediately, and Prinz Max told the Kaiser that there was no longer room at the head of the German government for both himself and Ludendorff. The Erster Generalquartiermeister's increasingly erratic behaviour proved his final undoing. The Kaiser summoned Hindenburg and Ludendorff to Berlin on 25 October, and the following day he informed Ludendorff that his resignation would be accepted. In his memoirs, however, Ludendorff claims he offered his resignation first. The following day Groener replaced Ludendorff at the OHL, but he never developed the bond and the level of trust that his predecessor had had with Hindenburg.

After Ludendorff's departure, Groener tried to hold the pieces together at the OHL. The Germans then had some 80,000 wounded troops to be evacuated back to Germany; at the same time their useable rail lines were being cut off by the Allies one at a time. The political situation in Germany only served to complicate matters at the OHL. As the pressures to abdicate mounted on the weak and vacillating Kaiser, he decided to run away from the problems. Abandoning Berlin, Wilhelm and his entourage of royal camp followers arrived unannounced at OHL headquarters in Spa on 30 October. The Kaiser announced his intention to 'lead his troops' personally, which was the last thing that Hindenburg and Groener needed to deal with.

By 7 November strikes and organized violence were rampant everywhere back in Germany. Bavaria was on the verge of breaking away from the Reich and declaring itself a free state (*Freistaat Bayern*). Believing that only he could restore order, the Kaiser ordered Groener to prepare the operations orders for the Supreme Warlord to march back into the homeland at the head of his troops. But Groener understood only too well that the troops back in Germany had already gone over to the revolution in large numbers, and that the army in the field would not follow the Kaiser against them. The Supreme Warlord apparently never stopped to consider what the Allied armies would be doing in the meantime. Groener was able to convince the vacillating Hindenburg of the reality of the situation, but the old Generalfeldmarschall refused to tell his king and emperor that the army was no longer loyal to him. Hindenburg passed the buck to Groener.[46]

The usually implacable Hindenburg was completely unnerved when he and Groener met with Wilhelm and his aides on the morning of 9 November. Hindenburg asked the Kaiser for permission to resign; but Wilhelm refused. Hindenburg then ordered Groener to give the Kaiser the blunt truth, that it was the considered opinion of the senior officers at the OHL that the army would not follow him back to Germany, and that any attempt to use military force would result in full-scale civil war. Ironically, it was Groener who, during the years of the Weimar Republic, was held up as the scapegoat for Hindenburg's inability to carry out his responsibility to the nation. As the Generalfeldmarschall blurted out to a group of nationalist political leaders after the war, 'You all blame me, but you should blame Groener.'[47]

Once faced with stark reality, the Kaiser then tried to convince himself that he could abdicate as German emperor but still retain the crown of the Kingdom of Prussia. He also announced that he would transfer formal command of the German armies to Hindenburg. But the train of history had already left the station, leaving the House of Hohenzollern behind on the platform. Shortly after 1400hrs that day the government of Chancellor Prinz Max in Berlin announced the Kaiser's abdication, without even consulting Wilhelm.[48] Prinz Max then resigned and was replaced as Chancellor by Friedrich Ebert, the leader of the Social Democratic Party (SPD).

On the morning of 10 November, the Kaiser boarded his private train and left for exile in neutral Holland, never to return to Germany. One day short of one year after the Mons Conference, the 500-year old Hohenzollern Dynasty of Brandenburg–Prussia collapsed. Wilhelm did not see Hindenburg that day, and he never did issue a formal abdication.

Hindenburg retired in July 1919, but he had one more final word to deliver on the German Army, a word that would have fatal implications for the course of German and world history. That November he appeared before a special investigative committee of the Reichstag, where he testified that the German Army had not been defeated on the battlefield. Invoking the story of the hero Siegfried, who in the *Nibelungenlied* had been struck down by the treacherous Hagen, the Field Marshal insisted that the German Army too had been 'stabbed in the back' by a cabal of Jews, Marxists, pacifists, and socialists in the homeland. Thus, he unwittingly gave credibility to the myth that the nationalists, especially Hitler and the Nazis, would use to destroy the Weimar Republic, and ultimately lead Germany into World War II.

CHAPTER 3

THE FRENCH ARMY IN 1918

Dr David Murphy

Late in 1915 and 1916, Allied military and political leaders had met to discuss strategic plans for the next year. In a broad sense, they came up with what was essentially the same plan both times. In the spring and summer of the following year, there would be a massive effort on the Western Front, while ancillary attacks would be developed in Italy and Salonika. These plans also envisaged a large-scale offensive by the Russians in the East. The logic was simple: the combined pressure on all fronts would force a collapse of the Central Powers. The Allied leaders of late 1917, however, faced an operational situation that was totally changed. Their combined offensives of that year had not brought a decisive victory, and the failed Nivelle and 3rd Ypres offensives had been particularly damaging. The French and Italian armies had come close to collapse, and Russia had effectively dropped out of the war. For France, these developments were extremely worrying. The French Army ended 1917 very badly damaged and largely unfit for major offensive action. Général de Divison Phillipe Pétain, commander of the French field armies, had faced a daunting task in keeping the army intact and in a position to defend France. France now faced the prospect of being confronted with large numbers of German troops freed up from the Eastern Front, while at the same time trying to rebuild and retrain the army in the hope of engaging in decisive action in 1918.[1]

The strategic context

As the Germans and the Russians began discussing an armistice in late 1917, the French Army began developing plans to face a fresh German offensive. Pétain's headquarters staff formed strategies based around a number of likely scenarios. They decided that a massive German operation was equally possible in either Italy or Salonika. It was more likely, however, that an offensive would develop on the Western Front with the aim of knocking France and Britain out of the war. Within this scenario, it was recognized that the German Army might invade via neutral Switzerland. In a series of meetings of the French War Committee, Pétain emphasized the need to adopt a defensive stance and, above all, to keep casualties low. By this point in the war, the French Army had suffered around one million fatal casualties. The army was, like the British and Italian armies, simply running out of men.

There were various means employed to try to mitigate this reality. In 1917, the army structure had been reformed and the number of men in divisions reduced. Infantry companies were reduced from 250 to 200 men and, as a result, a division now numbered 13,000 rather than 15,000 men. So, while the number of divisions remained high, they were now smaller.[2]

Manpower predictions anticipated a need for 110,000 new recruits each month up to late 1918, but, even with this influx of new troops, the French Army would still fall short. In the summer of 1916, the army had stood at over 2.2 million men, but the Verdun battles and actions of 1917 had resulted in a casualty rate of around 40,000 men per month. Faced with these rapidly dwindling numbers, staff officers at the Grand Quartier Général (GQG) and also Pétain's headquarters developed assessments of how these losses would impact on the army.[3]

A report of October 1917 predicted that the French Army would suffer over 920,000 casualties between October 1917 and October 1918.[4] These troops needed to be replaced, and there was also a further need for additional troops to expand the artillery, military aviation, tank units, engineers etc. The final total for troops required stood at over one million men but the expectation was that only around 750,000 could be supplied. In this calculation, the expected shortfall stood at at least 250,000, while other estimates cited 320,000 as a more accurate assessment of the deficit. In early 1918, Pétain himself estimated that the requirement would be for over one million new troops during 1918 but that only 836,000 could be expected. This would leave a deficit of around 25 divisions, Pétain argued, leaving him with just 77 divisions in the field to face a growing number of German divisions.[5] Ultimately, the figure of 750,000 potential new troops proved to be realistic, and French commanders argued over how this shortfall could be mitigated. Divisions would be dissolved and their remaining manpower incorporated into the remaining divisions, but sourcing further manpower continued to be a problem. Russia had provided men in the past, but this was no longer an option. There was discussion of bringing thousands of Chinese soldiers to serve in France, but this came to nothing. Polish and Czech units were formed based on recruitment among prisoners of war (POWs). Within France, a number of further strategies were employed. The draft of 1919 was called up early in April 1918, and men released for industrial work and also some reservists were called back to the army. The high casualty rates of 1918 ensured that manpower remained a key issue for the rest of the war, and this was only mitigated by the gradual deployment of American troops to the front line.

Command

The discussions on the manpower issue also highlighted French difficulties at senior command level and facilitated a power-play between the two key personalities. Even at this late stage of the war, the French had no overall strategic-level commander; Général de Division Ferdinand Foch occupied the position of Chief of Staff, while Pétain was commander of the field armies. French politicians had come to recognize the dangers of giving generals total control of all military forces and strategy. While this was seen as a democratic safeguard, the existence of the positions of both chief of staff and land commander effectively created a situation where unity of command, in the French Army's case, was not possible. The question of strategic level command was further complicated by the appointment of Foch as the French military representative on the *Conseil superieur de la guerre* (Supreme War Council) in November 1917. This council was composed of the French and British premiers and war ministers and also military representatives. The British representative was General Sir Henry Wilson (later Chief of the Imperial General Staff). As the Supreme War Council was tasked with the overall direction of war strategy, this encouraged Foch in his efforts to be appointed as the Allied Supreme Commander. The institution of a special committee in January to organize an Allied general reserve also facilitated Foch's wider plans. Yet his rise to the position was by no means certain.[6]

In reality, the French Premier, Georges Clemenceau, was extremely hesitant about the Supreme Commander concept and also about Foch, whom he personally disliked, as a potential candidate. Foch had been a candidate to succeed Maréchal Joseph Joffre in December 1916 but had been passed over due to his devout Catholicism and, perhaps more importantly, his strategic ideas. These discussions also played out in the midst of a wider and more complex political and strategic backdrop. France, having fielded the largest force on the Western Front for the entire war thus far, would see its dominance reduced in 1918. Clemenceau realized this but wanted France to direct the overall war strategy. The French Premier needed to carefully pick the right general to shape strategic discussions within the Supreme War Council for the remainder of the war.

Within the French general staff itself there was further disunity. The other dominant figure was Pétain, whose opinion on future strategy differed totally to Foch's ideas. While Foch still entertained the idea of offensive action, or rather counter-offensive action, Pétain was wedded to concepts of defence. He had experienced the fragility of the French Army throughout 1917 and was convinced that a defensive posture should be adopted, even relinquishing terrain during the German assault that he was sure was coming. Pétain's opinion was simple: when the Germans attacked, the French Army should utilize a defence-in-depth system that consisted of a lightly-held forward zone and then a battle zone with heavier defences and with reserves deployed locally. Then they would use concentrated firepower to kill the Germans in large numbers as they attacked. It was a simple but brutal and potentially very effective defensive concept.[7]

Throughout the early months of 1918, Foch and Pétain clashed at a number of successive meetings and on a number of issues. They differed fundamentally on strategy, how reserves were to be controlled and deployed, and how the American forces would eventually be deployed along the front. Field Marshal Haig agreed with Pétain and disagreed with Foch's proposals to form a centralized Allied reserve. Both Haig and Pétain were slow to release divisions for Foch's planned central reserve as they both tried to complete their defences in expectation of a German offensive. Pétain had maintained Nivelle's infantry and artillery reserve formations after his departure but was now reluctant to split them up and not have forces to hand for his own use. The central reserve idea was shelved following a stormy meeting of the Supreme War Council in London on 14–15 March, as a German attack seemed imminent. Pétain and Haig convinced both Clemenceau and the British Prime Minister David Lloyd George that they needed to retain control over their reserve formations. At that moment, it seemed that Foch would not emerge as the Allied Supreme Commander. However, Lloyd George and Clemenceau were increasingly convinced that the position was required, and this discussion became urgent after the outbreak of the German Spring Offensive on 21 March. In the days that followed there was huge pressure to resolve the issue.

In the final analysis, Pétain's utterances at various meetings were pessimistic, and he informed Clemenceau that the Germans would beat the British and then the French in turn. Such discussions focused the French Premier's mind. Whatever Foch's failings, he was charming, energetic, organized and focused on winning the war. At the Doullens Conference on 26 March, Foch was tasked with coordinating the Allied armies, forming a central reserve and developing plans to plug the growing gap between the French Army and the British Fifth Army. Clemenceau and Lord Milner, the British War Secretary, signed an agreement charging Foch with 'coordinating the action of the Allied armies on the Western Front'. His powers were extended to that of Supreme Allied Commander at a conference at Beauvais on 3 April and he was later granted the title of 'generalissimo'. In May, Foch was granted authority over the Italian Front. To outward appearances, the Allied forces now had unity of command for the first time in the war, but the cooperation required to make this system work was slow in coming.[8]

The command relationship between Foch, Haig and General Pershing will be discussed in due course, but it is worth pointing out that within the French command system there was a frequent lack of cooperation. Pétain was not averse to placing his own interpretation on some of Foch's later instructions, and on occasion he ignored them completely. The same can be said for more subordinate generals, such as Général de Divisions Marie-Eugène Debeney and Émile Fayolle. In reality, Foch was administrating a system of 'mission command'; he could issue general directions and identify objectives, but local commanders formulated the operational plans based on their own local assets. While there was much room for disagreement, the character of the French command was totally changed compared to that of 1914. The majority of poor commanders had, by this time, been removed. Those who remained were largely highly professional and fully immersed in the brutal realities of early 20th-century warfare. To take one example, Général de Division Charles Mangin had displayed a ruthless efficiency throughout the war but had fallen from grace following the failure of the Nivelle Offensive in 1917. By 1918 he had returned to favour and his Tenth Army would play a crucial role at the Second Battle of the Marne in July and August. Professional, highly organized and totally dispassionate, Mangin was perhaps typical of the generals of 1918. He had no illusions about the glory of war and knew that victory would only come following a hard and bloody slog. He later summed up the reality of modern warfare with 'whatever you do, you lose a lot of men'.[9]

Excellent staff work would also be a feature of 1918, and in this both Foch and Pétain were aided by very capable chiefs of staff. Foch was ably seconded by Général de Division Maxime Weygand, a brilliant organizer who also possessed an uncanny ability to anticipate his chief's intentions. This pairing would form a highly competent team for the remainder of the war and Foch's headquarters at Beauvais became a model of efficiency. Equally important within Foch's headquarter system was his artillery chief, Général de Division Pierre Henri Desticker, who anticipated artillery requirements at army group level. In his turn, Pétain was aided by a succession of chiefs of operations, Général de Divisions Maurice de Barescut, Julien Dufieux, and Duval, all of whom were highly capable, as was his artillery expert, Général de Division Edmond Buat. By 1918, there had been significant improvements in French Army staff work in general. Improved communications allowed for forces to operate more effectively and good use was made of air force couriers to convey orders more quickly.[10] The French intelligence system was also now highly efficient. All of these systems would be greatly challenged by the German operations in 1918.[11]

Strategy and doctrine

The pressing question for senior French commanders was just how to utilize the remaining French forces in the field. As the Germans and Russians progressed with their armistice arrangements in December 1917, it became increasingly obvious that considerable German forces would soon be free to act on the Western Front. In an operational sense, how should the French respond to an attack on the Western Front or an offensive through Switzerland?

What was certain was that something was about to happen. French intelligence was tracking the build-up of German divisions through radio intercepts and the interrogation of prisoners and deserters. The numbers were extremely concerning. In December 1917 they identified 151 German divisions on the Western Front. By February this had risen to 171, and in mid-March they had positively identified 188, with a possibility of further divisions incoming.[12]

A series of War Committee meetings were held in early December 1917 and, perhaps predictably, Pétain advocated a 'tactic of waiting'.[13] This would allow the French and their British allies to develop their defensive systems while awaiting the arrival of the Americans in numbers. Pétain also recognized the need to build up reserves in men and materiel and sought greater levels of cooperation with Haig and the BEF. In terms of defensive doctrine, Pétain was essentially proposing the adoption of German defence-in-depth methods. This was a system that the French had acquired bitter experience of in 1917. On the ground, he advocated multiple lines of defence, and also felt that the front line should be lightly held in order to avoid casualties in preliminary German bombardments. A crucial sticking point for Pétain's fellow generals, and also politicians, was his willingness to yield territory and withdraw in order to absorb an offensive and draw the enemy onto French reserves.

Foch, on the other hand, advocated offensive action and the two senior commanders clashed at a series of meetings of the Supreme War Council in the early months of 1918. Foch felt that the Germans might launch another attritional battle similar to Verdun, and in such an event, the Allied needed to be in the position to launch a counter-offensive to draw German forces away. There was some strategic logic in this and Foch cited the role the Somme offensive had played in reducing German pressure at Verdun. However, the language that Foch used to communicate this principle was alarmingly reminiscent of 1914 as he urged French commanders to 'seize every opportunity to impose their will on the adversary by resuming as soon as possible the offensive – the only means of obtaining victory'.[14] Foch communicated these concepts in a series of memoranda, and Pétain's marginal comments in his surviving copies are reflective of the vastly different mindsets of the two senior generals. Beside Foch's comments regarding the need for 'counter-offensives for disengagement', Pétain had grimly commented 'With what?'.

Both Foch and Pétain tried to enlist the support of Clemenceau and Lloyd George and also their British military counterparts, especially Field Marshal Haig. Foch would gradually qualify his remarks and emphasize that he was suggesting counter-offensive rather than offensive action. However, by February the possibility of the Allies mounting a major offensive had receded, and this was expressed in 'Collective Note No.12', which envisaged a defensive posture in the West with offensive action occurring against the Turks on the Egypt–Palestine front. There was also increased discussion about returning British and French troops from Italy, but Foch's proposals to form a central reserve would eventually come to nought. This was covered by 'Collective Note No.14', and on 6 February, Foch requested that Haig release nine to ten divisions and Pétain 13 to14, while a further seven would be returned from Italy. Both Haig and Pétain simply refused to comply, citing their need to retain control over their own reserves for immediate use. The extension of the BEF's responsibility for a further 54 kilometres of front also took considerable negotiation.[15]

The incorporation of American troops into the Allied order of battle also resulted in considerable debate. General Pershing obviously wanted to field American troops as a coherent and single formation. He has been much criticized for this, but, in his defence, the performance of British and French generals up to this point in the war would not have been an encouragement for him to place his troops under their command. But the American troops needed to be equipped and trained. Having initially resisted the amalgamation idea, Pershing agreed to release American regiments to serve for a month with French divisions in order to gain the necessary combat experience. Some African-American regiments were released to French command on an indefinite basis. Discussion continued as to the best method of incorporating this new manpower throughout January and February, with Pétain pushing for more integration with French forces, while Pershing saw this as for training purposes only. While Pétain felt that this insistence for an autonomous American force would mean that they would not be ready until 1919, the German Spring Offensive accelerated American deployment, and the US Army played a crucial role throughout 1918. The American forces needed to be supplied with heavy equipment, and this was provided by the French, who contributed aircraft, tanks, artillery and machine guns.

So, despite the appearance of a move towards unity of command, the respective commanders had significantly difficult views on how to respond to the expected German offensive, and various issues occupied their time in early 1918. Considering this level of debate, how did they communicate intent and doctrine to the troops on the ground? Foch essentially communicated to his subordinate commanders through memoranda, and these addressed broad strategic principles. Pétain and his fellow army commanders issued general orders and communiques, and while these often were general tactical statements and were aimed at encouraging the troops, they also contain specific tactical directions. For instance, Pétain discussed the use of tanks and infantry tactics in his communications in the run up to, and during, the Spring Offensive. In doctrinal terms, all branches of the service had developed their methods considerably, and these were communicated to the troops in a series of pamphlets and manuals, which appeared in increasing frequency during 1918. There was also much more emphasis on realistic training and rehearsal, and by 1918 there had been a total shift in the methods of all branches. In terms of artillery, the French had shown increasing proficiency in artillery fires and were more effective at coordinating suppressive barrages, creeping barrages and counter-battery fire. From 1917, there had also been an increased use of machine guns in the suppressive fire mode. For the infantry, there had been a total shift in tactical emphasis. In 1914, the main tactical unit was the battalion, due to the attacking ethos of the army. By 1918, the main tactical unit was the half-platoon: two sections of infantrymen armed with light machine guns and grenades and trained to use the ground to cover their advance. Although most of the cavalry had been dismounted to serve in the infantry role, some were retrained and served in armoured car units.

Perhaps the big question that remained regarding the effectiveness of the French Army concerned morale. The senior commanders were well aware that the army had been badly shaken in 1917, and postal censors were alert for signs of discontent. Trench newspapers also gave a good indication of the sentiment of the troops and were monitored by regimental officers and the GQC. The cumulative effect of years of war was found to be taking its toll, yet surprisingly morale was considered to be good on the eve of the Spring Offensive and remained high during its initial phases. French soldiers were extremely sensitive to issues on the home front and expressed anger at the treatment of industrial strikers, especially women workers. There was also contempt for politicians and industrialists who were seen as prolonging the war. The familiar criticism of British soldiers and generals was also expressed and the poor performance of the BEF in the early phase of the offensive was frequently mentioned by disgruntled French soldiers. Despite the huge efforts of the BEF in 1917 and the resultant casualties, many French soldiers seemed to think that the British were not doing their share of the fighting. Soldiers' letters and newspapers also noted the special transport arrangements made for the American troops; the US troops were provided with lorries while the French soldiers slogged along the road on foot. This was a subject of much discontent. Yet such feelings did not result in a major breakdown once the Spring Offensive started. Although there were some serious lapses in discipline and morale and some units did break and flee under the German onslaught, in general, the average *poilu* seems to have decided to persevere and to fight it through to the end.[16]

Weapons: artillery and tanks

The potential war plans for 1918 would be carried out by a vastly changed French army. Following the French collapse in 1917, Pétain had instigated a range of weapon production programmes while also expanding existing ones. The primary focus was on artillery, and by 1918 the artillery arm had been expanded to a huge degree. During the course of the war, there had been a shift in emphasis from light field artillery to guns in the medium and heavy range. The classic French 75mm field gun had been shown to have limited utility in trench warfare due to its flat trajectory and the small size of its shell. The army of 1914 had around 300 guns in total. In 1918 alone, over 5,700 guns were added to the artillery strength. These included 720 155mm field guns, 1,980 155mm howitzers, 144 120mm guns, and 576 105mm guns. There had been a total shift in artillery doctrine due to the growing realisation that heavier guns with a greater ability to provide indirect fire and creeping barrages were what was required. There was also an increase in the numbers of mortars with more tubes in the 45mm, 60mm, and 150mm ranges. The smaller calibre mortars (45mm and 60mm) could be operated by infantry teams, and alongside an increase in the numbers of the portable 37mm cannon, the introduction of these weapons increased the firepower within infantry formations to a significant degree.[17]

The venerable 75mm still played a role, however, and at the beginning of the year there remained around 140 batteries of these field guns. Some modified guns had a range of 11 kilometres, and in the opening phases of the Spring Offensive they proved particularly effective against attacking formations. Alongside this overall upgrade of the artillery potential of the army, further efforts were made to increase the effectiveness of the artillery. During the course of 1918, increasingly sophisticated artillery methods were introduced, and a range of creeping barrages, flash barrages, counter-battery fires, interdiction, and suppressive barrages were organized to facilitate operations. This necessitated a significant increase in time devoted to training and rehearsal and there was an increase in the number of courses run at the various artillery schools.

Communications and coordination had always proved problematic, but by 1918 over 350,000 field telephones and 30,000 wireless sets had been introduced. These enlarged the communications nexus across the Western Front and greatly facilitated the implementation of complex artillery plans and cooperation between the branches in general. Staff work had also become more effective, and each formation had a dedicated staff to coordinate the efforts of its associated artillery. There was an increased emphasis placed on aerial reconnaissance and cooperation. There was also a significant refocusing on the use of France's dwindling manpower. In 1914, the French Army had been predominantly an infantry army, with artillery strength standing at around 420,000. This represented around 20 per cent of the army. By 1918, the artillery branch stood at over one million troops, representing almost 40 per cent of the entire French Army.

The French tank force was also a major focus in campaign plans for 1918. The French tank programme had its origins in 1915 and was initially driven by one visionary, Colonel Jean-Baptiste Estienne. In late 1915 permission was granted to begin tank development, but for a series of reasons, this had resulted in two actual tank programmes. One programme produced the Schneider, a six-man tank armed with a shortened 75mm gun. The initial procurement programme of January 1916 ordered 400 of these machines, but numerous setbacks delayed production and the first units were not equipped with these tanks until late 1916. The second French tank programme produced the St Chamond, and design and production problems also delayed the delivery of this model in large numbers until late 1916. Ultimately, both programmes were competing for production capacity, and this delayed the introduction of these '*chars d'assaut*'.[18] Both suffered from being underpowered and had poor armour protection; the Schneider in particular had to undergo a process of armour modification. In terms of armament there were further problems due to the limited traverse of the main weapon. Also, due to their short track length, both tanks had a limited trench crossing capability, and it became practice to send combat engineers to accompany these tanks on operations in order to fill in trenches and create routes for them to cross. Classed as *Artillerie spéciale*, they were organized in 'groups' of 16 tanks. Their technical difficulties led to considering concerns regarding their deployment, as they had limited use as a breakthrough weapon. Their success in 1917 was very limited and usually accompanied by high casualties. Yet both the Schneider and the St Chamond continued in service in 1918 and needed to be factored into future plans.

The significant shift in French tank plans came with the development and production of the Renault FT-17 tank. The FT-17 was a lighter, two-man design with greater cross-country capabilities and, significantly, a turret capable of rotating through 360 degrees. By 1918, orders for the FT-17 were increasingly removing the Schneider and the St Chamond tanks from the production processes, and by that summer there were over 500 in service. By the end of the war, there would be around 3,000. Armed with either a 37mm cannon or an 8mm Hotchkiss machine gun, the FT-17s served well as mobile gun platforms and could suppress enemy machine guns and also clear routes through barbed wire. Estienne envisaged 'bee swarm' tactics, while Pétain advocated using Schneiders and St Chamonds to clear routes through the wire, leaving the FT-17s to suppress the enemy and exploit. By 1918, eight tank regiments had been formed, each with a group of Schneiders or St Chamonds and three battalions of FT-17s. Apart from their offensive potential, all of the tanks could play a significant role in defence and in several cases played a key part in shutting down German attacks during the Spring Offensive. However, the formations of large tanks were still dogged with high casualty rates in operations during the summer of 1918.[19]

As the French Army moved further towards developing a system of what we would refer to today as 'combined arms warfare', increasing emphasis was placed on airpower. The *Aéronautique Militaire* (the French air service) had expanded to a considerable degree during 1917, and in 1918 further numbers of more modern aircraft came into service. There were increasing numbers of the SPAD XIII, operating in the fighter role. Highly regarded by French pilots for its speed (over 130mph) and durability, by the end of the war over 8,5000 had been constructed. While they were also supplied in quantity to the US and Italian air forces, the majority of these went to the 74 French fighter squadrons. The two-seater Breguet XIV also played a significant role in air operations during 1918. Produced in large numbers it was the first aircraft to use a predominantly metal construction, which gave it considerable durability in combat. The Breguet would equip 71 squadrons by war's end. Officially classed as a bomber and reconnaissance aircraft, further versions were developed for long-range photo reconnaissance, as floatplanes, air ambulances and also as single-seat bombers. In addition, French pilots realized that the Breguet's construction, performance and armament allowed it to be used more aggressively in air fighting and ground attack. The Aéronautique Militaire also retained some aircraft that were classed as 'obsolescent', such as the outdated Voisin and Cauldron bombers. These could still be used in night bombing operations due to the comparative lack of fighter opposition.

All of these aircraft would play a key role in stopping the Spring Offensive and would facilitate offensive operations later in 1918 flying in the fighter, reconnaissance, bomber, and ground-attack roles. The latter function would be key in assisting French Army operations, and squadrons equipped with SPADs, Breguet, Samsons and other aircraft would be called in to serve in this role. This function brought with it an increased emphasis on ground-to-air signalling, and various visual signalling methods were used to focus aircraft on ground targets. Unlike the Germans, who had developed specific aircraft for ground attack, such as the Halberstadt CL.II and the Junkers J 1, the French did not introduce aircraft designed specifically for this role but preferred to task existing fighter and bomber squadrons with ground-attack operations. In some cases, aircraft were modified with armour protection, but this practice was not widespread.

By the autumn of 1918, the French air commander, Colonel Charles Duval, had essentially reorganized the force into an independent air force under centralized command. The service had a division and brigade format, which included 66 fighter squadrons and 19 day bomber squadrons. However, some squadrons remained under local command.

Despite having been challenged operationally and in morale terms during 1917, the French Army of 1918 had undergone a considerable transformation. While numbers of every type of equipment had increased and France's war industry got into full swing, there was an emphasis on new weapon designs in terms of artillery, tanks, and aircraft that reflected the changing nature of the battlefield. These new weapons and the associated doctrine would be tested in the early months of 1918 before the final offensive operations could begin.

Defensive operations

While French intelligence had noted the arrival of German divisions from the Eastern Front throughout the early months of 1918, German operational security ensured that the location of the planned attack remained a mystery. Haig focused on the Albert–Arras area, while French commanders concentrated on the Champagne front, in the area around Reims. Neither army, therefore, had its troops in the right location when the Spring Offensive began.

The opening blows of Operation *Michael* on 21 March fell mainly on the British Fifth Army and the right flank of Third Army. It would prove to be a disastrous day for the BEF, with over 50,000 killed, wounded, missing, and POW. Under this formidable German onslaught, the British troops began to yield ground and an alarming gap developed between Fifth and Third Armies. In this worsening situation, Pétain was faced with urgent requests for reinforcement, while also monitoring German activity in the Champagne area. Haig later criticized Pétain for the slowness with which he released reserves, but it can be shown that once he realized the attack represented the main German effort, French reserve divisions were sent to plug the gap. By 23 March, Pétain had ordered 12 divisions to move to the assistance of the BEF, and these were supplemented by a further 13 by 26 March. Pétain had, therefore, already begun sending reserve divisions before Haig had sent his original requests for help.[20] There is no doubt, however, that Pétain tried to control these formations tightly, as he feared a BEF collapse and retreat towards Dieppe, which would have to be covered by French forces. While Pétain had resisted Foch's plan for a central reserve, he had accumulated an impressive reserve contingent for his own purposes. This included five corps (39 infantry divisions, two cavalry divisions), 35 regiments of heavy artillery, and ten regiments of 75mm cannon. These were spread between the French Northern and Eastern Army Groups, while two infantry divisions were sent to bolster the Belgian Army. In pure artillery numbers, Pétain had access to over 6,500 light cannon and over 5,800 heavy and 417 long-range pieces. He had furthermore accumulated a large supply of reserve ammunition, including large supplies of gas shells. The artillery would play a key role in shutting down the German attacks, with 75mm guns engaging German forces over open sights, which had not been seen since 1914.[21] In the course of these actions, the 75mm guns alone would fire over four million shells.

Despite these accumulations of troops and equipment, the end of March 1918 developed into a desperate fight. For the French, it initially fell mainly to regiments from Third Army to respond to Operation *Michael* and the immediate crisis. In this situation, French commanders were aware of the desperate shortage of cavalry; the majority of French cavalry had been dismounted by this stage the war, while many of the remaining horsed units were countering strikes across France. Infantry units were fed rapidly into the line, many arriving without artillery or reserve ammunition, in a desperate attempt to stop the German advance. Casualties were high, and the force of the blow that had fallen on the BEF became immediately apparent to the French troops:

By the 24 March the Germans had crossed the Somme, and the following day both Bapaume and Noyon fell before the French could stop the German advance. In a 24-hour period, the Germans launched 15 further attacks on Général de Division Fayolle's Reserve Army Group, consisting of First, Third, and Sixth Armies. Pétain's instructions were not to become separated from the BEF, but while Pétain was assisting the British and the Belgians, he was also aware that the operational situation could develop and threaten Paris. His immediate priority became shielding Paris and stopping the Germans from pushing through Noyon and Montdidier. On 24 March, he and Haig had discussed the possibility of the two Allied armies losing contact, and it seemed that the situation would develop into two battles – the BEF fighting to control the Channel ports, while the French defended Paris.

It was against the backdrop of this worsening tactical situation that Foch was appointed as Allied Coordinator (26 March) and then Allied Supreme Commander (3 April). He immediately ordered 'Lose not another metre of ground'.[22] However, the atmosphere in Paris was less than confident and was not helped by the fact that the capital was now coming under shellfire from the 'Paris Gun'. This impressive 'supergun' began firing on Paris on 21 March, its shells travelling 130 kilometres and entering the stratosphere before falling on the city. By the time that Allied advances stopped its activity in August, the Paris Gun had fired between 320 and 360 shells (exact figures remain uncertain) and had killed 250 people. The worst single episode came on 29 March when a shell hit a packed Paris church during a Good Friday service, killing 91 people. This shelling, combined with Gotha bomber raids and news of the German advance, caused public panic and an exodus from the city, the likes of which had not been seen since 1914.[23]

After further withdrawals from the Somme and the loss of Montdidier by the French, Operation *Michael* began to run out of steam in early April. Troop exhaustion and supply difficulties had slowed down the German advance. These difficulties were compounded by Allied counter-attacks, including a major operation by Général de Division Denis Auguste Duchêne's Sixth Army. Having failed to reinforce his advantage over the BEF, Ludendorff called off the offensive on 5 April. The potential of French air power in ground operations also was fully realized. Capitaine René Fonck, the leading French air ace, later wrote of a major operation on 26 March designed to interdict German units on the ground:

I don't know who came up with this brilliant idea or how the High Command was persuaded to accept, but from the most distant points of the front, one squadron after another rushed to the danger zone. The roar of aircraft engines was louder than had ever been heard before. We flew so low that we were almost on the tips of their bayonets and our machine-guns rattled at point-blank range on the dense mass of troops below. The bombers were more heavily laden [and] dropped their missiles on the columns and convoys of marching troops. Our attack spooked the horses; they threw their harness into the ditches, creating [a scene] of unutterable confusion.[24]

As German pressure eased, Foch and his staff began planning for a counter-offensive on 9 April. On the same day Ludendorff launched Operation *Georgette* with 36 divisions of General Ferdinand von Quast's Sixth and General Friedrick Sixt von Arnim's Fourth Armies. This hammer blow fell on the BEF (First Army and associated Portuguese divisions) and was aimed at attacking the approaches to the Channel ports. Forces crumbled under the weight of the German attack, prompting Haig's 'backs to the wall' communiqué of 11 April. Yet after initial successes and pushing well into Allied lines, this offensive too began to stall by 18 April. Counter-attacks by the British Second Army and a five-division detachment of the French Armée du Nord began to stop the German advance. However, the loss of the strategically important Mount Kemmel by French troops on 25–26 April came as a serious blow. In this sector, three French divisions had moved into line on 18 April, with the 28th Division holding Kemmel itself. There were indications of a potential German attack, and the French were aware that the elite Bavarian Alpine Corps had moved into the line opposite, but the 28th Division had previously suffered serious casualties and could not withstand the attack. Following an intense German barrage that included large quantities of gas shells and an aerial bombardment by over 90 aircraft, the French lost the hill during the morning of 26 April. The loss of this important observation point with seriously criticized by British commanders and troops and tainted the relationship between Britain and France for some time.[25]

Bolstered by a further eight infantry divisions and two cavalry corps from Fayolle's reserve army group, the French line was stabilized by the time Ludendorff shut down Operation *Georgette* on 29 April. By this time the Germans had suffered over 340,000 casualties – many of these were from assault units, and were irreplaceable. Despite this, Ludendorff launched another operation, *Blücher-Yorck*, in the hope of drawing troops out of Flanders to allow him to restart Operation *Michael*. While Foch was expecting a further attack north of the Somme, Ludendorff turned his attention to the Champagne area, in particular the Chemin des Dames, and on 27 May opened an attack on a 45-kilometre front between Reims and Soissons using Kronprinz Rupprecht's Army Group (General Max von Boehn's Seventh Army and General Oskar von Hutier's Eighth Army). In total this force deployed 43 divisions, 4,000 guns, and a number of tanks. Facing them was Duchêne's Sixth Army and three British divisions that had been moved from Flanders and Picardy as they were deemed to be in an exhausted state. Following an intense artillery barrage, which again used large amounts of chemical shells, the Germans made good progress, threatening Reims and crossing the Marne. Duchêne has since been criticized for packing his troops into the front lines, leaving them susceptible to attack and also denying himself reserves. In his defence, he knew that his troops would not favour withdrawing from territory so hard-won in the spring offensive of 1917.

German barrages resulted in high casualties, and in the panic to withdraw, the French failed to destroy vital bridges over the Aisne. Stiff resistance before Reims and the transfer of troops from Picardy slowed the German advance as Pétain scrambled to re-deploy divisions to meet this new threat. BEF divisions were not available due to an expected attack in Flanders but two American divisions put in a spirited attack at Château-Thierry.[26] On 3 June, Ludendorff shut down Seventh Army's attack in the face of mounting casualties. On the French side, Général de Division Mangin became the unlikely hero of the hour. Having been returned to command by the Clemenceau government, Mangin put in a successful counter-attack on 12 June along the River Matz with six French divisions and also American troops. By 14 June, *Blucher-York* had also been halted.

Concurrently with *Blucher-York*, Ludendorff had launched Operation *Gneisenau* on 9 June in an effort to exploit tactical success at that time. French intelligence had warned of this attack, and the opening bombardment was less effective.[27] Nevertheless, the Germans made an impressive gain across a 37-kilometre to a depth of 14 kilometres. A surprise French counter-attack started by Mangin at Compiègne without preliminary bombardment stopped the advance, and the operation was called off on 12 June.[28]

The final offensive, Operation *Marneschutz-Reims*, followed a now familiar pattern. Launched by First, Seventh, and Ninth Armies on 16 July, this was effectively Germany's 'last throw of the dice'. Interestingly, this operation was also referred to as the *Friedensturm* or 'peace offensive'. Again, this was aimed at drawing reserves from Flanders, but German forces were now much-depleted due to casualties and the first outbreaks of Spanish flu among the army. The lack of fuel supplies restricted the activities of the German *Luftstreitkräfte* (the German air service), and French intelligence confirmed that the attack would take place in the Champagne area. In preparation, Général de Division Paul Maistre's Army Group Centre (Fourth, Fifth, Sixth and Seventh Armies) was reinforced with further American divisions. Despite these preparations, and due to the deployment of French troops into the front lines, the German attack inflicted casualties and broke through between the French Sixth and Seventh Armies. French divisions and some Italian divisions fell back before a series of defensive actions at Nanteuil-Pourcy and east of Reims stopped the German advance.[29]

These mid-July defensive actions and counter-attacks formed the preliminary stages of the Second Battle of the Marne. The next phase of operations would see the initiative pass to the Allies and began a phase of offensives that would continue to the Armistice in November. By the end of the Spring Offensive, the Germans had suffered over 680,000 casualties killed, wounded, missing and POW. They had made significant territorial gains but had not achieved decision. Furthermore, the German Army was now exhausted and exposed in some dangerous salients. Allied losses had not been insubstantial. The total figure numbered over 430,000 French and 418,000 British troops. Yet, despite being so hard-pressed, their transport systems had managed to move

The Second Battle of the Marne, July – August 1918

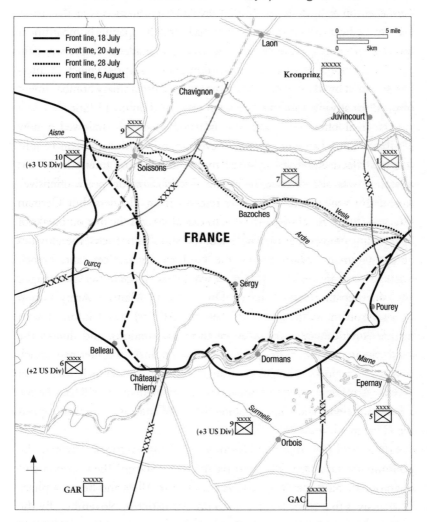

troops, under pressure, to meet attacks as they emerged. Regarding materiel, it was apparent that the Allied now had the advantage in terms of numbers and quality, and operational methods, communications and intelligence and were producing success. The growing American force was increasing in proficiency. These factors would prove decisive in the coming months. While France would play a lesser role in terms of manpower as the war neared its end, its industry would prove essential for equipping the US Army.

Offensive operations

While the last of the German offensives was still in the process of being shut down, the French began a series of counter-attacks. Foch had long awaited the chance to respond to a German attack with a major operation. By the end of Operation *Marneschutz-Reims*, the Germans had established a bridgehead over the Marne some 12 kilometres in length and 7 kilometres deep. Foch determined to destroy this bridgehead, and this would feed into a series of counter-attacks that is now referred to as the Second Battle of the Marne. This phase marked the beginning of the major French operations that would continue to advance into German-held territory until the end of the war. In the literature of World War I, the battle of Amiens is usually cited as the beginning of the 'Hundred Days' phase of operations that ended the war, but this is an Anglo-centric viewpoint. For France, this phase began earlier with the Second Battle of the Marne.[30]

Having absorbed and repulsed the final phases of the German attacks, Foch ordered the start of the counter-offensive for 18 July. Due to his recent successes, Mangin was chosen to spearhead the attack with his Tenth Army, which incorporated two American and two BEF divisions. Mangin also had 345 Renault tanks and 500 aircraft at his disposal and the focus of his attack fell between the Aisne and the Ourcg rivers. Général de Division Jean-Marie Degoutte's Sixth Army would attack between the Ourcq and the Marne with nine divisions, 145 tanks, and 350 aircraft. Artillery provision for both attacks numbered over 3,000 guns, and this combination of focused and highly controlled artillery fires and the use of armour and air support would be the preferred model for the rest of the war. Also, while a creeping barrage was used, there was no preliminary bombardment.

Progress was good but came with high losses; units in Mangin's Tenth Army suffered up to 75 per cent casualties. Also, supporting and flanking attacks were not organized in a timely fashion to exploit the German withdrawal. For their part, the Germans withdrew in tolerably good order, using rear-guard units and gas bombardments to slow the Allied advance. Nevertheless, the battle was hailed as a great Allied victory. A considerable foothold had been gained in the German lines and over 29,000 Germans had been taken prisoner with 793 guns and 3,000 machine guns captured. In the aftermath, Foch was made a Marshal of France on 7 August.

Foch now turned his mind to coordinating a series of offensives that could follow up on this initial success. In a format that he would return to, he envisaged launching massive pincher attacks with the British as the northern (left) arm of the attack and the Americans forming the southern (right) arm. The French Army would attack the central zone in any such attack. Haig's plan to focus on Amiens fitted into Foch's overall scheme, and he released elements of Général de Division Debeney's French First and Général de Division Georges Louis Humbert's Third Armies to take part in the battle of Amiens (8–12 August).[31] This decisive action saw the BEF, with French and American support, create a significant gap in the German lines in a model combined arms action. This resulted in panic among the German defenders and Ludendorff, recognising this as the 'black day of the German Army', suffered a nervous collapse. The Allies now had a system that they could repeat with success until the final defeat of Germany.

There then followed a serious of Allied offensives throughout August. Mangin attacked between the Aisne and Oise on 20 August, followed by attacks by combined BEF and French forces on the northern end of the Hindenburg Line on 23 and 26 August. Later in the month, Mangin forced the Germans out of their winter positions north of the Aisne, while the Americans (III Corps) and II Corps Coloniale began the St Mihiel offensive on 12 September.[32] This major American operation was a success, although German forces had managed to withdraw. Pershing pressed for further exploitation, but this was refused by Foch. On 26 September a massive French–American offensive began in the Argonne Forest with 31 French and 15 American divisions, 4,000 guns and 700 tanks. Despite this huge concentration of force, they advanced just a few kilometres due to the dogged German defence and their own logistical problems. However, Foch's strategy of keeping the Germans under pressure was followed and resulted in British attacks at Cambrai (Canal du Nord) and St Quentin on 27 and 29 September respectively. On 30 September, the French began a further major offensive on the Aisne. The combination of negative reports pouring into German headquarters resulted in a further nervous collapse for Ludendorff.

While German resistance continued, pressure now mounted on all fronts, with offensives in the West, Italy, and against the Bulgarians. There were increasing reports of unrest in Germany, and, on 30 September, Bulgaria signed an armistice. This was followed by a combined German and Austro-Hungarian appeal to President Wilson for an armistice on 4 October. Perhaps unsurprisingly, with the final defeat of the Central Powers in the offing, Allied politicians and commanders refused to countenance an armistice on conditional terms.

Thereafter, operations gathered pace. BEF forces and the French First Army attacked and breached the Hindenburg Line, near Cambrai, on 8 October. This was a decisive moment in the war and resulted in a general German withdrawal along the entire line. Despite growing logistical difficulties and the impact of influenza on the Allied armies, the French and British forces maintained the pressure throughout October. A combined French–American attack cleared the Argonne by 10 October, and the Belgians and BEF had cleared Lille by 14 October. In the south, Mangin took Laon while Général de Division Adolphe Guillaumat's Fourth Army cleared the Chemin des Dames and pushed for Mazières. By the end of the month, the BEF and Belgian forces had cleared the Channel ports and advanced to the Scheldt.

For the final phase of the war, the French maintained the offensive. This was later criticized due to the casualties incurred this late in the war but it marked a determination on the part of Foch and his subordinate commanders to continue to push the Germans from French soil. The French Army would remain in action right up until the Armistice. While the Americans remained on the offensive on the Meuse and the Sedan area, and the British advanced to the Sambre-Oise Canal, the French mounted a series of attacks on improvised German positions north of the Aisne. Day by day, they continued to reclaim patches of French territory in series of small, but bitterly fought actions. On 3 November,

Austro-Hungarian representatives signed an armistice. Thereafter, the German collapse accelerated and with naval personnel in a state of mutiny at home, Germany submitted armistice terms to the allied Supreme War Council on 5 November. On 8 November, Armistice negotiations opened at Compiègne.

Maréchal Foch, as Allied Supreme Commander, headed the Allied delegation for these negotiations. He had already formulated plans for further military action in 1919 and he adopted a hard line at the talks in the knowledge that the Germans faced total military annihilation if hostilities continued. Foch met the German representatives, led by Matthias Erzberger, only twice – at an initial meeting and then to oversee the signing process at the end. While the other members of the Allied staff met with the German delegation, Foch continued to direct military operations.[33]

The terms of the Armistice demanded the Germans withdraw from all occupied territory and effectively called for the demilitarisation of Germany. The articles for the cessation of hostilities called for the surrender of the materiel of war – artillery, machine guns, planes, naval vessels, tanks, trains, etc., while the Rhineland was to be occupied. If the conditions were not met, war would be renewed. Despite registering a formal protest at the terms, the Germans were in no position to negotiate, the Kaiser having abdicated on 9 November while Hindenburg sent a message urging them to sign regardless of the conditions. Signed at 5am (French time) on the morning of 11 November, the armistice would come into effect at 11am.

French troops remained in contact with German forces and on the offensive until this deadline. At Vrigne-sur-Meuse, a river-crossing operation was begun late on the evening of 10 November, consisting of around 700 troops. Of these, around 90 soldiers were killed in the attack. The last French soldier believed to have been killed was Soldat Augustin Trebuchon, of the 415th Infantry regiment. A regimental runner, he was killed while bringing forward a message that read 'muster at 11.30 for food'. In the nearby cemetery, Trebuchon's grave cross records his date of death as 10 November, as indeed do the crosses of all those killed in this action on the last day of the war.[34]

In the final analysis, despite their often violent disagreements, the divergent strategic visions of Pétain and Foch both had a part to play during the campaigns of 1918. Pétain's dogged tenacity in defence, his ruthless use of firepower, and his ability to shift reserves speedily had preserved France during the onslaught of the Spring Offensive. In Foch's turn, his ability to organize and synchronize a series of simultaneous operations had allowed the French Army to keep the pressure on Germany during the final months of the war.

Legacy – the 'poverty of victory'

Technically speaking, France emerged from World War I as one of the victorious nations. At the war's end and in 1919, there were a series of victory parades in Paris and other French cities. Having survived this devastating conflict, there was much to celebrate, but in many ways this was an empty celebration, as France had emerged from the war a fundamentally damaged nation. In human terms, France had suffered over 1.3 million fatal casualties with a further 3.2 million wounded. Of the wounded, over a million of them had been permanently disabled, many of them classed as being '*mutilée*' – mutilated by their injuries.[35] Such losses had created over 700,000 war widows and innumerable children who would now grow up without fathers. In sheer demographic terms the war had killed off a whole French generation, if not generations. The effects would be felt for the remainder of the century. While there was a large number of marriages in 1919 as troops were demobilized and returned home, marriage rates and birth rates would decrease in the 1920s and 1930s. During the 1920s, many small rural towns were predominantly populated by women, children and old people, and some eventually became deserted ghost towns as the remaining population moved away.

In physical terms, a huge scar stretched across the surface of France, marking the battlefields of 1914 to 1918. It would take many years to repair towns and infrastructure and remove the debris of war. Many locations, Verdun in particular, still have cratered landscapes as a reminder of the war and un-exploded ordnance still shows up each year across France.

In terms of commemoration, travellers in France will notice the war memorials in every town and village. Also, even the smallest city or rural church seems to have a depressingly long list of names of local men who did not return from the war. The national place of remembrance for World War I is the *tombe du Soldat inconnu* at the Arc de Triomphe in Paris, but commemorations take place across the country every Armistice Day. The recent centenaries have seen a number of major commemorations at significant locations and a number of new memorials.

Sadly, France also has many large cemeteries for its war dead, several with huge ossuaries containing the interned remains of many soldiers. During the 1920s, the French government allowed families to repatriate the bodies of their loved ones to their home towns. While this was a great comfort to the relatives, it also ensured that the grieving process would continue through the 1920s.

By the time World War I ended, France was also already committed to further campaigns abroad. Many soldiers who had expected demobilisation were instead sent to Russia as part of the Allied intervention against the Bolsheviks, or to Salonika as Bulgaria descended into chaos. The successful campaign in the Middle East had brought France control of Syria and Lebanon, and sporadic fighting continued in Syria during the 1920s. Alternatively, a French soldier could be sent to North Africa or to join the occupation forces in Germany. Finally, industrial and political unrest in France was a feature of the 1920s and occasionally necessitated military intervention. While the world war may have ended, conflict at home and abroad would be a feature of the 1920s.

Many of the main personalities on the French side, such as Foch and Pétain, have undergone phases of evaluation since the war's end. Foch, who died in 1929, had a reputation that waxed and waned in the post-war years, but today he is largely remembered as an efficient and effective commander who possessed a considerable strategic facility.[36] Pétain, on the other hand, was unfortunate not to die until 1951. Although having been recognized as the 'saviour of France' on at least two occasions and elevated to the rank of Marshal of France, his association with the Vichy regime during World War II permanently damaged his reputation. As a result, it is difficult to objectively see Pétain in his World War I context.

For French officers and men, the war had proved to be a dangerous and harrowing experience. By the end of the war, the French Army had fielded almost nine million soldiers. The worst fatalities occurred, as might be expected, among the infantry at 22.6 per cent. The war that emerged in 1914 was entirely unexpected by the French commanders and its character continually evolved. Any soldier who survived the whole war would have recognized that the war of 1918 was fundamentally different to the methods employed at its onset. Like the British, the French had developed the tank and had, by 1918, developed a combined arms doctrine of warfare. In the inter-war years, against a backdrop of turbulent domestic and international politics, the hard-won lessons of World War I were largely forgotten. France's successful methods of 1918 were ignored, and from the late 1920s, the Maginot Line emerged as the embodiment of the new defensive strategy. While the Germans returned to the concept of mobile warfare, France would dig in and defend against any future German attack through a strategy of fortification. It was a lesson that was based on the battle of Verdun and the experiences of 1916 rather than the operational lessons of 1918. The bitter defeat of 1940 would prove that it was the wrong lesson.

CHAPTER 4

THE BRITISH ARMY IN 1918

Dr Jonathan Boff

1918 was the most successful year in the history of the British Army.[1] Never before or since has it exerted such strategic weight and advanced Great Britain's foreign policy aims so completely. It helped defeat the Central Powers, ending World War I, and ensured Britain had a crucial seat at the Paris peace conference, all the while safeguarding and reinforcing her imperial position around the globe. The focus of this chapter is resolutely on the Western Front, where the army, for the first and last time in its history, played a leading role in the defeat of the main enemy in the primary theatre of operations. British soldiers and airmen, with their American, Belgian, and French allies, fought a series of battles which broke the spine of the German Army, shattered the nerve of its leadership, and so helped to force Germany to beg for peace. They did so by achieving an extremely rare operational feat. Three times in the 20th century British forces have managed to make the extremely difficult transition from theatre-level defence to successful offence. In 1942, Eighth Army held Rommel in the Western Desert before Montgomery led it over to victory with his attack at the second battle of El Alamein. In 1944, Slim's Fourteenth Army withstood ferocious Japanese attacks at Imphal and Kohima and then launched the counter-offensive which cleared Burma. Both were brave and well-handled campaigns, but neither matches the achievement of Sir Douglas Haig's British Expeditionary Force (BEF) during March–November 1918 in either scale or significance. First, in the spring, the British, retreating, fought a series of heavy German assaults to a standstill. Then, during the late summer and autumn, the BEF, alongside its allies, went on the attack, overrunning multiple successive lines of defence and liberating swathes of Belgium and France until the German High Command was left with no option but to request an armistice.

This chapter explores what underpinned this rare military achievement. It comprises four sections. After first outlining the situation around New Year 1918, it will secondly analyse the defensive fighting undertaken by the BEF in the spring. A third section looks in detail at the autumn offensive, often known as the 'Hundred Days' campaign. A recurring theme is how the historical record has been distorted in particular by the German official historians between the wars and then by the Cold War concerns of Western soldiers and military analysts. The chapter concludes with a brief case study of the 46th Division attack on the Hindenburg Line which demonstrates the capability of the British Army by late 1918. It argues that the BEF owed its victory to a variety of factors. These included improved tactical and operational skill, resilient morale, and improved leadership at every level, but also, crucially, weaker opposition from a German army which had run out of men, materiel and ideas.

Background

The BEF's successes in 1918 were especially remarkable because it had begun the year in something very close to crisis after a year of disappointments. The battle of Arras (9 April–16 May 1917) had opened with promise but the successes of the first day could not be exploited and the fighting soon degenerated into a bloody attritional slog. Innovative use of artillery and mines had brought success at

Messines (7 June 1917) but the follow-up offensive had taken weeks to set up. When the British did finally open the Third Battle of Ypres, on 31 July, progress in critical sectors was much less than hoped and poor weather soon slowed the advance to a crawl. A series of limited-objective attacks, carried out according to the operational method known as 'bite and hold' in September and early October, got the offensive moving again but progress was slow and casualties high, even before rain and mud turned the battlefield into a swamp. It took the Canadians until November to get onto higher ground and seize the ruins of Passchendaele village. In London, Prime Minister David Lloyd George was growing increasingly uneasy at Haig's conduct of the campaign. 1917 would claim over 800,000 British casualties and, despite the Commander-in-Chief's repeated protestations that the German Army was on the brink of collapse, Lloyd George could detect little sign that it was closer to breakdown than it had been a year earlier.[2] Any optimism raised by the initial success of an attack using massed tanks and innovative artillery tactics at Cambrai on 20 November soon evaporated as exploitation once more failed and Haig repeated his old mistake of repeatedly throwing tired troops against strengthening defences.[3] Worse, a neatly executed German counter-attack caught the British off balance and recaptured much of the ground lost. As the generals involved scrambled to pass the buck, Lloyd George decided to purge the army command. Politically, Haig was untouchable and there were in any case no obvious candidates to do much better. His staff at General Headquarters (GHQ) in France, however, was another matter and several of Haig's closest subordinates, including the head of intelligence, the Quartermaster General, and even the Chief of Staff, Launcelot Kiggell, were replaced. At the War Office, the place of Sir William Robertson as Chief of the Imperial General Staff and main military advisor to the government was taken by Sir Henry Wilson.

These personnel changes were designed to send Haig a message, which Lloyd George now underlined by refusing to agree to GHQ's demands for another 650,000 men to fill gaps in the establishment and allow for foreseeable wastage. Lloyd George thought he could see better uses for manpower at home in the factories, in other theatres, or indeed in the future, than in another probably futile slaughter under Haig on the Western Front in 1918. Indeed, any use seemed better than that. GHQ received only 100,000 men. In consequence, the War Office decided to reorganize the BEF and broke up a handful of infantry and cavalry divisions. More importantly, the old 'square' infantry brigades were restructured on a 'triangular' basis, dropping from four battalions each to just three. Divisions which had been used to fighting with 12 infantry battalions now disposed of only nine. Some 134 battalions were disbanded, amalgamated, or converted. In principle, the idea of reducing reliance on manpower in favour of firepower was sensible. However, the timing of the reorganization, which disrupted almost every formation in the BEF as units were transferred in or out, proved unfortunate. The process was not complete until 4 March.

A second consequence of the manpower shortage was that no thought was given to any kind of pre-emptive attack to disrupt the German offensives planned for the spring. Allied intelligence knew that the German *Oberste Heeresleitung* (OHL) under General Ludendorff and Generalfeldmarschall Hindenburg were shifting divisions from the Eastern Front to France in the wake of the October Revolution in Russia almost at once, although GHQ was still underestimating overall German strength well into 1918.[4] By mid-February 1918, analysis was pointing to an attack in March, possibly against the right centre of the British line in the sector held by the Third and Fifth armies between Arras and St Quentin. By 19 March, the BEF correctly expected an imminent attack against its right, stretching all the way down to La Fère. The British had only recently taken over this area from the French, leaving them holding 30 per cent more of the line and so being more thinly spread than before. In these conditions, no one seems to have considered any attempt at a spoiling attack, as the Germans had launched along the Belgian coast in July 1917 and as would become common practice in the next world war. Nor did Haig concentrate his reserves in the threatened area. Instead he parcelled them out equally all along the line, probably because he was more concerned about protecting the Channel ports than he was about his right flank, where there was more strategic depth to retreat into and the French might be able more easily to help.

The manpower shortage had a third consequence: it undermined the British attempt to establish a solid defence. The BEF had little experience of fighting defensively. Since the end of 1914 the British had largely been on the offensive, at least operationally speaking. Such defence plans as had been worked up in 1915–17 tended to be local tactical schemes designed to frustrate German raids and local assaults rather than to withstand large-scale onslaughts. Cambrai highlighted the fragility of British defences and, together with the possibility of the Germans seizing the initiative in the spring, concentrated BEF minds on how to fight defensively. On 14 December 1917 GHQ issued instructions on organizing the defence, apparently based on German tactics and built around three zones. A 'forward zone' would be relatively lightly held in dispersed but mutually supporting outposts rather than a single continuous line of trenches. The garrison here would disrupt any attack, identify the enemy's main thrust, and buy time to alert the main defences. If enemy pressure dictated, the defenders of the forward zone would pull back into the 'battle zone', a mile or two back, where the main fighting would take place on carefully prepared ground at least 2,000–3,000 yards deep. Counter-attacks would win back any ground lost. A further four to eight miles to the rear another position would constitute the 'rear zone', a backstop to which the defenders could retreat if circumstances dictated. One problem with this scheme was that the labour to build all these defensive positions was not available. Combat soldiers were set to digging, at the inevitable cost of fatigue and foregone training. Even so, the extent to which all these fortifications had been completed by March varied wildly. North of the Scarpe River and Arras, much had been accomplished, but, while Fifth Army's forward zone was well developed, its battle zone still lacked dugouts and it had barely begun construction of a rear zone. Inevitably, commanders tended to concentrate their troops where they could best be protected, in the forward zone: a tendency reinforced by the pressure to cover wide fronts with insufficient strength. In theory, no more than a third of the defenders' strength should be deployed in the forward zone, although the proportion may well have been much higher in practice.[5] Concentrating forward exposed more of the garrison to suppression or worse by enemy artillery. It also meant there were few or no reserves to counter-attack and relieve outposts isolated in the forward zone, with inevitable consequences for the morale of those holding out.

In addition to lack of manpower, at least two further problems undermined the British defence-in-depth. First, and most obviously, the unfamiliarity of the approach left many uncomfortable. This not only contributed to the tendency to unbalance the defence as noted above, but was also exacerbated by a lack of practice in command, communications, and counter-attacks, all essential elements of a successful elastic defence. A second and even more fundamental problem existed too, however: one which concerned not merely the implementation in practice of defence-in-depth, but the very concept. The German official histories written between the wars exalted defence-in-depth and contributed to a narrative which argues that by 1917 years of experience had taught the German Army that defence-in-depth was best. Modern military historians see a straight line from the Western Front, through the resilience of German defensive tactics in 1943–45, to NATO's reliance on variants thereof as the only conventional hope of stopping a Soviet drive on the Rhine during the Cold War.[6] They thus assume that the concept of defence-in-depth was the answer in 1918. Any defensive failures, therefore, must have been the result of a failure either to understand the concept, or to apply it properly. In their view, the BEF just got it wrong in March 1918. Their assumption, however, is flawed. The German official histories were not a dispassionate historical record but composed by ex-members of the General Staff as a resource for officer training during the 1920s and 1930s, during most of which period the army's most urgent task was how to defend the Reich with a tiny professional force.[7] To them, mobility and defence-in-depth seemed the obvious answer to the problems they faced, so that is what they focused on in their history. By doing so, they flattened out a much more complex process which saw vociferous debate within the German command about the merits of elastic defence right to the end of World War I. Much of the apparent success of defence-in-depth during World War II and NATO exercises depended on much greater battlefield mobility, better communications, lower force-to-space ratios, and more favourable terrain. It was thus highly contingent, and not the result of such tactics being inherently superior at all. Indeed, without the benefit of hindsight, the German or British officer of early 1918 thought defence-in-depth was far less obviously the solution than it seems to us today. It could not have saved Vimy Ridge in April 1917 or Messines in June. It had proved incapable of halting the 'bite and hold' advances of the BEF at Ypres during the autumn and had provoked a panic about defensive doctrine in late September. It was rain, terrain, and logistics which ultimately stopped the British push in Flanders, not German tactics. Even the highest expression of defence-in-depth, the Hindenburg Line, had buckled at Cambrai. It was not surprising, then, that many British commanders did not wholeheartedly embrace the new GHQ doctrine. Only after months of debate was consensus achieved and a comprehensive doctrinal document published. Stationery Service (SS) pamphlet 210, 'The Division in Defence', which enshrined the new approach, did not come out until May 1918.[8] The British Army was, therefore, a long way from being ideally prepared to withstand the offensive Erich Ludendorff launched on 21 March 1918.

Defence

The battles of spring 1918 exerted intense pressure on the British Army. It was forced to give up most of the ground it had spent 1916 and 1917 capturing and suffered heavy casualties in the process. Between March and May the BEF lost 366,937 men, or one in four of the front-line fighting troops. Over 150,000 of those were confirmed dead or went missing. In the infantry, who bore the brunt of combat, losses were inevitably higher. In 16 sample infantry divisions, 55 per cent of men became casualties. The British Army took a beating: 55 of its 60 divisions were heavily engaged, 29 of them twice; and six divisions found themselves in full-scale action three times that spring. Among the last, unfortunate group was 21st Division which suffered 110 per cent casualties in just three months.[9]

The first blow the Germans struck, on 21 March, was the strongest. In three waves, Ludendorff deployed some 68 divisions, or about a third of his troops on the Western Front, against the 18 British divisions holding the front. About 10,000 guns and trench mortars fired 3.2 million shells on the first day alone. This bombardment destroyed British communications, unstringing efforts at combined arms cooperation and leaving guns blind. Resistance, even where stout, was disjointed. Many units, left isolated with little chance of relief, faced little choice but to surrender. Initial results were impressive by Western Front standards; the Germans captured more territory on 21 March than the Entente did in 140 days on the Somme. By 23 March the pace of the German advance was picking up amidst growing reports of confusion in the BEF's rear. The Germans cleared the British out of all three of their defence lines, seized bridgeheads across the Somme River, and drove a wedge between the Third and Fifth armies. More British soldiers became prisoners of war in three days than in the previous three and a half years: some 40,000 men.

By 26 March, however, the balance of advantage had begun to swing away from the Germans and back to the British and French. Four factors played a part in this. First, the British had received a severe knock but were not out of the game yet. They were still offering resistance, especially up toward Arras where German progress had so far been minimal and a full-scale attack on 28 March (Operation *Mars*) was easily repelled. This contributed to the second factor: the attackers were becoming exhausted. The railheads had been left far behind and transport was scarce, so food, ammunition, and even water were in short supply. Ludendorff had lost 90,000 men in five days and fresh reserves were running out: eight of the 37 German divisions in action had already been thrown back into battle for the second time in a week. Thirdly, Ludendorff grew overconfident and dispersed his forces in an attempt to finish off the British while simultaneously defeating the French. Lastly, and perhaps most significant in the long run, a solution was found to the mutual mistrust which had characterized relations between Haig and the French Commander-in-Chief, Pétain. The appointment of Ferdinand Foch to unified supreme command enabled the dispatch of French reinforcements to protect the crucial rail junction at Amiens. This maintained contact between the allies and prevented the battle from disintegrating into two separate fights. French units soon began to make their presence felt and the German push had completely stalled by 30 March. Attempts to get it moving again achieved little and on 5 April Operation *Michael* was suspended for good. Both sides had suffered heavily. The BEF lost 177,000 men and the French another 77,000, for 254,000 in all. German casualties were nearly as bad, however: 239,000. In all, 90 German divisions had been used up, including nearly all those trained and outfitted to lead an assault.

The next major German attack on the BEF, Operation *Georgette*, began on 9 April, with some 29 divisions committed to an attack in the valley of the Lys River, close to the border between Belgium and France. Once more, the early days saw considerable success. Haig had to evacuate Armentières and give up the ground won so painfully around Ypres the previous autumn. Worried that he risked losing the important railway junction at Hazebrouck, he issued a melodramatic order of the day insisting that, 'with our backs to the wall', every position must be held 'to the last man' and each soldier should 'fight on to the end'. Again, however, German success gave way to frustration after a few days as tired troops reached the limits of their endurance and logistics broke down. Even the capture of Mount Kemmel, high ground dominating the roads and railways leading into Ypres, could not be exploited. *Georgette* was finally suspended on 29 April, by which time a last attempt to renew the push south of the Somme at Villers-Bretonneux had also collapsed. British casualties in *Georgette* were 82,000, German 86,000, and French 30,000. Apart from a few unlucky British divisions which, after being sent to the French sector for a rest, found themselves in the path of other German attacks, by the end of April the worst of the German offensives was over for most of the BEF.

There is a deceptive apparent symmetry to these battles which ignores the many real differences between them and entrenches an over-simple narrative among military historians. According to the consensus, the operations of spring 1918 all adhere to a common pattern of brilliant German tactics outthinking and outfighting brave but weak British defenders. The mobility and aggression of 'stormtroop' tactics, where command was decentralized, momentum was key, and enemy strongpoints were bypassed and mopped up by follow-on forces, overran a system of defence the British had cribbed from the Germans and failed either to grasp or apply properly. British command and control were paralysed while the soldiers of the BEF, often cut off in small units, fought bravely but in vain and seemed unable to stem the field-grey tide. British commanders, beset by communications breakdowns, failed to coordinate effective counter-attacks. Instead, they too often fell back to avoid encirclement, leaving gaps in the line for stormtroops to exploit with glee. Eventually, despite their excellent tactics, the Germans were only let down by their logistic frailty and by Ludendorff's operational and strategic errors.

This narrative is primarily one about the German Army. It assumes that the Germans would have succeeded had they not made certain mistakes. It underpins a view that the attack tactics employed in spring 1918 served as forerunners of Blitzkrieg and established the template for attack tactics in modern manoeuvre warfare. The problem with this narrative is twofold. First, the reality was considerably more nuanced. Further, German failure was the result, not only of things the Germans did wrong, but also of things the British and French did right. Even on 21 March, tactical success had been far from uniform: the German left wing had, it was true, stormed eight miles into the British lines. The right, however, had fared much less impressively, struggling to make 5,000 yards and falling five miles short of their objectives. Nor were all the German assault troops capable of operating at the highest level. Operation *Mars* on 28 March was badly botched: the bombardment was less thorough than it had been the previous week; counter-battery fire was less effective; the barrage rolled forwards too quickly. Not all the troops had been trained in stormtroop tactics, and in any case the enemy positions in this sector around Arras were well established and complex, so that many units reverted to traditional close order tactics rather than small-group manoeuvre and infiltration. With little fog to mask the assaulting troops, British forward crust defence methods worked well: defenders in the front line had little trouble repelling the attack without needing to give ground at all. By early afternoon the operation had clearly failed and was suspended. On 9 April, however, with a slower barrage, fog aiding infiltration, and some of the defending units still recovering from fighting *Michael*, once again the Germans quickly overran the British defences. Throughout March and April, even where the new tactics were employed, troops repeatedly seemed unable to shake the habits of trench warfare and keep up with the tempo of mobile operations. Although some units used the so-called Pulkowski method of firing artillery by the map with little or no prior registration in an effort to enhance surprise, others again did not and no common doctrine was applied until the end of May. Finally, far from leaving subordinates free to use their initiative within a decentralized model of command, corps and army headquarters, and indeed Ludendorff himself, had been trying to exercise too much control, micromanaging far down the hierarchy. In other words, whatever the shortcomings of German logistics and strategic decision-making, any initial success depended at least as much on other contingent factors, such as terrain, weather, and the strength or weakness of the Entente defence, as it did on German tactical excellence.

With the benefit of a hundred years of hindsight, we now know that the BEF had survived the worst by the end of April, that Ludendorff's attempts to break the French over the early summer would come to nothing, and that, at the Second Battle of the Marne, the initiative shifted for the last time from the Germans to the Allies. To Haig, Pétain, and Foch at the time, of course, none of this was evident. All they could see was that the tempo of enemy offensives was declining, but that the German Army remained poised within 40 miles of three key objectives: Paris, Abbeville, and Calais. One good victory might see the German Army at any of these, with possibly disastrous consequences for the Allies. Loss of the Channel ports might force the BEF to evacuate the continent. The fall of Paris might drive France out of the war. And German troops in Abbeville would, as in 1940, cut the British and French forces in two. At late as mid-June, Allied intelligence estimated the Germans still had some 25–30 divisions in reserve, the majority opposite the British sector. The threat still seemed both real and imminent and the BEF remained on a defensive footing through May and June, replacing the losses in its ranks, rebuilding lines of communication and networks of supply, and organizing new defences. By late June, however, Haig and Foch began planning counter-offensives against a German army which was beginning to suffer from the first wave of the famous Spanish flu pandemic.

Offence

The first sign of renewed British aggression came on 4 July with a small but perfectly designed attack by Australian and American troops to mark Independence Day. Tanks, infantry, artillery, and aircraft all worked together to excellent effect. They captured the village of Hamel and over 1,000 German prisoners within 93 minutes. Further small-scale operations followed, for example at Méteren later in the month, but the next large-scale attack came on 8 August at Amiens, in a battle which marked the beginning of the campaign soon known in Britain, with a nod to the Waterloo campaign, as the 'Hundred Days'.

Foch's overall intention, outlined to Haig, Pershing, and Pétain at his headquarters on 24 July, was, as a first step, to clear the Germans away from important French rail networks and nodes, freeing up Allied transportation all along the front. The British Fourth Army, commanded by Sir Henry Rawlinson, was to begin by pushing the Germans back east, away from the junction and marshalling yards at Amiens. Meanwhile the French First Army would liberate Montdidier. Rawlinson detailed the Australian, Canadian, and British III Corps to launch a surprise assault after no preliminary bombardment. Some 3,500 British and French artillery pieces neutralized enemy guns, interdicted communications, targeted strongpoints and headquarters, and delivered a creeping barrage to cover the infantry advance. Nearly 2,000 Allied aircraft ensured air superiority and attacked ground targets, although attempts to isolate the battlefield by destroying the bridges over the Somme proved an expensive failure. Over 500 tanks supported the infantry advance. At Cambrai in November, the BEF had learned that the same troops could not be relied on to capture multiple objectives: they grew too tired and disorganized. This time, fresh troops leapfrogged through to maintain the momentum of the advance. The first day, 8 August, saw stunning success: Rawlinson's men advanced seven miles, capturing almost all their objectives and at least 12,000 German prisoners. Altogether, the Germans lost 27,000 men. Ludendorff was so disgusted by the defenders' performance that he famously dubbed it 'the black day of the German Army'.[10] Over the next few days Allied momentum slowed and results dribbled away as resistance solidified and the familiar

World War I entropy set in. By 11 August only 38 tanks were still fit to take the field and the British infantry were exhausted. After minimal progress that day Haig accepted the recommendation of Rawlinson and his corps commanders to suspend the Amiens offensive. Instead, General Sir Julian Byng's Third Army, next door to Rawlinson on the north bank of the Somme, was warned to begin preparations to capture Bapaume.

The decision to call a halt at Amiens marked a significant shift of approach on the part of Haig and the BEF High Command and set a pattern for the rest of the war. From now on, the old bull-headed insistence on hammering away repeatedly at the same place with increasingly tired troops in the hope that the enemy might break was largely abandoned. Instead, each time diminishing returns set in, the offensive was closed down and a new attack begun elsewhere. In June–July 1917 seven weeks had elapsed between the battle of Messines and the launch of the Third Battle of Ypres, a lag largely driven by the need to build up transport capacity and other infrastructure, to relocate guns and to stockpile the munitions required for another major push. A little over a year later, with materiel more plentiful and logistics improved, Third Army was in action within only ten days of Rawlinson's pause. On 23 August Fourth Army attacked once more, and three days later General Sir Henry Horne's First Army also swung into action. Plentiful supplies and efficient transport made possible coordinated operations on a scale rarely attempted before. The fighting of late August was hard, casualties were heavy and progress slow: it took the New Zealand Division eight days to drive seven miles and liberate the ruins of Bapaume, for instance. By early September, however, with his defences on the Drocourt–Quéant Line and at Mont St Quentin both neutralized and his troops in danger of encirclement, the German army group commander Kronprinz Rupprecht von Bayern had no choice but to order a retreat into the Hindenburg Line, giving up all the ground gained since 21 March.

It took the BEF three weeks to close up to the Hindenburg Line, clear its outworks, and prepare a set-piece assault as part of Foch's plan for a series of coordinated offensives all the way from the Meuse River to the Channel. Between 26 and 29 September, no fewer than eight armies, from Belgium, France, Great Britain, and the United States of America, would seek to pose

The Allied offensives, 1918

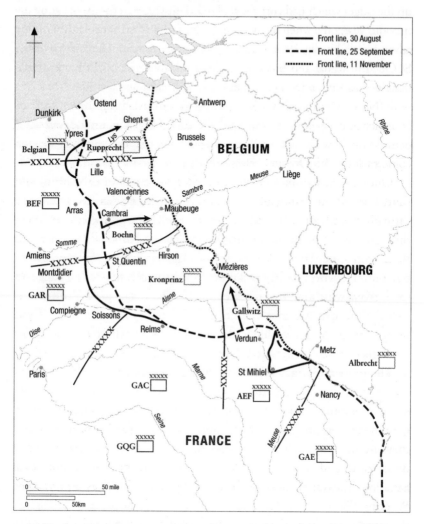

more problems than Ludendorff could ever solve, sucking in reserves here before striking there, breaking through the enemy defences and inflicting a victory that would win the war. British operations began on 27 September with an audacious combat crossing of the Canal du Nord by the Canadian Corps while Third Army cleared the main Hindenburg Line and drove on Cambrai. General Sir Herbert Plumer's Second Army, alongside Belgian and

French troops, attacked at Ypres the next day. Within 48 hours Plumer rolled up the ridges which had cost the BEF more than three months of agony the previous year: only when the weather broke and his logistics collapsed did his advance stall. Finally, 29 September saw Fourth Army seize crossings over the St Quentin Canal and break into the Hindenburg Line in what has been described as 'one of the greatest feats of British military history'.[11] Notably, 46th (North Midland) Division captured the Riqueval Bridge and the village of Bellenglise, opening a way into the heart of the enemy defences and demonstrating what well-led British troops could achieve by 1918. We shall come back to 46th Division below.

Once again, German resistance proved ferocious in the second and third lines of the Hindenburg Position, but the British slowly chewed through it and, on 8 October, another set-piece attack carried them through the last prepared defences the Germans possessed: the so-called Beaurevoir Line. From now on, Rupprecht's army group would have to rely on improvised positions hurriedly scratched behind the canals and small rivers which lay across the British axis of advance. This was just as well for the British, since the difficulty of rebuilding rails, roads, and bridges made it increasingly difficult to bring up the heavy guns and tanks needed for set-piece assaults on properly fortified positions.

The most important consequence of the defeats on the Hindenburg Line was that, together with the actual, or obviously imminent, collapse of all Germany's allies, they broke the spirit of the German High Command. On 28 September Hindenburg and Ludendorff agreed that they needed an immediate armistice. Otherwise the army might disintegrate and not be available if needed to oppose any Bolshevik agitation. The Kaiser appointed a new government which asked President Woodrow Wilson for peace talks on 5 October. While proper negotiations remained some time off, now for the first time an end to the war seemed at least a possibility. We shall examine the effect on the motivation of soldiers on both sides below, but the fighting, now in less open terrain, remained fierce and casualties heavy.

By early November the British had fought their way across the Lys and Selle rivers, had liberated Lille, Ghent, and Valenciennes, and were preparing another deliberate attack on German positions behind the

Sambre River. When they launched this on 4 November the result was resounding victory: the Germans began a headlong retreat, covered by skilful rearguards which delayed the British so well that by 8 November the two sides had completely lost touch. By the morning of 11 November, when news of the Armistice arrived, Canadian troops were famously in Mons, back where the BEF's war had begun.

The way military historians have tended to explain British success during the 'Hundred Days' displays interesting parallels with their analysis of German stormtroop tactics in March 1918. In both cases, the application of hindsight and a search for the roots of Blitzkrieg has tended to flatten out the history, smoothing out nuance and downplaying the importance of contingency. British and Commonwealth historians, keen to react against a long-running popular 'lions led by donkeys' myth, have highlighted how much the BEF learnt as the war went on. They suggest that in 1915 and 1916 the army had been forced to expand too fast on too narrow a base of experience and to adapt to new ways of war, all the time struggling against a ferocious and highly dangerous enemy as well as shortages of trained troops and materiel. By 1918, however, they argue, it had become the equal of, or even superior to, the best continental militaries. They have placed particular emphasis on the BEF's tactical development, stressing the integration of new weapons such as the aeroplane, tank, and poison gas, together with the adoption of innovative ways of using traditional ones, such as artillery, trench mortars, and infantry, weaving the whole into a combined arms weapon system capable of overcoming any defence the Germans were capable of mounting. At the operational level, not only had lessons been learnt about the importance of breaking off offensives before they reached culminating point and about exploiting laterally, using the width of the front, rather than vertically in depth, as we have seen, but British command had, we are told, been made considerably more flexible. In place of the unwieldy top-down 'restrictive control' management style of the war's middle years, an approach closer to modern ideas of 'mission command' was adopted. Authority was delegated and more latitude was given to the man on the spot to exercise his initiative according to the situation as he interpreted it. This improved response times and led to better decision-making in the more freewheeling 'semi-mobile' warfare which characterized the 'Hundred Days'.

There is much truth to this picture. The British Army of 1918 was a much more capable instrument than it had been even a year earlier, never mind on the first day of the Somme, despite the inevitable heavy casualties consequent on more of the army being in action at once, and more mobile fighting taking the place of trench warfare. The BEF as a whole was 30,000 men stronger on 1 September than it had been at the beginning of March, but the aggregate figures conceal a continuing shortfall in trained infantrymen. The number of infantry other ranks in the field fell by 16 per cent between 1 March and 1 November, from 515,000 to just under 434,000. Infantry battalions with establishment ration strengths of 900 were only 700 strong, and frequently sent 400 or fewer men into action. When replacements could be found, they were often young: 36 per cent of soldiers were aged 21 or under, where the average for the war as a whole was 28 per cent. Not all were, though. Some reinforcements, men who had been combed out or medically re-graded, were green but others were experienced men returning from convalescence: about half of one draft reaching 1st Battalion Gordon Highlanders in October 1918 had served in France before.[12] Inevitably, some of the new men became good soldiers while others did not.

To some extent, shortfalls in infantry mattered less by 1918 than earlier in the war because firepower was taking the place of manpower and men were increasingly necessary only to support the machines. For example, battalions which had gone to war with two Vickers machine guns each in 1914, four years later had 36 Lewis guns on the establishment: it took 200 men, or half the unit's combat strength, just to keep them firing. By 1917 and 1918 industry was geared up to provide those machines and everything else the soldiers needed to fight. Written-off aircraft were rapidly replaced: despite heavy losses, by 8 April 1918 the RAF had more aeroplanes in action than on 21 March. All the guns lost during the spring offensives had been replaced, and then some, by July. The weight of shells fired off by British artillery during the week of the attacks on the Hindenburg Line in 1918 was three times what had been possible on the Somme two years previously. Where the BEF had been living from hand to mouth in 1914–16, by the Armistice it had enough munitions immediately on hand to fight for another three weeks.

Possessing all the weapons in the world was of limited value without knowing what to do with them. There is no question that, often via a process of trial and error, the British Army had ascended a range of individual learning curves and developed experience and new skills. By the summer of 1918, for instance, the RAF had discovered and was executing all the principal roles for aviation in war that have been used forever since.[13] To fire an artillery shell with the increased accuracy possible by 1918 depended on improved techniques and new inventions in a range of fields including: survey, aerial photography, meteorology, metallurgy, fuse and propellant technology, communications, command, control, and intelligence. To then employ that shell to the best possible effect required a sophisticated grasp of tactics and operational art. And nothing was possible at all without mastery of the logistic skills necessary to transport the shell to the gun and ensure the gun was working, with the crew fed, clothed, and watered, and ready to fire.

The army had learnt, not only how to fight but also how to learn. A process evolved to capture lessons learned, distil the most important and revise best practice through new doctrine. Sometimes, the new approaches were codified and published in documents such as the SS pamphlets and other instructions. The most famous of these were the *Fourth Army Tactical Notes* distributed by Rawlinson to the troops about to attack on the Somme in 1916: SS 135 *The Division in the Attack*, which covered combined arms warfare and operations and went through four editions between 1916 and 1918; and SS 143 *The Infantry Platoon in the Attack*, which concentrated on small-unit tactics. Other doctrine was disseminated through the many informal channels of communication which linked the army within and between theatres scattered all over the world.[14] Consciously or by fortunate accident, the army managed to construct a highly flexible and effective system of learning systems, operating simultaneously down multiple different channels, each characterized by varying degrees of formality and central control, to spread the word and ensure innovation and adaptation was as effective and efficient as possible.

To see how much more potent a weapon the British Army constituted by the end of 1918, all we need do is compare the BEF's position at the beginning and end of the year. In January and February, as we saw, it squatted on the defensive, apparently paralysed by the high command reshuffle and swingeing reorganization of its ranks, awaiting a German offensive which it expected to be able to contain but had no thought of pre-empting. By the end of the year, in contrast, the BEF had launched multiple major offensives employing up to five armies at once in less time than it had taken to plan an attack by just one in 1916 and had defeated the German Army time and again, outfighting it in trench warfare and more mobile operations alike. All this had been achieved while continually advancing as Haig and Foch employed, with great success, a form of 'rolling attrition' designed to chew through German reserves of manpower while slowly but continually forcing them back. The logistic achievement was no less impressive than the fighting performance. The BEF played a leading role in defeating the most feared army in the world, the military which had set the standard worldwide since the 1860s.

This central and important fact of British improvement should not blind us to two other realities, however. First, the German Army of late 1918 was a much weaker opponent than it had been earlier in the war, largely as a result of the attrition imposed by the British and French in 1916–17. Second, while the improvement in the British Army was considerable, it would be a mistake to regard the BEF as a paragon of military virtue which had unlocked the secret of success in modern warfare and applied the recipe consistently throughout the 'Hundred Days'. Indeed, its victory was founded at least as much on mobilizing its traditional values and ethos as on new conceptual insights and ways of war. Let us take these two issues in turn.

The German Army of 1918 was, without a doubt, a weaker force than it had been earlier in the war. It lagged behind the Allies in increasingly important materiel, for instance: by summer 1918 it was outnumbered nearly two to one in aircraft, six to one in tanks, and ten to one in lorries, although it managed to preserve rough parity in artillery strength. The manpower situation was also a concern. Three and a half years of war had already seen the deaths of around 1,750,000 soldiers. Nonetheless, the

Germans began 1918 with as many men as the Allies on the Western Front. The ranks were only kept relatively full, however, by drafting in young men who often proved less resilient. Fewer than one in 12 German combat soldiers in 1914 was under 21 years old; by August 1918 more than one in five was, although that proportion remained lower than in the British Army, as we have seen. During 1918 German wastage occurred faster than at Verdun, the Somme or Third Ypres: casualties exceeded a million. Replacements could not keep up, so the ration strength of the average infantry battalion fell from 807 men in February to 630 in August and 463 by the Armistice. Training became increasingly rushed and difficult, not least due to high loss rates of NCOs and officers. The strength of many divisions fell by nearly 80 per cent and 32 had to be disbanded altogether. By November, the German Army had only two fresh divisions in reserve, down from 43 at the end of June and 74 on 20 March. Discipline began to fall away, however, especially from the summer of 1918 onwards, with insubordination, desertion, and surrenders to the enemy all on the rise. Hope of victory was a key determinant of morale until the evident failure of the spring offensives. Thereafter, the prospect of a quick end to the war (and survival) became more important, with significant consequences for motivation.[15]

The most serious problems confronting the Germans in 1918, however, did not concern materiel, manpower, or morale, but the army's very ability to think. It lost its ability to adapt to the changing situations in which it found itself. An organization which had always prided itself on its flexibility of command became increasingly arthritic. As the problems confronting it multiplied and intensified, ideas of delegated command, with the subordinate on the spot encouraged to exercise his initiative within the framework of his superior's intent, evaporated. Ludendorff set the tone with his micromanagement. He was quick to blame and slow to praise, treating his subordinates with increasing disdain and aggression. The insecurity Ludendorff felt about his position, dependent as it was on the goodwill of an unpredictable Kaiser, transmitted itself down through the ranks of command and spread fear through a structure of already inherent instability. The consequence, inevitably, was that too often after-action reports told the boss what he wanted, not what he needed, to hear. In particular, the staff officers were unwilling to admit the weakness of the German Army to Ludendorff.[16] As a result, inconvenient truths remained untold, objectivity fell away, and decisions became made on the basis of increasingly flawed information.

A good example of the BEF's tactical improvement was in the realm of combined arms. The way it integrated armour, artillery, aviation, infantry, and even on occasion cavalry, could be devastating, as, for instance, the first day of the battle of Amiens demonstrated. Rarely, however, were the British able so effectively to draw on their whole panoply at once in this way. Amiens was an exception, not a rule, for three main reasons. First, key assets, such as tanks, were in short supply. Even in August there were not enough to go around and by October heavy casualties and poor transportation facilities reduced armour support considerably. On 21 August, 183 tanks supported the attack of Third Army; by 4 November, only 25 could. The problem of shipping forward shells, especially for heavy guns, along extending supply lines reduced the level of artillery support possible. Second, nature intervened: terrain was sometimes unsuitable for combined arms, particularly once fighting moved into more built-up areas from October onwards; and as the autumn went on, fog and longer hours of darkness inhibited inter-arm communications and, increasingly frequently, weather kept aircraft grounded. Third, inter-arm coordination remained problematic at times, especially when carefully thought out set-piece attacks gave way to more improvised fighting. The level of comfort of different units and formations with the latest tactics varied widely. Fundamental techniques such as 'fire and movement' were misunderstood or misapplied almost as often as they were properly employed. GHQ-led attempts to standardize doctrine had only limited success and practice remained highly diverse. Indeed, in 1918 there was a move away from standard formations and one-size-fits-all solutions and back towards a more flexible approach dictated primarily by the specific situation faced. The attack of 10th Canadian Brigade on Mont Houy on 1 November was atypical in the weight of fire support made available at this stage of the campaign: seven tonnes of high explosive fell every minute on a front less than two miles wide. But, it did reflect the best of a British tactical method primarily based, not on all arms, but on a highly refined form of close infantry–artillery cooperation that not all units of the BEF could manage.[17]

Whatever the reality of British combined arms tactics, however, the threat of them, and in particular of tanks, undoubtedly destabilized the German defence. Tanks were neither in fact nor potentially the war-winning weapon that apostles of armour such as J. F. C. Fuller and Basil Liddell Hart claimed between the wars. But neither were they an irrelevance, as some, such as the British official historian, have claimed.[18] Tanks posed two particular threats to the Germans. First, they could cut barbed wire for the infantry, removing the need for a preparatory bombardment and so reintroducing the possibility of surprise. Second, the mobile firepower they offered, and the moral impact they had on defending infantry, helped the attacker break through relatively quickly and gave him the chance of overrunning German artillery positions. There was a solution to both problems, however, and the Germans were quick to find it. The most effective way of knocking out enemy tanks was to position field guns in forward positions where they could engage them over open sights. By mid-September at least a third of German field artillery was deployed forward in this way and succeeded in inflicting heavy losses on British armoured units. By October the Tank Corps had lost nearly half the men, and 130 per cent of the tanks, with which it had begun the campaign.[19] The proximity of anti-tank guns also stiffened the morale of the infantry in the front line and prevented 'tank panic'. Solving one problem merely created others, however. Guns detached to the front line were very vulnerable to being overrun by infantry assault, especially when visibility was poor. Losses were consequently high. The other problem was that the guns left to the rear were not only fewer in number, but often deployed further back to reduce the risk of being captured by a tank break-in. Inevitably the artillery could not deliver the same weight of indirect fire support any longer, weakening the defensive barrage, leaving the infantry feeling abandoned and so undermining their morale in a different way. The failure of the German Army to identify, and alter its tactics to reflect, the declining British armour threat from October onwards is an excellent example of the rigidity of its responses by this stage of the war.

The German Army did not spontaneously lose the ability to think straight in 1918. The main cause of its cognitive breakdown was enemy pressure. The speed and violence of the Allied offensive exhausted not only the material and moral, but also the mental capacity of the German Army to react and exposed its underlying weaknesses. Its rigid and overcentralized response stands in contrast to the flexibility demonstrated by the BEF. The German command structure ossified further with every setback, while the British one became more relaxed as confidence grew they were on the right track. This is clearest in British attempts to decentralize decision-making in an effort to improve reaction times and increase tempo. Having passed through a phase of centralized restrictive command in the structured and carefully choreographed set-piece battles of 1916–17, the BEF in 1918 began to move to delegate more authority, allowing the 'man on the spot' the maximum possible initiative. This did not always work: many commanders at all levels found it hard to adjust to the looser command arrangements semi-mobile warfare demanded. Some, inevitably, used to receiving or issuing dozens of pages of neatly typed instructions, never grew comfortable with verbal briefings later corroborated by a few paragraphs scribbled in pencil on a page torn out of a notebook. Senior commanders proved as reluctant to relinquish control as junior ones were to assume responsibility. Nonetheless, overall, greater delegation was one factor underpinning a tempo of operations much faster than anything previously achieved on the Western Front.

This delegation was partly the result of a higher level of expertise throughout the whole BEF. As Robin Prior and Trevor Wilson argued in their seminal work on Sir Henry Rawlinson, the importance of higher command withered away.[20] But it was as much a reassertion of traditional values as a reaction to new realities. Also at work was the British Army's pre-war principle of letting the 'man on the spot' get on with it.[21] Active service all over the globe, frequently dispersed in small units with very poor or non-existent communications, placed a premium on initiative in the Victorian and Edwardian army and reinforced an even older tradition of gentlemanly independence dating far back in the army's history. Officers were expected to do the right thing without having to be told. Such expectations were perhaps unrealistic with the inexperienced men of 1915–16, and in any case the intricate choreography of the set-piece trench battles of the war's middle years militated against allowing individuals much leeway. As the fighting lost structure in 1918, tried and tested commanders were once more, within limits, accorded some of the autonomy their predecessors had been used to on the frontiers of Empire.

The traditional ethos of the British Army reasserted itself in another important manner: its approach to learning and adaptation. We saw above that the BEF had got better at fighting and learning by 1918, but that it did not always either fully internalize or implement the lessons it had learnt. The efficiency with which information was disseminated around the organization varied widely and some units seem to have been unable to process new information sufficiently well to change their approach. It is certainly possible to see the British Army of 1914–18 as a very imperfect learning organization incapable of generating uniform change in any systematic fashion. At first sight, the British certainly look haphazard next to the French and, especially, German armies, both of which employed a more centralized process within which the centre played a much more active role in promoting adaptation. Modern Anglo-American military analysts have also become accustomed to seeing innovation implemented in a centralized and process-heavy way due to the very particular requirements of post-war NATO interoperability, where innovation was often led by the very large US military, and where clarity and uniformity were essential if troops from many different countries were to work together in mutually predictable ways. Again, the British Army of World War I can seem amateurish by such standards. It is questionable, however, whether such standards are appropriate. The British Army had a long tradition of laissez-faire in the spheres of tactics and doctrine. Pre-1914, within broad and generally accepted principles of war, it preferred to leave as much latitude as possible to commanding officers to train the men they would lead into action, rather than impose centrally devised programmes. The flexibility this engendered seemed better suited to the wide range of environments British soldiers were likely to find themselves operating in than the uniformity instilled in the conscript armies almost exclusively designed to fight on the continent. It also fed into the way British officers tended to perceive themselves as pragmatists and skilled improvisers. In a distaste for theory and prescriptive rules they saw one of the features which set themselves apart from their French and German counterparts, who seemed, in contrast, keen on abstract ideas, elaborate doctrine, and programmatic solutions.[22] Between 1914 and 1918 the tension between central and local solutions to problems was a feature common to all three armies' experience. It certainly remained unresolved in the British case but the BEF tended to allow more free play to the periphery than its allies or enemy, and there were times in 1918 where this helped, rather than hindered, operations. As a result, the British proved a sometimes unpredictable opponent. The Germans, however, were not. Indeed, British 'bite and hold' tactics were designed precisely to chew up the German counter-attacks which were bound to come in as soon as ground was lost.

The British Army in 1918 was able to combine modern techniques with traditional values and strengths to good effect. The best way to demonstrate this general truth is to study the particular; the operation carried out by 46th (North Midland) Division to seize crossings over the St Quentin Canal and break into the Hindenburg Line on 29 September.

Case Study: 46th Division attacks the Hindenburg Line[23]

This case study is an excellent example of how far the British Army had come, not least because this was a division with an, at best, extremely average reputation. A Territorial Force formation, it was felt to have performed poorly at Loos in October 1915 and during the diversionary attack at Gommecourt on 1 July 1916. It was primarily used to hold the line thereafter until it marched south to join the Fourth Army's IX Corps and was committed to the huge set-piece battle to break the Hindenburg Line.

The divisional commander, G. F. Boyd, was typical of the tough-minded, talented, and experienced officers who had come through by 1918. He had been commissioned from the ranks during the Boer

War and flourished as an officer. The confidential report his CO wrote on Boyd in 1913 described him as

> loyal, cool, self-reliant. He possesses in a marked degree the valuable characteristic of a good staff-officer in dealing with many minor matters on his own initiative without giving offence, and at the same time keeping me informed where necessary. He is very quick, thorough and active in mind and body. A good horseman. He has considerable professional knowledge, which he is able to apply very quickly and accurately in the form of orders. I have formed a high opinion of his character and capabilities and would be glad to have him with me on service. I recommend him for accelerated promotion.

Accelerated promotion was definitely what he got. A captain in 1914, after successful service as a staff officer at brigade, division, and corps level, he was given brigade command in July 1918 and two months later was promoted to major general. He was clearly an impressive soldier. His confidential report at the end of the war spoke of his being 'a disciplinarian, a tremendous worker, at all times cheerful and optimistic ... and he can, and does, breathe his own indomitable spirit into his men'. 'Major-General G F Boyd had a most attractive personality', recalled a regimental historian who served under him.

> He was young. He was handsome ... He had a smile for everyone. He had a brain like lightning and an imagination as vivid ... When the 46th Division was placed in his hands he seized it as an expert swordsman seizes a priceless blade. This was just the weapon he had been looking for. He would wield it as it had never been wielded before. He would breathe his luck upon it; with it he would leap to victory.[24]

After the war he rose to Military Secretary and might have gone further, had he not died young. Above Boyd, the commander of IX Corps, Walter Braithwaite, was similarly highly rated by this stage of the war, having commanded the 62nd (West Yorkshire Division) to good effect for nearly two years before his promotion.

Along half of Rawlinson's Fourth Army front the canal ran in a tunnel. American and Australian troops were to strike here. Further south, though, the canal, 35 feet across, ran in places between banks up to 50 feet high and contained water or mud six feet deep. It was the job of 46th Division's 137th Brigade to fight forwards 1,000 yards, through well-wired German trenches and machine-gun posts, to reach the west bank of the canal, cross under fire, clear the far bank and the village of Bellenglise, and establish a bridgehead for the other two brigades of the division to then pass through and exploit, before they in turn were leapfrogged by another division. Over 3,000 life-belts and rafts were requisitioned from cross-Channel leave steamers to help men float or swim across the canal. A brick bridge, wide enough for a horse and cart, which the Germans had left intact at Riqueval to help supply their men on the west bank, would be the focus of special attention, as we shall see.

The 137th Brigade was made up of Staffordshiremen and commanded by Brigadier General J. V. Campbell, 41 years old. He had won the DSO and been mentioned in dispatches twice in South Africa while still in his twenties. He was awarded the Victoria Cross for his leadership of a battalion of Coldstream Guards at the battle of Ginchy on 15 September 1916, where he achieved fame as the 'Tally-Ho V.C.' for using his hunting horn to rally his men. Daunting as the task now facing his men was, they had four advantages. First, the intelligence picture was as full as could be hoped. Detailed plans of the German defences in this sector had been captured during the battle of Amiens and the British positions overlooked the German defences and the canal. Second, on the brigade's right flank, where the canal bent eastwards, the guns of 1st Division would be able to support the attack on Bellenglise village. Third, the preparatory artillery bombardment in places had broken down the walls of the cutting in which the canal ran, creating ramps down which troops could reach the water relatively easily. Lastly, when they advanced to the attack at 0550hrs on 29 September, they did so through thick fog which masked their advance and reduced the effectiveness of German firepower.

Covering the infantry attack were eight brigades of field artillery and three battalions of machine guns. One shell fell every four yards of front every minute for eight hours.[25] They delivered 'a barrage which was one of the finest under which troops have ever advanced during the war', mixing smoke, gas, high explosive, and shrapnel which kept the Germans in their dugouts while heavy artillery targeted known enemy strongpoints, headquarters, and reinforcement routes.[26] The three battalions of 137th Brigade swept forwards, catching the defenders by surprise and overrunning many before they had a chance to get out of their dugouts and man their defences. Moving with speed and resolution, all three reached the west bank with relatively little trouble. On the right, 1/6th Battalion South Staffordshire Regiment found the canal largely dry. They rushed across it in the fog, overwhelming the machine guns on the east bank, stormed a German trench line, and seized the village of Bellenglise. They captured more than 1,000 enemy troops who were sheltering in a tunnel nearby.

In the centre, the canal was full of water so the men of 1/5th Battalion, South Staffordshire Regiment, had to swim across. In thick fog, small-unit leadership proved crucial: Corporal A. E. Ferguson, for example, led a party of 15 men which captured 98 Germans and ten machine guns. Meanwhile Sergeant W. Cahill, who could not swim, struggled across the canal somehow and captured the four enemy machine guns holding up the advance in his sector. Eventually, the battalion was across and advanced to its objective on schedule.

On the left, one of the tasks assigned to 1/6th Battalion, North Staffordshire Regiment, was to seize intact the bridge at Riqueval, a mission delegated to Captain Arthur Humphrey Charlton's A Company. Humphrey Charlton was born in 1892, the son of the vicar of Abbots Bromley in Staffordshire. He was a farmer by occupation who had emigrated to Canada in 1911. When war broke out he returned to England and volunteered in December 1914, joining the Army Veterinary Corps as a private soldier, with special responsibility for horses. He had been commissioned in November 1915 and by 1918 was an experienced soldier and officer. As his men advanced down a ravine leading to the bridge they came under fire from a machine gun on the western bank. At once, Charlton charged the machine gun with a party of nine men. Lance Corporal J. Smith from Burton-on-Trent bayoneted the machine-gun crew, whereupon Charlton charged the bridge itself. German pioneers and a couple of sentries who had been sheltering in their blockhouse, ready to blow the bridge, came racing out just as Charlton and his men arrived. Lance Corporal F. Openshaw, a Royal Engineer from Bury, killed two Germans and took the surrender of a third while Charlton cut the wires and threw the demolition charges into the water. He had captured the Riqueval Bridge in under half an hour. Engineers set to work at once to reinforce it. A Company then drove through the trenches east of the canal, taking 130 prisoners in a single trench. By 0830hrs, after two and a half hours of combat, all objectives had been achieved and 137th Brigade had taken some 2,000 prisoners at a cost of 25 officers and 555 men. The tanks promised in support had not been able to fight their way through the German lines in the Australian sector around Bellicourt. For his achievement, Humphrey Charlton was awarded the DSO. A few days later he also won the MC. Openshaw received the DCM and Smith a bar to his DCM.

At least as impressive as 46th Division's tactical achievement was its operational-level follow-up. As soon as 137th Brigade began to consolidate its hold on its objectives that morning, 138th and 139th brigades began moving through to continue the attack. The fog which had helped the assault waves proved a considerable hindrance to the traffic controllers trying desperately to get the right men and materiel to the right places when no one could see where they were going and when communications, as always during a World War I advance, collapsed. Nonetheless, by 1400hrs 46th Division had achieved all its objectives and 32nd Division in turn began to pass through and continue the push. The Hindenburg Line was not quite broken that day, but IX Corps made a big dent in it and helped set Fourth Army, and the BEF in general, up for the victories that followed. The British had plenty of men and supplies, and had worked out how to feed them in to battle to maintain a fast tempo of operations. The same could not be said of the Germans, who were continually being asked to do more and more with less and less until eventually they found they could no longer do anything at all.

The action of 137th Brigade on 29 September, according to one post-war assessment, offered 'not much to be learned tactically … but it is a good example of what can be done by good organization, fine leadership and fighting spirit'.[27] Luck, good intelligence, and the outstanding quantity and quality of artillery support also helped. The 46th Division operation also demonstrated some of the problems their opponents were struggling with by this stage, however. The German 2nd Infantry Division, responsible for the defence of Riqueval and Bellenglise, concentrated 30 of its 36 rifle companies in or near the forward positions, leaving almost no reserve.[28] This was partly because its companies were so worn down that it was necessary to maintain the integrity of the front line. Additionally, however, this was because the Germans exaggerated, and became fixated on, the strength of the defensive position offered by the canal, while underestimating the tactical ability of the BEF. An important lesson of 29 September is that, by this stage, it was not just elite formations which the Germans had to fear tactically.

Conclusion

We have seen that a range of factors underpinned British success. Much of it was the result of mistakes and institutional weaknesses by and within the German Army. Historians, often because they were seeking answers to the urgent questions of their day, have tended to downplay those. This has led in turn to an overestimation of the British Army's capabilities by this stage of the war. This chapter has demonstrated that the British Army of 1918 was far from a new model army of uniform excellence. The British troops of 1918, like those of 46th Division, were a mixture of the green and the hard-bitten. Mainly citizen soldiers serving only for the duration, many had become skilled warriors, as or more adept at the highly technological new ways of fighting than their enemies. Others, inevitably, lacked the experience or training to reach the same level. The peaks of performance were high, the troughs depressingly familiar. By the end of the year, however, the profit and loss ledger contained more pluses than minuses, and that was all that mattered. They only had to be good enough. Success was built on a mix of new sciences and old arts. Modern machines and techniques, married to old-fashioned virtues such as leadership and courage, delivered a year of the largest victories British land forces have ever won. About one in three of the Allied troops in

France at war's end were British, and they captured nearly half of all the Germans taken prisoner between the middle of July and November.[29] Their efforts on the Western Front for the first time made the British Army as valuable to its allies as Britain's sea power and financial resources had been for centuries.[30] The fact that Great Britain was able to fight and win in France, while simultaneously conducting active campaigns in East Africa, central Asia, the Middle East, Russia, the Balkans, and Italy, and also maintaining garrisons worldwide, vividly demonstrates the superpower it remained even after the most terrible war to date. Ultimately, that superpower was built on the backs of men like Charlton, Openshaw, and, appropriately, Smith.

CHAPTER 5

THE US ARMY IN 1918

Professor Mitch Yockelson

Introduction

When the United States joined its British and French comrades in their fight against Germany by entering the Great War on 6 April 1917, tremendous optimism erupted among the Allied commanders who assumed that the raw, inexperienced doughboys soon to be mustered for service in the American Expeditionary Forces (AEF) would amalgamate into their armies for training and combat. They were sorely mistaken. America would essentially fight under its own terms. President Woodrow Wilson considered the United States an 'Associated' partner and not an 'Ally', so that America was not bound by pre-existing agreements among the Allies. One month after declaring war Wilson and his Secretary of War, Newton D. Baker, drove home this point when they selected General John J. Pershing to lead the AEF. Wilson and Baker gave Pershing much latitude in his role as Commander-in-Chief, and one simple order: that he cooperate with the Allies in conducting military operations, but that his soldiers must fight as an independent, American command.

Pershing and his small staff headed to Europe in June 1917 on board the *Baltic* to meet with the Allied commanders and organize the AEF. The American commander was hindered by the fact that he had inherited a force that would literally have to be built from ground up and would not be ready for combat until the next year. Miraculously, Pershing did build the AEF in relatively short order, but to the dismay of Allied leaders such as Ferdinand Foch and Sir Douglas Haig, the doughboys would not make their presence known on the battlefields until spring 1918. To better understand Pershing's army, it is helpful to glance back to the beginning.

No officer in the US Army was more qualified to lead a fighting force in Europe than Pershing. Much of his military career had been spent abroad, where he represented his country as a soldier and a politician. A West Point class of 1886 graduate, Pershing served with a cavalry regiment on the frontier in New Mexico, taught military science at the University of Nebraska, and was cited for bravery during the Spanish–American War, and in the Philippines; his impressive work as both a department commander and a military governor helped him catapult over a long list of other junior officers for promotion to brigadier general. Pershing's stellar military career was marked by tragedy when a fire at the Presidio in San Francisco on 27 August 1915 took the life of his wife and three out of four of his young children. Now more than ever he was dedicated to army service and in March 1916 was tapped to lead the Punitive Expedition in pursuit of the Mexican bandit Pancho Villa. Secretary of War Baker also recognized Pershing's leadership ability and never expressed any regrets in selecting him to lead the AEF. After the war Baker revealed the ideal partnership between a war secretary and his commanding general: 'Select a commander in whom you have confidence; give him power and responsibility, and then ... work your own head off to get him everything he needs and support him in every decision he makes.'[1] Baker and Pershing maintained a solid, respectful relationship throughout the war.

On the afternoon of 16 June 1917, Pershing met with Général de Division Henri Philippe Pétain, the hero of Verdun and now *commandant en chef des armées françaises*, to discuss how US soldiers would support the Allies in their struggle against the German forces on the Western Front. Pershing made it known his troops would fight as an independent army with their own sector and chose Lorraine, a region stretching between the Argonne Forest and the Vosges Mountains. To supply the AEF, the Americans were provided access to the ports of St Nazaire, La Pallice, and Bassens on the western coast, as well as French railways that converged in the Lorraine region.

Organization of the AEF in 1917

Over the summer and early autumn of 1917, Pershing and his staff laid the foundation for the AEF and how it would be deployed for combat on the Western Front. Every aspect of the AEF's operation and organization – from training and tactics to troop strength and shipping – had to be deliberated. Pershing initially had few troops to draw from. The regular US Army had an aggregate strength of 127,588 officers and men; the National Guard could count another 80,446. Together they totalled just over 208,000 men; a paltry sum when compared to the Allied and German forces. Just as problematic the US arsenals were mostly bare of artillery and machine guns, now the primary tools of modern warfare.

To grow the AEF with new recruits, US Congress passed the Selective Service Act. Conscription was used for the first time since the Civil War and it proved highly successful, providing the army with about two-thirds of the soldiers who served in 1917–18. All males between the ages of 21 and 30 (later extended to include ages 18 to 45) were required to register. Ten million men complied, and the army eventually drafted 2.7 million.[2]

The War Department General Staff organized the soldiers into divisions, which consisted of just under 28,000 officers and men; twice the size of an Allied or German division. Regular Army divisions (professional soldiers) were numbered from 1 to 25. Numbers 26 to 75 were reserved for the National Guard (state units federalized by President Wilson) and higher numbers for divisions of the National Army (drafted and volunteer troops).

Exactly how large an army the United States needed depended primarily on General Pershing's plans and recommendations to meet the operational situation on the Western Front. In July 1917, Pershing and his staff called for a field army of about one million men to be sent to France before the end of 1918. By the end of the war the US Army had actually formed 62 divisions, all but 19 were sent overseas.

Amalgamation issue

Toward the end of 1917, an urgent Christmas Eve cable from Secretary of War Baker arrived at Pershing's Chaumont headquarters.[3] It informed Pershing that 'both the English and French are pressing upon the President their desires to have your forces amalgamated with theirs by regiments and companies'. Baker also indicated that 'we do not desire loss of identity of our forces, but regard that as secondary to the meeting of any critical situation by the most helpful use possible of the troops at your command'. He added that 'the President desires you to have full authority to use the forces at your command as you deem wise in consultation with French and British commanders-in-chief'.[4] Pershing was in no hurry to respond and waited almost a week to do so.

On 1 January 1918, Pershing finally replied to the Christmas Day cable by writing to the American Supreme War Council representative, Major General Tasker Bliss, not Secretary of War Baker. His long message assured Bliss: 'I do not think an emergency now exists that would warrant our putting companies or battalions into British or French divisions'.[5] Pershing echoed his long-held conviction that if American troops were amalgamated, they would lose their national identity, and that the methods of instruction in the Allied armies might interfere with AEF training doctrine. 'Attention should be called to prejudices existing between French and British Governments and Armies,' he wrote, 'and the desire of each to have American units assigned to them, and the exclusion of similar assignment to the other.'[6] A cable to Bliss three days later showed he was beginning to soften his views, albeit slightly. He now entertained the idea of the British transporting and assisting in the training of American troops, as long it was 'strictly supplementary to our own regular program' of fielding an American army.

Pershing recognized that British help was needed to transport troops to France, and he had to make a concession.[7] To discuss this matter, General Sir William Robertson, Chief of the Imperial General Staff, met with Pershing on 9–10 January 1918. The two men had last conferred in November 1917, but that discussion had accomplished little. Now it was a new year and a fresh start for both. Robertson brought a proposal that offered to transport 150,000 troops (150 battalions) from divisions still in the United States that were not already scheduled for overseas duty. He also suggested breaking them up as the British had done with some Territorial Force and New Army divisions in 1915 to supply reinforcements and lines of communication troops. The proposal, he reiterated to Pershing, related only to infantrymen and machine gunners needed by the British to reinforce understrength units. Robertson also sought to reassure Pershing by reminding him that he in no way wished to interfere with the build-up of an independent American army.

Accordingly, Pershing and Bliss met with Lloyd George, Lord Milner, Robertson, and Haig on 29–30 January 1918, and after two days of tense discussion, both sides accepted an 'agreement between the commanders-in-chief of the American and British forces in France regarding the training of the American troops with British troops'.[8] They settled on the American plan for the British to transport six complete divisions, less artillery, to France for a ten-week training programme. The artillery units would be trained in American camps located in the French sector, while the British took responsibility for feeding and supplying the Americans. Pershing emphasized that the American divisions were on loan to the British Army and could be recalled at his discretion.[9] Soon after the agreement was sealed the number of divisions sent to the British sector was increased to ten and they would be organized as American II Corps under the eventual command of Major General George W. Read.

Pershing made sure the agreement clearly outlined how training would proceed. Perhaps the most important proviso of the agreement stated that once platoons, companies, battalions, and regiments of each division completed training, they would be designated ready 'to take the field ... and would then be handed over to the American commander-in-chief, under arrangements to be made between the various commanders-in-chief.'[10] This gave Pershing the assurance he insisted upon – that American divisions were only temporarily assigned to the British. The British also enhanced the agreement by proposing that American commanders and staff officers be attached to corresponding British headquarters for additional instruction. Also, this clause benefited Pershing since it gave his inexperienced officers the training they never would have received in the US.

Mostly forgotten during the negotiations were the French, and their reaction to the British proposal was one of disappointment. Since December 1917, Pétain had requested transfer of AEF divisions in France to his army for amalgamation. He was anxious to strengthen his divisions before the impending German attack. Pershing, of course, rejected this request. Nevertheless, he had great fondness for Pétain and wanted to ensure that good American–French relations continued. As a matter of courtesy, Pershing met with Pétain on 21 January to inform him of the British proposal. He refused to say why his troops were headed to the British, but he did indicate that he hoped this decision did not hurt their friendship, or show any lack of respect toward the French Army. It was a necessity to accept the British offer to transport troops since the Americans lacked shipping, he explained.

Once they began arriving in Europe Pershing promised his troops would then go to the French Army for advanced training. He also immediately offered them four black infantry regiments that were formed into the 93rd Division. This included the 369th Infantry, which had trained briefly at Wadsworth until racial tension with the citizens of Spartanburg forced the unit from the Jim Crow south. In France, the 'Harlem Hell Fighters', as they were called by the French, would distinguish themselves in combat during the spring and summer of 1918.[11]

Training at home

To train American divisions before they deployed overseas the US Army established 32 camps or cantonments throughout the United States. US soldiers would spend six months learning the rudiments of war from officers, who in many cases knew only slightly more than they did. Both the British and French helped out by sending officers across the Atlantic to assist with the instruction. It was an eye-opening experience for the foreigners, some of them veterans of Verdun and the Somme. They travelled from one training camp to another, preaching trench warfare to young recruits who carried wooden guns and were without proper uniforms and equipment. It was hard to point out the benefits of grenades, flamethrowers, and artillery when it would be months before many American troops would actually see combat.

Training was hampered by the fact that many of the new recruits had not yet received a full complement of equipment. For instance, the commanding general of the 30th Division complained to the War Department that it was two months before all units had been issued with rifles for the infantry. The infantry rifle was the heart of what Pershing preached in his open warfare doctrine. He criticized both the British and French armies because they had 'become mired in trench warfare', and, as a result, their offensive capabilities were diminished to a defensive posture on the Western Front.[12] Pershing was fearful that if his own army adopted trench warfare, it would also lose the offensive spirit. He envisioned aggressive movement and pursuit to force the enemy into the open. His thinking drew from experiences of the old frontier army during the Indian wars, when part of the infantry consisted of expert marksmen and scouts. Much to his dismay Pershing heard that training in the US at camps focused on trench warfare with little emphasis on open warfare tactics. He found the news distressing and repeatedly cabled the War Department to complain that training with the rifle was not being sufficiently stressed at home and when the divisions arrived in France, they would be re-trained to his liking.

First combat

Two weeks after the United States passed the one-year mark of entering the war, an AEF division saw combat for the first time. On 20 April 1918, a German bombardment, then infantry assault, surprised the

26th Division in a so-called quiet sector near the village of Seicheprey. That morning veteran German stormtroopers quickly captured the village. But by afternoon the American doughboys counter-attacked, re-occupied the village, and drove German forces into the surrounding woods. Fighting continued the next day when the 26th Division massed rifle power and forced the enemy to scatter. Although the Germans intended the attack as a limited operation to test American fighting capability, it was a costly affair for both sides. Around 160 German troops were killed, while the Americans suffered 634 casualties and the loss of 136 men as prisoners.[13] In the months ahead more American units became engaged in combat, albeit in minor operations. Two regiments of the 1st Division had attacked the village of Cantigny on 28 May. And on 4 July, elements of 33rd Division, attached to the Australians, fought at Hamel.[14]

The AEF in the Aisne–Marne campaign, July–August 1918

Through most of June and July the Germans struck Allied positions along the Aisne and Marne rivers. Général de Division Foch countered with his own offensive to include 1st, 3rd, 4th, and 26th US divisions. By the end of May Ludendorff's troops had reached the Marne at Château Thierry and threatened the French capital, less than 50 miles away. In response to the crisis Pershing offered Foch five American divisions. By nightfall of 31 May, the machine-gun battalion of 3rd Division had motored to Château Thierry and was positioned to help the French keep the Germans from crossing the bridge. The remainder of 3rd Division was advancing towards a position to hold the river line. The next day 2nd Division prepared defensive positions north of the Marne and west of Château Thierry along the main highway to Paris.

For two days German troops hammered the American lines and encountered stiff resistance. Beginning on 6 June, 2nd Division attacked enemy positions against Belleau Wood and the villages of Bouresches and Vaux with the fighting continuing for three weeks. The Americans suffered 9,777 casualties, including more than 1,800 dead. But it was a moral victory for the Marines.

On 17 July, the Allies launched a counter-offensive to cut the highway leading from Soissons to Château Thierry, the main German supply line in the Marne sector. The troops moved into position on 17 July in the pouring rain, which helped conceal their movements. A short, but intensive artillery preparation took place early on the 18th. Afterwards, Allied infantry moved to the attack from near Soissons in the north to Château Thierry to the south. American infantry was supported by 359 French tanks.

On 18 July, a Franco-American attack surprised the Germans. To keep the attack secret, there was no preliminary artillery preparation. Infantry jumped off with support of over 550 tanks; on 18 July both American 1st and 2nd divisions made notable progress, advancing over three miles and achieving their objectives by early morning. The next day the corps renewed its attack. The Germans, however, had been heavily reinforced with machine guns and artillery during the night; the French and American infantry found the advance slower and more costly. Fresh from Belleau Wood, 2nd Division was in the thick of the fight and had advanced more than eight miles. During five days at the front 1st Division captured 3,800 prisoners and 70 guns from the seven German divisions. For these gains, the division paid a heavy price, losing 7,000 casualties, including 1,000 killed. With the American 26th Division, I Corps pushed beyond the old Belleau Wood battlegrounds and advanced about ten miles between 18 and 25 July. For the next three weeks, the corps made steady gains against the tenacious German defenders. Advancing with the 42nd Division between 25 July and 3 August and then the 4th Division between 3 August and 12 August, the American corps crossed the Ourcq and then the Vesle, a distance of almost 15 miles.

At the end of the first week of August, the Aisne–Marne campaign came to a close. The campaign successfully removed the threat against Paris and freed several important railroads for Allied use. From mid-August to mid-September this advance included troops from the American III Corps before they withdrew southwards to join the new American First Army. From 28 August to 1 September, 32nd Division attacked north of Soissons, seizing the key town of Juvigny and making a two-and-a-half-mile penetration of the German lines.[15]

American II Corps with the British

Of the ten divisions that Pershing had loaned Haig in exchange for shipping and training, by August 1918 Pershing had taken back eight of them. The first five divisions (4th, 28th, 35th, 77th and 82nd) left in mid-July for training elsewhere. In fact, Pershing elected to take all ten, but encountered heavy resistance from the BEF commander. Haig did not hold back his bitter resentment over this decision.

> What will History say regarding this action of the Americans leaving the British zone of operations when *the decisive battle* of the war is at its height, and the decision is still in doubt ... I hope events would justify his [Pershing's] decision to withdraw such a large force of American Divisions (over 150,000 men) from me at the height of battle. For the present, I am convinced that if they had taken a part in this battle, they would, owing to the present tired and demoralized state of the Germans on this front, have enabled the Allies to obtain immediate and decisive results.[16]

Foch intervened on Haig's behalf and negotiated to allow the British to first keep five divisions, but Pershing protested and as a compromise allowed two to remain behind with the BEF; Haig selected the 27th and 30th. The other three (33rd, 78th, and 80th) moved to the east and joined First Army. The frustrated British Army commanders could do little but abide by Pershing's wishes. At least the British still had two American divisions, and they were good ones. During the final phase of their training, the 27th and 30th entered the line side-by-side in mid-August for their first taste of combat in the Canal and Dickebusch sectors near Ypres.

They were ordered to assist in the construction of the east and west Poperinghe defensive system, and from 31 August to 4 September the 27th and 30th divisions received their baptism of fire during the Ypres–Lys operation. The inexperienced Americans drove the enemy from Mount Kemmel and the adjacent high ground with the help of the British. Their breakthroughs south of the front prompted German withdrawals in the Kemmel area, thus assuring a successful campaign. Although a minor operation, the Americans gave a good effort and did much to prove to the British they could fight. The 27th Division lost one officer and 72 men killed, while 30th Division suffered two officers and 35 enlisted men killed. On 3 September, II Corps withdrew from the Canal sector and was placed in reserve of British forces for additional training.[17]

Hindenburg Line attack

The confident doughboys, with one operation under their belt, were about to receive a much larger challenge. On 20 September, the 27th and 30th divisions were released from GHQ reserve, where they had been training under the direction of British Third Army, and placed under British Fourth Army to operate with the Australian Corps. Two days later they received orders to move towards the front lines and make preparations for a significant part in the next offensive. Since 8 August 1918 the British Army was in the midst of an offensive to drive the German Army from its positions near the old Somme battlefield, where it had stalled during the Spring Offensive. By mid-September the Germans were forced back to their heavily fortified defensive zone, the Siegfried Position, which the Allies called the Hindenburg Line. The British, with help of the American divisions, were planning to conduct an offensive that would demoralize the enemy and destroy his defences, including wire and dugouts.

The II Corps' main objective was to break through the main line in the vicinity of St Quentin, a key line of German resistance, and eliminate the enemy entrenched on the canal and below the tunnel. They would spearhead the British Fourth Army assault on the trenches around the tunnel area with the Australian Corps following. This was a formidable task for any experienced army and the mission, in hindsight, had little chance of succeeding.

The 27th and 30th entered the front trenches on the night of 25 and 26 September, relieving the 18th and 74th British divisions, and the 1st Australian Division, respectively. The line assigned the doughboys faced the outer defences of the Hindenburg system, to the west of the entrance to the Bellicourt tunnel. The features of this outer line were positions situated on the high ground opposite the Quennemont Farm, Guillemont Farm, and the so-called Knoll. From this outer line the terrain sloped down toward the main defence to the east, rising again at Bony, which was included in the enemy defensive system. For the Americans to achieve their objective on 29 September, they would have to undertake a preliminary operation two days before to occupy the outer defences, including the farms and the Knoll. If successful, this would become the jumping off point for the attacks. That would not be any easy task either. British III Corps also failed to capture this ground after several attempts and now the far less experienced Americans were asked to do the job.

To prepare for the preliminary operation 27th Division entered the front line on the night of 24/25 September, relieving the 18th and 74th British divisions in the Gouy sector. The 30th Division relieved the 1st Australian Division in the Nauroy sector, west of Bellicourt, on the night of 23/24 September. Preceding the attack was an intense artillery bombardment; more than 750,000 shells lobbed at the German defences.[18] A unique element to the artillery attack was eight hours of 'BB', the British designation for mustard gas. The attack on the St Quentin Canal was the first use of mustard gas by the British during the war even though the Germans had introduced the gas 15 months before. The gas attacks put a number of German artillery batteries out of action and caused casualties.[19]

The preliminary ground attack in the 27th Division sector started with the 106th Infantry Regiment advancing towards the objective at 0530hrs on 27 September. They were successful until driven back by machine-gun fire. All three battalions of the regiment were in the line, each supported by four tanks. Elements of the regiment penetrated the German outpost system, but were too weak to cover a front 4,000 yards wide. Support came from the 105th Infantry Regiment, but was of little use. The enemy filtered through the many ravines and communication trenches into dugouts that obviously were unaffected by the artillery.

The following day a conference at 54th Brigade headquarters, with representatives of the 27th Division and Australian Corps in attendance, discussed the failure of the 106th to capture Quennemont Farm,

Guillemont Farm, and the Knoll. This was complicated by the fact that American troops, including wounded, still occupied portions of the trenches around the farms and the Knoll.[20] A proposal was to adjust the artillery fire to a line farther in the rear so those troops might advance under its protection.

After consulting the artillery commander, the conference participants learned that due to lack of time it would be impractical to change the barrage table and bring the barrage back. Fourth Army commander General Sir Henry Rawlinson and General Sir John Monash, commander of the Australian Corps, worried over the delicate situation, justifiably. Failure of 27th Division to secure the objective was the result not so much of inexperience, though that certainly was the case, but of a complicated battle plan devised by Monash and approved by Rawlinson. One writer correctly asserts, 'This proposal was not Monash at his best. He was expecting a longer advance from the Americans than he had ever demanded of his Australians.'[21]

On the 30th Division front, the doughboys were having more success. They launched the advance at 2130hrs on 26 September with the 118th Infantry establishing a line north of La Haute Bruyere.[22] With the benefit of trench bombardment, counter-battery fire, and a creeping barrage that cut the wire, they were able to catch the Germans in their dugouts. The Americans formed up to the east of the tunnel, but could not advance due to enfilade fire from the Quennemont Farm on the left. At this point the 5th Australian Division advanced toward the Americans, now in a defensive position. The advance was slowed when the Australians encountered fire from concealed machine-gun posts. Determined, both the Americans and Australians moved forward and captured Nauroy that afternoon.

The fight continued into the next morning with the 118th Infantry Regiment advancing toward its objective of securing the line of departure for the general attack. Resistance allowed only slight gain. Still, the 30th Division was in a position for the main attack on 29 September.[23] Despite the setbacks during the preliminary operation, Rawlinson still held out the hope that the main operation would be a success. In his diary entry of 28 September, he wrote: 'I feel pretty happy about the prospects as a whole, for, if the Americans are inexperienced, they are keen as mustard and splendid men.'[24]

Heavy fog and low visibility greeted the Americans as they launched their Hindenburg Line attack on the morning of 29 September. The 30th Division advance started at 0530hrs under the dreadful conditions of mist and low clouds. Mixed with smoke from the barrages the low visibility hampered their approach. It was a Sunday morning the doughboys would not soon forget, and one an Australian brigade commander thought a 'spectacle well worth watching'.[25]

While 30th Division gained most of its objectives, on its left 27th Division had a much more difficult time. The New Yorkers started their attack nearly an hour earlier, at 0450hrs, with infantry advancing towards the jump-off point that they had failed to reach during the preliminary attack. Reports received at division headquarters indicated the 107th Infantry and 108th 'going well'. At 0810hrs the 108th was reported to have crossed the Hindenburg Line and was on the way to the tunnel. But an hour later the situation had changed. Regimental messages indicated the 3rd Battalion had suffered heavy casualties from machine-gun fire at Guillemont Farm. By 1005hrs reports received from the 107th Infantry related casualties were heavy and one battalion was falling back. Reports from the 3rd Australian Division confirmed that many 'Americans were leaderless near Guillemont trench and Willow trench'.[26]

Despite such strong opposition, portions of the 108th Infantry Regiment crossed the main Hindenburg Line south of Bony at 0800hrs: a remarkable achievement against enormous odds. The regiment could not go beyond the line, but was able to hold until joined by the 3rd Australian Division. Together, they captured Quennemont Farm. There they came upon pockets of German troops, who appeared from underground passages of the tunnel behind the Americans. Casualties filled the battlefield. 'They'd just became figures going down', remembered one New Yorker, 'like pins in a bowling alley'.[27] Because of the fog and poor visibility the 27th had overrun their position and failed to clear the way for the Australians.[28] The Diggers secured most of the line in the 30th Division sector, but could not reach the German main line in the 27th Division zone.

On the extreme left the 105th Infantry Regiment, according to the plan, was supposed to march across the tunnel and turn to the north along the east bank of the canal and seize Le Catelet and Gouy. There the 3rd Australian Division would leapfrog them. They were following behind the 107th, but when that regiment failed to advance because of the fire at the Knoll, the 105th had to take up a defensive position. The 53rd American Brigade commander ordered it to hold against counter-attacks. In liaison with the 18th British Division, they captured the Knoll and Macquincourt Trench. The 105th regimental commander, Colonel James M. Andrews, blamed failure to proceed beyond the Knoll on 'the smoke barrage laid down by the Allied Artillery that proved very confusing to our troops; the direction of the march was hard to maintain and due to some as yet unexplained phenomena, our compasses were so unstable as to be practically useless'.[29] What Andrews fails to mention is that not all of the company commanders had a compass, a failure on his part to ensure that such valuable instruments were in ready supply.

During the evening of 29 September mixed troops of the 27th Division and the Australian Corps occupied trench lines in the vicinity of the Knoll, Guillemont Farm, and Quennemont Farm. During this fighting the 107th Infantry lost more than half its men, 377 killed and 658 wounded: the heaviest losses suffered by an American regiment during the war.[30]

By late afternoon the confidence Rawlinson had exhibited the day before the attack now turned to frustration. After reading field messages reporting fierce opposition encountered by the Americans, he reluctantly concluded they were in trouble. One of Rawlinson's diary entries records: 'the Americans appear to be in a state of hopeless confusion and will not I fear be able to function as a Corps so I am contemplating replacing them … I fear their casualties have been heavy but it is their own fault.'[31] To compensate for what he arrogantly concluded was American failure to mop up, he changed the plan and now ordered capture of the town of Bony and the northern end of the tunnel.

Such criticism of the American battle performance was exaggerated. In reality, the Americans had fought quite well against solid German positions in one of the most heavily defended sections of the Hindenburg

Line. While it is true that the doughboys were inexperienced, especially in the case of line officers who had not yet seen combat, the main problem they encountered was the failure of the BEF preliminary artillery attack to soften the German defences. Simply put, 27th and 30th divisions went up against a superior foe and, despite the chaotic moments in the attack, they still reached most of their objectives. On 30 September, they were relieved and sent to a rear area for rest.

From 2 to 19 October 1918, the 27th and 30th divisions made their final contribution of the war. After a brief rest, following the St Quentin Canal–Hindenburg Line operation, 27th and 30th divisions were back into line. The 30th took part in the 8 October Cambrai operation with the British Third and Fourth armies; a combined effort that forced two German armies to retreat to the Selle River. During the battle of the Selle, the 27th and 30th divisions assisted the Fourth Army in driving six divisions from their defensive position. Since September 27th the doughboys had fought almost continuously, suffering high casualties without replacements. Rawlinson finally relieved the divisions on 12 October 1918, and moved them to a rear area for a well-deserved rest. The Armistice was signed before the divisions would participate again.

By the end of what became known as the Somme Operation, the American divisions suffered more than 3,400 killed and over 13,000 wounded and missing. The 27th served 57 days on the front line and 30th Division 69 days. Both figures include both front-line training and battle.[32]

Pershing's independent American Army

By August 1918, Pershing had over a million troops in France. He could now set his sights – and American First Army – on an operation against the St Mihiel salient, a triangle formed between two rivers, the Meuse on the west and the Moselle to the east. Before emptying into the Rhine River, the Moselle flows through France, Luxembourg, and finally Germany. The salient overlooked the Woëvre Plain, a low marshland of ponds and streams surrounded by woods of varying size. The salient's three anchor cities were Verdun to the north, St Mihiel in the south, and Pont-à-Mousson 25 miles to the east.

Then, on 30 August Pershing's plan to attack the salient was about to be de-railed by Maréchal Foch when the two generals sat down for a meeting. Foch told Pershing, that recently, Allied victories in other fronts had made significant gains, and he now believed the Germans were on the verge of collapsing. Because of these battlefield developments, the Commander-in-Chief informed Pershing that he either had to reduce the scope of the St Mihiel attack or abandon it altogether. Furthermore, Foch declared that a better course of action would be a combined Allied offensive with the British converging on the German lines from north to south, and the French and Americans attacking from the west. An operation against the St Mihiel salient was still feasible, Foch assured Pershing, but only a limited attack on the southern face. It would then have to be followed up with a separate attack against German defences in the Meuse–Argonne, which Foch believed had more strategic importance than St Mihiel. Pershing disagreed vehemently and the meeting was adjourned. The following day Pershing sent Foch a written response, telling him that by no means would he allow the American army to be broken up, and would sacrifice the St Mihiel operation if necessary. If that were the case, he would comply with Foch and attack only in the Meuse–Argonne – but as a whole American army and nothing less.

On 2 September, Pershing and Pétain met with Foch at Bombon and presented their case. Foch was in a better mood and more reasonable – and for that matter, so was Pershing, perhaps because Pétain was there as a mediator. Foch agreed that the American First Army could execute a restricted attack on the St Mihiel salient, but they were not to push forward to Metz; they must stop after the salient had been reduced and prepare for a larger operation west of the Meuse. Foch insisted that the St Mihiel attack take place no later than 15 September, and the Meuse–Argonne operation would launch by 25 September.

Pershing had now committed his inexperienced army to undertake two large operations over the course of two weeks.

St Mihiel

On 12 September 1918, General John J. Pershing and his newly formed American First Army attacked the St Mihiel salient, a bulge in the Allied lines created by German forces in the autumn of 1914. Sixteen miles deep and 25 miles wide, the salient stretched between Verdun and Nancy and prevented rail transport between Paris and the Eastern Front.

At the St Mihiel operation First Army utilized 500,000 doughboys, 110,000 French Colonial troops, 1,500 planes, and 3,000 guns. Opposing them were 230,000 Germans who, unbeknownst to Pershing, were preparing to withdraw from the sector and were caught off guard when the attack was launched early on 12 September. The battle was essentially over on the first day, but lasted until 16 September, as First Army mopped up German resistance throughout the salient. It was an impressive showing for the Americans in their baptism of fire, inflicting about 2,000 German casualties (killed and wounded), and capturing more than 1,500 prisoners, 443 artillery pieces, and 752 Maxims and other machine guns. Two hundred square miles of formerly occupied territory went back to the French, including the Paris and Nancy rail lines. American losses were high compared to the German ones; around 7,000 killed and wounded.

Immediately after St Mihiel, attention shifted south to the Meuse–Argonne. The attack was set for 26 September and planning for the operation was placed in the hands of Colonel George C. Marshall. Between the American and French armies, the Argonne Forest ran northward for about six miles. The plan was not to make a direct frontal assault upon this forest but to force the enemy out of his defences by the threat of surrounding it. Pershing's ultimate objective in the battle was the city of Sedan, which the Germans had taken early in the war and turned into a vital railway hub to supply their troops. General Max von Gallwitz's army held the front with five understrength divisions.

If First Army could drive the enemy from Sedan and cut their rail line, German armies would be trapped between the Americans on the Meuse–Argonne front, French forces converging through the Aisne River valley on the left flank of the doughboys, and the British striking north-west in the Somme sector. Pershing would open the attack by advancing through the Aire River valley with the Argonne Forest on the left and the east bank of the Meuse on the right. To meet the objective, 225,000 doughboys in three corps made up of three divisions each would attack on a front 25 miles wide. Sedan was about 40 miles from where First Army would jump off, and along the way Pershing's soldiers had to traverse the six-mile-deep Argonne Forest and its assortment of jutting rocks, steep cliffs, and slippery ravines. If First Army's doughboys made it beyond these obstructions, the fortified barriers of the Hindenburg Line awaited them.

Pershing and his operations staff visualized the battle in two segments. During the initial attack, First Army would pierce the three German positions, advance another ten miles, then clear the Argonne and link up with the French Fourth Army on the left. The next attack would press forward ten more miles to outflank the enemy defences along the Aisne River, which would place the Americans in striking distance of Sedan and Mézières on the Meuse. Smaller attacks would clear the enemy from the heights facing the east bank of the Meuse.

Before the battle commenced Marshall first had to move 500,000 troops, 2,000 guns, and 900,000 tons of ammunition and supplies 50 miles into position for the attack on 26 September, but that could not be done until the 200,000 French soldiers left the area where the Americans were to jump off. All travel had to be made under cover of night, while aeroplanes, under command of Brigadier General William Billy Mitchell, moved either early in the morning or just at dusk to camouflage themselves. In the daytime, nothing was to be seen. By the evening of 25 September 1918, First Army with nine attacking divisions placed in three corps were ready to jump off early the next morning.

Following a three-hour artillery barrage the infantry jumped off at 0530hrs on 26 September. Results for the first day were mixed. Meanwhile 35th Division, including artillery officer Captain Harry S. Truman, took Vauquois Hill early in the day, which had seen fierce fighting between the Germans and the French in the previous years of the war. Then the 35th Division had trouble breaking out of the woods near Cheppy until they were rescued by tank units, including one led by Lieutenant Colonel George S. Patton who was badly wounded in the fight and knocked out of action for the remainder of the war. The 28th and 77th divisions made great strides crossing the Aire, but Montfaucon was Pershing's main objective that day and 79th Division was tasked with the tremendous responsibility of taking the heavily fortified high ground. By nightfall the division reached the outskirts of this landmark and, despite Pershing's instance that the 79th keep fighting, they ran out of steam. The attack resumed the next morning and Montfaucon was firmly in American hands by the afternoon of the 27th.

General Max von Gallwitz's army with five understrength divisions held the ground opposite First Army. Gallwitz was completely caught off guard by the American attack, and although he quickly bolstered the lines by calling up the 51st and 76th Reserve divisions and the 52nd Infantry Division, this was a temporary fix. Gallwitz feared that Pershing's attack toward the Argonne might have been a diversion to mask a more concentrated thrust in the direction of the Woëvre or Metz. Not until later in the day would he have a good sense of the American First Army's battle plan after Fifth German Army intelligence interrogated several French and American POWs. Just two days into battle the First Army struggled to advance while American casualties mounted and only got worse as German resistance stiffened after Gallwitz had brought up reserves. Compounding the accurate enemy fire power were clogged roads, poor weather, and the next wave of the influenza pandemic. Pershing saw no other choice but to stop the attack and regroup for a few days. On 4 October he sent the 29th and 33rd divisions to capture the Meuse Heights, but they struggled to drive the German machine gunners from the high ground and it remained in enemy hands for another week.

In the Argonne the 77th Division was also slowed by German defences that were hard to penetrate in the deep woods. Then a composite battalion from the 307th and 308th Infantry regiments got cut off and were trapped in the forest for five days. The tactical actions in the context of this episode are worth mentioning, not because they changed the course of history, but because they shaped the US memory of World War I to a disproportionate degree compared to their military importance. The composite battalion mentioned above became known as the 'Lost Battalion', a 550-man force of US soldiers. It was trapped by the Germans in the Argonne Forest on 2 October after having been separated from the main contingent of the 77th Division. The unit was neither lost nor a battalion, but consisted of six companies of the 308th Infantry Regiment, and a contingent of men from the 307th Infantry. Led by 308th Battalion commander Major Charles Whittlesey, for five days the so-called Lost

Battalion remained in the 'Pocket', a hill between the Charleveaux Brook and an old Roman road.

During its ordeal Whittlesey's men ran out of supplies, ammunition, and food while continuously subjected to German machine-gun and trench mortar fire that inflicted heavy casualties. Friendly artillery from 77th Division guns created added misery and, with communications cut off between the Lost Battalion and headquarters, Whittlesey had to rely on homing pigeons to deliver messages to the rear. On 7 October, the Lost Battalion was rescued after runners broke through the German lines and directed advancing 77th Division troops to the Pocket. Out of the 550 Lost Battalion troops who entered the Argonne, only 194 were rescued unharmed, while the rest were either killed or wounded.

While on an operation to rescue the Lost Battalion, corporal, later sergeant, Alvin York became the Hero of the Argonne.[33] On 8 October 1918, his unit, Company G the 328th Infantry, attached to the 82nd Division, entered the Chatel-Chéhéry sector in Argonne Forest. They were part of an operation to relieve enemy fire pouring down on the Lost Battalion. Corporal York and 16 other doughboys attacked German machine guns protecting a railroad line. After the Americans captured a large group of German soldiers, the Germans counter-attacked, and nine of the US soldiers became casualties. York took charge of the remaining doughboys, and with his skills as a marksman, single-handedly took a machine-gun nest and captured 132 German prisoners. For his heroism on 8 October York would receive more than 50 decorations, including the French Croix de Guerre and the Medal of Honor.

To the west of First Army the French Fourth Army was also struggling and the depleted force asked Pershing for reinforcements. He sent the 2nd and 36th divisions to help out and they fought with distinction at the Blanc Mont Ridge in the Champagne.

During the middle of October Pershing sent the 37th and 91st divisions to reinforce a French army division between the Lys and Scheldt rivers in Flanders. The next day both divisions attacked in the direction of the Scheldt between Waregem and Kruishoutem and received heavy fire from Germans troops protected by hedges and abandoned farms. Both divisions would remain under French command until the end of the war.

But as the battle in the Meuse–Argonne dragged on Pershing was heavily criticized by the other Allied commanders that First Army was in shambles and he was unfit to be its commander. In Washington the President, Secretary of War, and Chief of Staff stood by Pershing, but he also came to the realization that leading both an expeditionary force and a field army was more than one man could handle, especially since some of his division commanders needed more managing than he had thought. This was a steep learning curve for Pershing and his doughboys, and their success depended on having more independence for the corps and division commanders to make decisions on the ground; a fact already recognized by the Allied forces after more than three years of costly fighting.

Both the British and French high commands offered advice to the Americans from lessons they had learned after the bloody attacks at Ypres, Verdun, the Somme, and most recently the Chemin des Dames. Allied training publications and enemy intelligence reports were shared with the AEF on a regular basis, but there is little reason to suggest that American officers glanced at this ready information, much less digested what British and French officers had to say. Instead, Pershing's generals were encouraged to take their own initiative, and if they were not up for the task, then they were sacked and replaced. Called by one historian 'The AEF Way of War', division commanders 'adjusted their doctrine and operational methods as they fought' in the Meuse–Argonne. Attack plans became more comprehensive, 'employing flexible infantry formations and maximizing firepower to seize limited objectives'.[34]

A turning point for the AEF came on 12 October when Pershing reorganized First Army. He stepped aside as its commander and put Lieutenant General Hunter Liggett from I Corps in his place and also formed a Second Army with III Corps' Lieutenant General Robert Lee Bullard at the helm. Pershing retained command of the entire AEF, but was now essentially an army group commander on a par with other Allied leaders.

Liggett formally took charge of First Army on 16 October, but much to his dismay Pershing remained close by and interfered frequently with tactical and personnel decisions. Liggett inherited a fighting force that showed great promise, but the men had been in line for extended periods and were exhausted and prone to straggling when they lost contact with their units. Once he felt First Army was back in order he launched another offensive directed right at the Kriemhilde Position. He sent the 42nd Division against the Côte De Châtillon and the 32nd struck the Côte Dame Marie. Both obstacles were heavily protected with machine-gun nests and wire. But positions were pierced by the doughboys, although not until after days of severe fighting and counter-attacks. This key position was now held by First Army, but it took three weeks at the cost of around 100,000 casualties.

On 1 November, a two-hour artillery barrage preceded what became the third and final phase of Meuse–Argonne. The 2nd and 89th divisions crossed the Meuse against heavy German machine-gun fire. Liggett devised the operational plan into three stages: first, the attack on 1 November, then a pursuit as the Germans fell back, and last, the crossing of the Meuse. Liggett designed a frontal attack, straight at the German lines, just like the opening offensive on 26 September. The only difference was that First Army had come of age, and as Liggett pointed out, they were secure in their knowledge that the Germans were on their last legs. One last thrust would take care of the battle and the war. Everything was coming together.

During the final stages of the battle an embarrassing episode occurred between two First Army divisions when they both descended upon the city of Sedan. Pershing wanted the Americans to capture Sedan and hand it over to the French as a goodwill gesture, since France had lost the city during the 1870 Franco-Prussian War. Instead of an organized military operation, the pursuit to Sedan turned into a debacle. On 6 November, V Corps commander Charles P. Summerall decided that 1st Division, which was on the far left flank, would capture the city. This meant the 1st would have to cross the front and rear of two other divisions, the 42nd and 77th. Summerall wanted this accomplished at night and, along the way, the 1st Division became tangled up with other divisions. One group of soldiers thought another was the enemy and opened fire. Communications and traffic broke down. Sedan was not taken until a week later.

On 8 November, on behalf of the Allied commanders, Maréchal Foch and a British naval representative met with a German delegation to discuss a ceasefire. The Germans did not agree to Foch's armistice terms, which were in

The Meuse-Argonne offensive, 1918

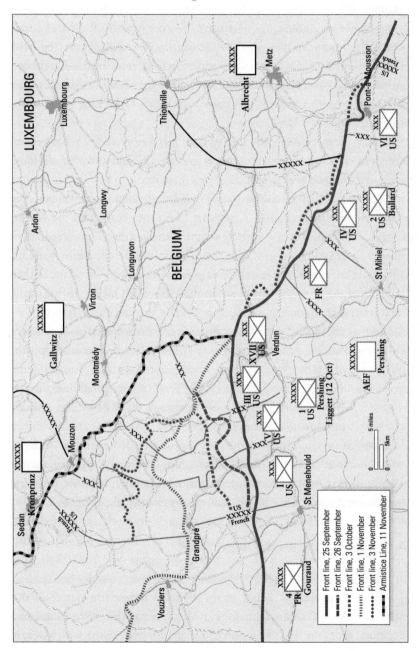

line with what Pershing wanted. Foch demanded that they surrender their weapons and war equipment, and evacuate their forces back to Germany, among other conditions. The Germans refused to give Foch an immediate answer, and in return he refused to grant a provisional armistice. They had three days, until 11 November, to consider Foch's terms. Until then the Allies would remain on the offensive. Along the Meuse, from the region of Sedan to Stenay, German machine gunners, clinging to the hills overlooking the river, fought as if they had never heard of peace talks, and prevented the Americans from crossing. At 0830hrs on the morning of 11 November, American commanders received orders to cease advancing 90 minutes later, as an armistice had been set for that exact moment.

Despite so many fits and starts, the Meuse–Argonne was an impressive effort by mostly untested American divisions, ultimately involving 1.2 million American and French troops who used 2,417 guns that fired off about 4,214,000 rounds of artillery ammunition. Brigadier General Billy Mitchell's 840 planes had managed to drop 100 tons of explosives on enemy lines. Yet the battle was fought mostly by soldiers who jumped off from trenches and exposed ground in the face of blistering machine-gun and artillery fire. First Army divisions, inexperienced as they were, penetrated over 34 miles and captured 16,059 German prisoners of war, 468 pieces of enemy artillery, and about 3,000 guns and mortars of all types. During the course of 47 days, 150 French villages and towns, many of them in ruins, were liberated by Pershing's doughboys at a cost of 120,000 Americans killed and wounded.

From the opening salvos in the early morning of 26 September until the clock struck at 1100hrs on 11 November, Pershing's warriors fought tenaciously and bravely, although at times recklessly, and they made an outstanding contribution to the Allies' victory on the field of battle.

American troops on the Italian front

In July 1918, Allied leaders received an urgent plea by the Italian government for troops to bolster its depleted forces. On behalf of the AEF, General Pershing contributed by sending the 332nd Infantry Regiment from the 83rd Division to the Italian front along with medical and supply units, For several weeks the regiment trained in mountain warfare in the vicinity of Lake Garda. Then in early October 1918, the 332nd moved to Treviso for placement as a reserve under command of the Italian 31st Division and prepared for the Italian Vittorio Veneto offensive. On 29 October, the 332nd entered combat in pursuit of the Austrians across the Taliamento River. On 3 November, the Americans attacked an Austrian rear-guard battalion protecting the river crossings. The following day the regiment's 2nd Battalion crossed the river on a narrow footbridge and skirmished with the Austrians. The Austrian position was taken and the battalion pushed forward along the Treviso–Udine railroad, eliminating several machine-gun nests and capturing a three-inch gun. At the town of Codroipo the Americans seized a large cache of enemy ammunition and supplies. At 1500hrs on 4 November, an armistice with Austria went into effect, and the war was over for the 332nd Infantry.

The American Army contribution in 1918

Among World War I's vast scholarship, the US Army's legacy has largely been overshadowed by historiography that stresses the BEF's role in forcing the Germans to capitulate. Yet, when the war ended there was no doubt that the AEF had played a significant role in the defeat of the German Army. Over the course of 200 days of fighting the AEF had taken about 49,000 German prisoners and 1,400 guns. Over one million American soldiers in 29 divisions saw active operations, while one million more served in support roles. During the relatively brief period of combat the AEF lost over 320,000 casualties, of which 50,280 were killed and another 200,600 were wounded in action. In October, during the midst of the Meuse–Argonne battle, the Americans held over 101 miles, or 23 per cent, of the Western Front. After reorganizing, First Army's improved staff work and coordination pushed the doughboys through the German defences. In November, as the front contracted with the German retreat, the AEF held over 80 miles or a fifth of the front line.

Such AEF achievements would not have been possible without Allied assistance. The French and British helped train and transport the

American soldiers and supplied much of the artillery, and all of the tanks and aeroplanes used in battle. The French were especially cooperative. Pétain frequently intervened on behalf of Pershing and the AEF to push for an independent American army fighting in its own sector of the front. More so than any other Allied commander, Pétain seemed grateful for the AEF and the Allied cause.

The AEF also served as a training ground for the generals of World War II. Three of the most notable were operations officer and later Chief of Staff George C. Marshall, tank commander George S. Patton, who later took Third Army across Europe in 1944–45, and Douglas MacArthur, a highly decorated brigade commander in the 42nd Division, who received greater fame while leading ground forces in the Pacific Theatre in World War II. This list also includes Major Terry de la Mesa Allen, who would lead the 1st Division as a general in North Africa and Sicily, and who had commanded a battalion of the 90th Division; Lieutenant Colonel Joseph 'Vinegar Joe' Stillwell, the sour-faced commander of the China Burma India Theatre during World War II, who in 1918 served as IV Corps' intelligence officer; and Captain Jonathan Wainwright, who in 1942 surrendered his command in the Philippines and served the rest of World War II in a Japanese POW camp, who in 1918 was the 82nd Division's chief of staff.

Besides its battlefield achievements, the two-million-strong AEF aided the Allies through its mere presence. Throughout 1918, as the German Army ranks depleted, the Allied military strengthened as Americans increasingly arrived on the Western Front. Had the war continued into 1919, Pershing's AEF would likely have made up the bulk of Allied forces since by November 1918, another two million men were ready for overseas deployment. As a commander, Pershing created the first modern American army that proved its capability to fight alongside the Allies, and against the superior German soldiers.

This was especially true during the 47-day Meuse–Argonne battle when during the first days of the attack the American soldiers showed more courage than skill. Much like the learning curve experienced by the British Tommies and French *poilus* earlier in the war, the doughboys and their commanders slowly learned how to fight against a well-entrenched enemy over unforgiving terrain. Through the leadership of Pershing's senior officers, such as Hunter Liggett, American divisions showed remarkable tactical skill during the difficult fighting in October and November 1918. At the higher command levels, many of Pershing's staff officers experienced their own learning curve and earned the respect of Allied counterparts.

CHAPTER 6

THE FORGOTTEN FRONTS IN EUROPE

Russia, Italy, and the Balkans in 1918

Professor Lothar Höbelt

In the historiography of World War I, the Western Front usually takes centre stage. There is no doubt that the Western Front is where the decisive battles took place during World War I, from 1914, when the Battle of the Marne ended German hopes of dealing a knock-out blow to France, to 1918, when the final German offensives ran out of steam and the Allies then drove the Germans back.

The famous musical *O What a Lovely War* has Douglas Haig praying, 'God grant me victory before the Americans arrive', but actually that was a line that might have been stolen from Ludendorff's prayer book. That was what the German campaign of 1918 was all about. Graf Ottokar Czernin, the Austro-Hungarian Foreign Secretary, realized that the Central Powers could never defeat Britain and the US but he reckoned that once the Germans had taken Paris – or Calais – the Entente might start talking about a reasonable peace settlement in earnest.[1] Yet, short-term fears about a massive German breakthrough in the West and a fight 'with our backs to the wall', were one thing; long-term anxieties about Germany dominating not just continental Europe, but most of Eurasia after the Russian collapse, were another. The Bolsheviks were widely regarded as German puppets. After all, Lenin had been repatriated in the famous sealed train in April 1917 courtesy of the Prussian General Staff. French Général de Division Henri Berthelot, the advisor to the Romanian Army, summed it up: 'The Bolsheviks are nothing but agents of the Boches.' Before 1914, Britain had been apprehensive about the growing power of Russia. Little wonder it was worried about the impact of a Russo-German combination. As the Chief of the Imperial General Staff, General Sir Henry Wilson, put it: 'It was a question of pulling Siberia out of the wreck, in order to save India.'[2]

This situation had the makings of an obvious dilemma for German planners. Short-term considerations, the necessity of making the best possible use of their window of opportunity, argued for a concentration of forces in the West. Long-term geopolitics for securing the Empire demanded an emphasis in the East. Ludendorff was the first to realize the supreme importance of the great push in the West; yet even he was tempted by the prizes to be won in the East where much could be gained in return for fairly minor investments. Some authors have criticized the frittering away of scarce resources in imperialist ventures in the East. More than 30 German divisions remained tied down on the Russian front, even after that front had officially ceased to exist.[3] However, a closer look at the composition of these forces detracts from the gravity of these charges. Heavy artillery and well-trained stormtroops moved West; what remained in the East was cavalry and lightly armed occupation forces that were of little use in the sort of warfare to be expected on the Western Front. 'What remained in the East was "fourth grade" material.'[4] Austria-Hungary had an even bigger proportion of its army engaged in the Ukraine, starting with something like ten or 11 out of 70 divisions. But, once again, few of the howitzers needed on the Piave front against Italy were deployed in the Steppe. In fact, half a dozen Austro-Hungarian batteries of heavy guns (12-inch mortars) took part in the German offensive in the West.[5]

The Russian Revolution and the 'Bread Peace'

On 7 November, Lenin had organized his *coup d'état* in Petrograd, the event that we now know as the 'October Revolution'. On 26 November, he proposed an armistice. Lenin's priority was peace at almost any price to consolidate his hold on Russia. Peace and land for the peasants were the two slogans that promised to win the hearts of the majority of Russians. While communism soon made a mockery of the second pledge, Lenin was determined to deliver on the first. In his mind, Russian territorial losses did not matter at all, as the imperialist order of things would soon be overtaken by world revolution anyway. According to the Marxist calendar, if revolution was possible in a backward country like Russia, it could hardly be far behind in heavily industrialized states like Germany or Britain. In turn, none of the capitalist regimes whose downfall Lenin confidently predicted expected the Bolshevik government to last long. That is why Czernin argued the Central Powers should jump at the chance to make peace with Lenin. He agreed that his regime would not last but argued that no Russian government that succeeded him would dare to reverse that decision and re-enter the war.

The Western powers were invited to join the peace conference that was supposed to start in Brest-Litovsk on 22 December 1917. They turned that offer down. They were not going to start negotiating in the wake of Russian defeat – and before the United States had made its weight felt in Europe. To counter Russian slogans of a peace without annexations and contributions, Wilson published a programme of his own, the celebrated Fourteen Points, on 8 January 1918. The Fourteen Points had not been discussed with his allies. At least one of them could be interpreted as a swipe at the Royal Navy's command of the high seas ('absolute freedom of navigation upon the seas'); others hinted vaguely at a kind of self-determination for the subject nations of both the Austro-Hungarian and the Ottoman empires ('freest opportunity to autonomous development'). The only nation that was promised independence in unequivocal terms was Poland. But Polish independence, of course, came largely at the expense of Russia. Germany and Austria-Hungary had already declared their commitment to an independent Poland more than a year before, in November 1916. Czernin did not reject Wilson's Fourteen Points but cautiously welcomed them as a starting point, at least.[6]

The Russian delegation to Brest-Litovsk, led by Leon Trotsky, tried to make best possible use of the Central Powers' dilemma. The Germans were in a hurry, the Russians were not. Trotsky's way of putting pressure on the Germans was to delay matters as far as possible. In a reference to Wilson's mistrust of secret diplomacy, negotiations were supposed to be held in public. The result was grandstanding on a grand scale. Trotsky and his two opposite numbers, Czernin and German Foreign Secretary Richard Von Kühlmann, engaged in brilliant rhetoric, swinging between learned discourse and flights of fancy. Russia was willing to sign a peace based on the principle of *uti possidetis* ('as you possess', i.e. at the end of a conflict the territory remains with the possessor or occupying force); in other words, the eastern borders of Russia should roughly follow the current front line. Thus, Trotsky was resigned to the loss of Poland, Lithuania, and Courland. The Central Powers in turn were quite willing to pay lip-service to the idea of self-determination. None of these countries would be annexed outright, but they would be turned into satellites and client-states. Poland would be linked to Austria-Hungary in a personal union; on 28 January 1918, the Polish Council of Regency decided to offer the crown to the Austrian Kaiser Karl I. In turn, Lithuania and Courland would be run by princes from the cadet lines of German ruling dynasties.

Poland belonged to the so-called historic nations, with a history of statehood and a long tradition of rebellions against the partitioning powers. The Ukraine did not. The fertile lands of the black earth, famous for their roaming bands of Cossacks, had long served as a buffer zone between Ottomans, Poles, and Muscovy before being integrated into the Tsarist Empire during the 18th century. The idea of the Ukrainians as a nation of their own had first flourished in Austria-Hungary. It was an invention of Viennese bureaucrats, their neighbours scoffed. Yet, in 1918, with revolution engulfing Russia, an independent Ukraine also suddenly seemed an attractive prospect, from the point of view of Russian Ukrainians. Thus, a junta (*rada*) of Kiev politicians declared their independence from Russia towards the end of December. With something like 30 million potential inhabitants, the Ukraine was a prize well worth fighting for. Whether the Kiev rada – or anybody else – was entitled to speak for all of them, was another matter.

Strangely enough, the new state was welcomed by almost everyone – except, of course, the Russian government (of whatever hue). The Entente was disposed to look upon the Ukraine with kindly eyes because it was opposed to the awful German puppet regime in Petrograd and might yet provide the Entente with a foothold in the East. Prussian generals were disposed to support the Ukrainians because they could serve as a counterweight to the Poles they distrusted (with or without Habsburg monarchs). The Ukraine could also provide the Germans with a stepping-stone to the Black Sea. The Russian Black Sea Fleet, including two fairly modern dreadnoughts, left Sevastopol before the Germans arrived. Foreshadowing events in Scapa Flow in 1919, most of the fleet was scuttled in July, following secret orders from Moscow. Only the one surviving dreadnought ended up in German hands in October.[7] Austrians were disposed to heap favours upon the new state because the Ukraine was famous as the breadbasket of Europe – and Austrians had been going hungry because of the British blockade (exacerbated by their own counterproductive policies). None of these friends proved to be stalwart supporters in the long run. They were at loggerheads with each other. They all harboured mental reservations. But right now they all helped to ease the *entrée* of the new state on the international scene.[8]

On 9 February 1918, the Central Powers signed the first peace treaty of World War I – strangely enough with a state they had never fought at all: the Ukraine. The treaty was immediately styled the 'Bread Peace' by the mayor of Vienna. Indeed, in one of its clauses the Ukrainian government pledged to send no less than a million tons of grain to the Central Powers within six months. In return, the Ukraine was not just recognized as a player on the international scene but promised the province of Cholm (hitherto reserved for Poland); a secret clause also bound the Vienna government to create an autonomous province for Ukrainians in Galicia. However, all these promises were null and void if the Ukraine did not succeed in delivering the stipulated million tons of

Field Marshal Sir Douglas Haig (1861–1928) was Commander-in-Chief of the British Expeditionary Force from December 1915 until the end of the war. (Hulton Archive/Getty)

General John J. Pershing (1860–1948), commander of the American Expeditionary Forces during World War I, pictured at the general headquarters in Chaumont, France, 19 October 1918. (Interim Archives/Getty)

Maréchal Ferdinand Foch (1851–1929) was appointed Supreme Allied Commander in the spring of 1918. (FPG/Archive Photos/Getty)

General Henri Philippe Pétain (1856–1951) was Commander-in-Chief of the French Army during 1917–1920. (adoc-photos/Corbis/Getty)

Generalfeldmarschall Paul von Hindenburg (1847–1934), pictured here on his 70th birthday, was appointed Germany's Chief of the General Staff in 1916. (Hulton Archive/Getty)

General Erich Ludendorff (1865–1937) was appointed First Quartermaster General in 1916. (Hulton Archive/Getty)

On 3 March 1918, Prinz Leopold von Bayern signed the Treaty of Brest-Litovsk with Russia, which outlined terms for their coexistence following World War I. (© Hulton-Deutsch Collection/Corbis/Getty)

The main French light bomber of 1918 was the Breguet XIV, one of the best bombers produced in the war. (USAF Historical Research Agency)

Men of the 20th British Division and of the 22nd French Division in hastily dug rifle pits covering a road in the Nesle sector at the actions at the Somme crossings, 25 March 1918. (Topfoto.co.uk)

Past a twisted iron bed frame, a relic of the civilian world that once existed here, and the body of a French soldier fallen on the edge of a shell hole, German troops advance through smoke and fire during the first of Ludendorff's great spring offensives in 1918. This photograph, probably staged, including the action of a man about to hurl a potato masher grenade, was taken at Villers-Bretonneux in April, as Hindenburg's Eighteenth Army overran Allied lines near the Somme. (Bettman/Getty)

In an image reminiscent of John Singer Sargent's famous painting 'Gassed', British troops blinded by tear gas wait outside an Advance Dressing Station near Bethune, 10 April 1918. (2nd Lt T. K. Aitken/IWM/Getty)

Renault FT-17 tanks in the Aisne region. The FT-17 was used by both the French and US armies, and first saw action on 31 May 1918. (Roger Viollet/Getty)

German soldiers sleep in their positions at the front outside of Arras during a break in the fighting, spring 1918. (ullstein bild/Getty)

This busy scene shows Mark V tanks of 10th Battalion going forward alongside New Zealand and British infantry following the capture of Grevillers, west of Bapaume, 25 August 1918. (2nd Lt T. K. Aitken/IWM/Getty Images)

ABOVE In this photograph, probably staged, American soldiers of the 23rd Infantry Regiment, 2nd Division, are seen firing a 37mm machine gun at a German position in the Argonne Forest, autumn 1918. (US Army Signal Corps/American Stock/Getty)

LEFT Men of the 137th Brigade, 46th Division, are addressed by Brigadier General J. V. Campbell on the Riqueval Bridge over the St Quentin Canal, which formed part of the Hindenburg Line, broken on 29 September 1918. (2nd Lt D. McLellan/IWM/Getty)

As other soldiers run for the cover of slit trenches, an Indian Lewis gun team engage an enemy aircraft, Mesopotamia 1918. During the long and arduous Mesopotamia campaign, over 29,000 Indian soldiers perished in what was their most significant contribution to the war effort. (Ariel Varges/IWM/Getty)

American soldiers of the 64th Infantry Regiment, 7th Division, celebrate the end of the war in Jaulny, France, 11 November 1918. (PhotoQuest/Getty)

21st November 1918: Seen from a British ship, the SMS *Hindenburg* surrenders at Scapa Flow in the Orkneys, the principal British Naval base. *Hindenburg* was the last capital ship built for the German navy during World War I and it was scuttled by the Germans at Scapa Flow on 21 June 1919 (A. R. Coster/Topical Press Agency/Getty)

grain. Doubts whether the Kiev rada would be able to do so were given a new lease of life when it became known they had lost their capital to a Bolshevik attack the day before they signed the treaty.[9]

Trotsky had been willing to sign away Poland and part of the Baltic. He drew a line at the Ukraine. The day after the signing of the Bread Peace, 10 February 1918, he left Brest-Litovsk. No peace treaty had been concluded. Trotsky simply declared the war to be over, unilaterally. German and Austrian diplomats were willing to be content with that result because it gave them a free hand to do whatever they wanted in their respective zones of occupation. But the German High Command's appetite had been whetted. It chose to interpret Trotsky's move as an infringement of the armistice. This time, the generals were supported by the Kaiser and his Chancellor, Bavarian Graf Hertling. The Kaiser dearly wanted to take the Baltic Barons in Livonia and Estonia under his protection, too; maybe even do away with his unsavoury Bolshevik allies at the same time. Thus, on 18 February, the German Army resumed its advance in the East. Within a few days, the Germans reached Reval (modern-day Tallinn) and Minsk. In Austria-Hungary, Karl I did not want to encourage any expansionism by his German allies but had to acquiesce when the Ukraine issued a call for help against the Bolsheviks. In fact, both armies vied with each other over who had been first to reach Odessa.

The German advance became known as the *Eisenbahnvormarsch* (advance by rail). There was no organized resistance. The Germans simply took the train to the nearest towns in the Russian hinterland. A more sinister explanation sometimes added was: the faulty logistics of the remnant of the German Army in the East did not leave them with any other choice. After all, one of the crucial shortcomings of the German Army in 1918 turned out to be a lack of horses that could keep the army on the move in time-honoured fashion. Anyway, the Eisenbahnvormarsch turned out to be a brief affair. Less than a week after it had started, Lenin gathered his Politburo for a crisis meeting on 23 February. Lenin stood his ground in no longer relying on guns. In a line-up that maybe foreshadowed future conflicts, Trotsky opposed accepting the German ultimatum, while Stalin supported it. Lenin stated he would sign the treaty without even reading it – and had no intention at all of keeping any of its clauses longer than strictly necessary. What he wanted was simply a breathing-space that would enable the Soviet regime to survive 'until the Western revolution matures'. In the meantime, appeasement of the Germans was crucial as they were potentially a far bigger danger to the Soviet regime than the Western powers.[10]

Brest-Litovsk has often been characterized as a manifestation of German hubris, an imperialist venture that justified the equally drastic peace of Versailles. While moralists might argue endlessly over the merits of both treaties, none of the territories the Soviets were forced to cede in 1918 were ethnically Russian. In the West, Foreign Secretary Arthur Balfour even wondered whether Germany would be content with an 'unacknowledged protectorate' over the Baltic provinces.[11] What Britain was really worried about was not the fate of the Russian borderlands but the prospect of the whole of Russia becoming a giant satellite of Imperial Germany, with all its possible effects on the balance of power – not just in Europe, but also in Asia. From that perspective, the exact delimitation of the respective spheres of influence between the Germans and their Russian collaborators did not matter all that much.

The Treaty of Brest-Litovsk was signed in a hurry on 3 March 1918. Soviet troops promised to leave not just the Ukraine but also Finland, which had also declared its independence in December 1917. Bolshevik sympathizers who continued to fight in either the Ukraine or Finland could no longer rely on the conventions of war but were regarded as rebels liable to be shot at sight. The Finns, under their Swedish-speaking ex-Russian General Mannerheim, managed to defeat the Reds with a little German help in April 1918; in October they invited a brother-in-law of the Kaiser, Friedrich Karl von Hessen, to serve as their monarch. Livonia and Estonia remained part of Russia for the time being but were occupied by German troops who did their best to encourage secessionist movements. In late August Lenin finally left them to their devices.[12] Except for Belorussia (and the Viborg district), the Russian borders of 1918 resembled the current ones. German and Austro-Hungarian POWs – no less than a million and a half of the latter – were going to be repatriated. At first sight, statistically speaking, this mass release should

The Treaty of Brest-Litovsk, 1918

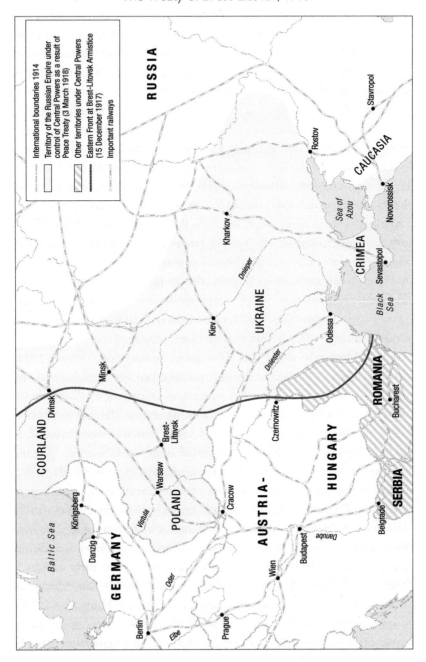

Legend:
- International boundaries 1914
- Territory of the Russian Empire under control of Central Powers as a result of Peace Treaty (3 March 1918)
- Other territories under Central Powers
- Eastern Front at Brest-Litovsk Armistice (15 December 1917)
- Important railways

RUSSIA

Stavropol

Rostov

CAUCASIA

Novorossisk

Sea of Azov

Kharkov

Dnieper

CRIMEA

Sevastopol

UKRAINE

Kiev

Black Sea

Odessa

Dniester

Minsk

Dvinsk

Czernowitz

ROMANIA

Bucharest

COURLAND

Brest-Litovsk

Warsaw

Vistula

POLAND

Cracow

AUSTRIA-

HUNGARY

SERBIA

Belgrade

Königsberg

Danzig

Baltic Sea

Oder

GERMANY

Budapest

Danube

Wien

Berlin

Elbe

Prague

have given a huge boost to the war effort of the Central Powers. In practice, Austria-Hungary did not derive any great benefit from the return of her prodigal sons. Army administration suspected them of having picked up dangerous Bolshevik ideas in Russia. The way they were debriefed after their return to the fatherland did little to encourage their patriotism. In fact, most of them arrived too late to take part in the last stages of World War I.[13]

A German empire in the East? The Russian Civil War

In fact, some of the Austro-Hungarian POWs in Russia created one of the most dramatic stories of 1918. Roughly 15 per cent of Austro-Hungarian troops consisted of ethnic Czechs who had never shown any great enthusiasm for the fight against Russia. The awful living conditions within Siberian POW camps persuaded many of them to change sides and join the Czechoslovak Legion that volunteered to fight for the Entente powers in order to win independence from Austria-Hungary for Czechs and Slovaks. The Legion had first seen action in July 1917 and acquitted itself well. Its numbers reached 60,000 men. When Russia started to drop out of the war, Thomas G. Masaryk, the leader of the Czechs in exile, travelled to Russia and arranged for the Legion to be transported to the Western Front. The only way such a transfer could be effected was either by way of Archangelsk or via the Trans-Siberian railway, a trip reminiscent of Sir Phileas Fogg's journey around the world. (In fact, it promised to last much longer than 80 days.)[14]

The Western powers were in two minds about their reaction to the Soviet take-over. Some of their men on the spot advocated a policy of bowing to the inevitable and making the best of it. The French Army desperately wanted a second front in the East, with or without the Soviets. Their priority was to support whoever was willing to continue fighting the Germans. That kind of mostly ineffectual pledge was easier to extract from opposition groups than from the Soviet government. On 8 February 1918, the British War Cabinet debated whether Lenin should be recognized as the legal government of Russia at all. Even though both Prime Minister Lloyd George and Foreign Secretary Balfour supported recognition, there was sufficient opposition (e.g. from Parliamentary Under-Secretary of State for Foreign Affairs Lord Cecil and the leader of the House of Lords Earl Curzon) to produce deadlock. Even so, Trotsky initially tried to avoid a complete break with Russia's former allies. He consented to the British landing a detachment at Murmansk on the Arctic Sea to safeguard the supplies they had sent earlier. However, when the Soviets moved the Russian capital to Moscow in March, Western diplomats did not follow suit but retreated to Vologda, a railway junction on the way to the Arctic.[15]

Once Lenin had openly aligned himself with the Germans, in British eyes at least, the Western powers began to have second thoughts about sending the Czechs on a grand tour around the globe. In that case, they would only be competing with US troops for scarce resources of shipping. Maybe the Czechs could be of more use if they stayed in Russia and tried to rally the anti-Bolshevik forces willing to fight Lenin – and the Germans. Thus, the Legion could be turned into an embryonic 'second front'. Before any of these musings had crystallized into coherent plans, events in far-away Siberia had taken on a life of their own. In mid-May, the Czechs travelling East had started fighting Hungarian POWs returning West along the Trans-Siberian railway. When the Russian authorities insisted that the Czechs hand over their weapons while crossing Russia (i.e. by now neutral territory), the Legion took matters into its own hands. Within a few weeks they had taken over most of the railway from the Urals to the Pacific Ocean, an achievement sometimes compared to the miraculous Spanish conquest of Mexico in 1519.

Uncertain rumours reached Europe of the strange fight with ideologically inverted fronts that was taking place along the shores of Lake Baikal. Conservative German or Austrian POWs were allegedly fighting for the Bolsheviks to help their fatherland, even if authorities back home disapproved of that connection. Left-wing Czechs were supporting Russian counter-revolutionaries to impress the Western powers with their prowess. Edvard Benes, Masaryk's representative in Paris, made the most of the occasion when he told the French that the Czechs were willing to fight for the Entente but they would do so only as an army in the employ of an internationally recognized Czechoslovak government. As a result, Britain and France at least awarded the Czechoslovak Committee the status of a belligerent in July. At the same time, the Legion outdid the wildest expectations when it crossed the Urals and reached the Volga River in late July 1918. While millions of men and thousands of guns fought for a few square miles in the West, no more than 12,000 Czechs sufficed to throw Lenin's regime into a state of crisis. 'Soviet Russia had shrunk to the size of the medieval Muscovite state.'[16] On 1 August, Lenin declared that a state of war existed with the Entente and officially asked for German help but the Germans hedged their bets. They were willing to fight the British in Murmansk but only if they were granted free transit through Petrograd. The Soviets could only stabilize the situation once they managed to divert a few of the destroyers of the Baltic fleet to the Volga via the Russian canal system, once more demonstrating 'the influence of river power' upon world history.[17]

In fact, the Germans were recruiting their own sort of counter-revolutionaries, too. Von Kühlmann commented ironically that 'all our new friends' seemed to have served their apprentice years as guards officers or adjutants of the Tsar, from Finnish Marshal Gustav Mannerheim and Ukrainian President Pavlo Skoropadskij to some of the Cossack leaders operating in the Don area. The Baltic barons who flocked to the German colours as a reaction against communism had always prided themselves on their loyalty to the Tsar even if they had increasingly been eyed with suspicion by Russian nationalists, alongside the German-born Tsarina. But far more potent than ideological factors, the Germans, too, thought the Bolshevik regime an unreliable partner, first and foremost because it was unlikely to survive. To preserve the sort of influence the Germans had started to enjoy in the East, they needed to ingratiate themselves with the successors in time. The army toyed with the idea of marching on Moscow and putting an end to it all. But the diplomats in the German Foreign Office were unwilling to upset the status quo and preferred the unholy alliance with Lenin, at least for the time being. 'The present regime is a safeguard against the creation of a new front in the East.' As Kühlmann explained: 'We must try to prevent Russian consolidation as far as possible and, from this point of view, we must therefore support the parties furthest to the Left.'[18]

A good pointer to that sort of tacit understanding came in late August when the Germans actually sided with the Soviets who were defending the oil wells of Baku against their Ottoman allies. During the controversy, German and Turkish troops even clashed along the border. The Turks only came into their own once the British 'Dunsterforce', launched through Persia, linked up with dissident Russians in mid-August. The presence of an Entente force on the shores of the Caspian Sea served to concentrate minds wonderfully: Germans and Ottomans patched up their quarrel. Nuri Pasha, the brother of Enver, re-took Baku on 14 September. The Transcaucasian region was informally partitioned between the Central Powers: the Ottomans gained control of Azerbaijan (and a free hand in central Asia), the Germans occupied Georgia along the shores of the Black Sea. Austria-Hungary had to be content with a diplomatic mission to beleaguered Armenia (led by Baron Georg Franckenstein, who went on to become Austrian Minister to London for 18 years). The British had to be content with a foothold in Turkmenistan, on the eastern shore of the Caspian Sea.[19]

In the Far East, Japanese forces had in the meantime landed in Vladivostok on 7 July 1918. That move had first been mooted at the turn of the year, but been endlessly postponed because of US opposition. Woodrow Wilson's reaction to the Russian Revolution was famously tolerant: 'Let them sort it out themselves.' The United States was prejudiced against Japan, to be sure. Yet, there was something to be said for its argument that no number of Japanese troops in Siberia was going to do a lot of harm to the Germans – especially when they stated they would certainly not advance any further than Irkutsk and Lake Baikal. In the end, the Japanese force was increased to more than 70,000 men but still proved ineffectual in helping the counter-revolutionary Russians, just as their intervention did little to further their own ambitions in China.[20]

The Austro–Italian duel

The future of a whole continent seemed to be at stake. All the warring kings – or presidents – were playing for high stakes in Russia. Like

Ludendorff, they were all fascinated by the prospect of long-term gains to be won at the expense of tiny immediate down-payments. The Soviet regime, of course, had a crucial impact on the shape of the post-war world, in more ways than one. Yet, paradoxically, for all these momentous consequences, nothing of what went on in the East after Brest-Litovsk had any great impact on the war itself. Germany's chances of winning the war rested with the 200-odd divisions it had managed to assemble on the Western Front in the spring of 1918. Neither could any of the other fronts rival the importance of the Western Front. But as it turned out, at least they could serve as a catalyst.

The Eastern Front had forced the Central Powers to coordinate their efforts, culminating in the *Oberste Kriegsleitung* (Supreme War Command) created for the campaign that defeated Romania in late 1916. In late 1917, German help had been instrumental in delivering an almost mortal blow to the Italians at Caporetto. But after the collapse of Russia, it seemed, each of the Central Powers went their separate ways again. The Ottomans turned towards the East, back to the roots, the mythical homeland of the Turkish tribes. The Bulgarians defended their Macedonian gains against the motley collection of the Salonika-based Entente forces known as the *Armée d'Orient*. Austria-Hungary concentrated on fighting the Italians.[21] The Salonika front (plus Albania) kept some two dozen Entente divisions occupied (vs. 14 oversized Bulgarian ones and an Austrian corps); the trenches along the Piave front (and the mountains of the Tyrol) were manned by 50-odd Italian and Austro-Hungarian divisions each. Partly for reasons of climate and geography, neither of these two theatres of war saw any trace of action in the early months of the year. April 1918, which saw some of the most intense fighting in the West, was the month when the Austro-Hungarian Army suffered fewer casualties than at any other time during the Great War.[22]

After Caporetto, Britain and France had sent a dozen divisions to bolster the Italians; half of them were recalled in early 1918. The Germans obviously favoured diversionary attacks by the Austrians that might help to tie down as many Entente troops in Italy as possible, while the crucial battles were fought along the Western Front.

The Austrians needed little prompting. The successful defence along the Isonzo, followed by Caporetto, had imbued them with a strange sense of superiority. Rather than see their task as a sideshow, they had high hopes of winning a decisive victory themselves. One of their cabinet ministers – a famous economist – noted in his diary what an honour it was for the Austrians to be able to land the decisive blow.[23]

Austria-Hungary's last great offensive was a good example of how not to do things. Conrad, the ex-Chief of Staff, who commanded the Tyrolean front, and Svetozar Boroevic, the martinet who aspired to be created Count of the Isonzo, both wanted to be the ones to win eternal laurels. Conrad's successor as Chief of Staff, Baron Arthur Arz von Straussenburg, was overawed by his subordinates' inflated egos and unable to impose a decision on them. The Italian Army had been reduced to 33 divisions in the weeks after Caporetto; by the spring of 1918 it was back to 58. Thus, the Austrians were still slightly inferior to the Italians in numbers, let alone in reserves of food – or air power. Both sides fielded roughly 7,000 guns (but far fewer heavy ones than on the Western Front). Neither Conrad's nor Boroevic's front presented the attacker with promising terrain. Conrad had always dreamt of erupting into the Venetian plains from the mountains and cutting off the bulk of the Italian Army. However, Tyrol could only be supplied by a single railway; in Alpine terrain there was also little chance of moving the heavy guns forward once the advance got going. Boroevic, on the other hand, was severely handicapped as he had to cross the Piave River in the face of the enemy. His solution was not to put all his eggs in one basket but to try his luck at as many points as possible. Once again, the principle of concentration of force went overboard.

The Austrians launched their attack – which Gabriele d'Annunzio christened the Battle of the Solstice – on 15 June 1918, a little too late to help the Germans who had already shot most of their bolts by that time. They need not have worried too much about the strategic dilemma created by their wilful commanders. Along both main lines of attack, the offensive ended in a clear-cut tactical failure, anyway. Conrad's thrust had to be suspended within 24 hours; Boroevic fared only marginally better. Only on the extreme flanks of his army group, on the Montello in the north, and towards the mouth of the Piave in the south, did the Austrians actually manage to cross the river, build a few bridges, and advance a few miles beyond the river. To make matters worse, torrential rains started the next day that made any further crossings almost impossible by washing away many of the pontoons. The Austrians were lucky to conduct their retreat without leaving any of their forces behind on the wrong side of the river. Even so, their losses at 115,000 were considerably higher than Italian ones (85,000). The bad weather at least provided a ready-made excuse. Italian folklore adopted the same tune: a Neapolitan created a popular song, *La Leggenda del Piave*, which celebrated nature's contribution towards the defence of the homeland.[24]

The soft underbelly of the Central Powers

The failure of the Austrian summer offensive coincided with the height of the hunger crisis in Vienna, as townspeople plundered the fields in search of food. One week later, on 24 June, Kühlmann openly admitted that the German offensives in the west, too, had not been sufficiently successful. At that point, Ludendorff still insisted on Kühlmann's dismissal but privately admitted that he was right. In the middle of July, the Germans started to suffer their first setbacks in the west. A couple of Austro-Hungarian divisions were now actually sent to the Western Front: equipped with captured British machine guns, they were sent to a quiet sector that suddenly became the butt of US attacks in September.

Public opinion in Berlin and Vienna was not yet resigned to notions of defeat; but the fond hopes that all that was needed was one last final push had evaporated. The statesmen of the Central Powers realized they would now have to start negotiating from a weak hand. In September, Graf Leopold Berchtold (who had started it all) still wistfully talked about the war ending in a draw.[25] The German armies in the West were forced to retreat, but the fronts in Italy and the Balkans remained stable. It came as a surprise to almost everybody when the trigger that led to the collapse of the Central Powers was pulled in an area that had been regarded as the most expendable of sideshows by almost all the belligerents, with few exceptions. In fact, the British Army had for a long time argued for a withdrawal from the Salonika front. Even Clemenceau made fun of the 'gardeners of Salonika' who had not done any real fighting for over a year. Supplying the Armée d'Orient – composed of roughly half a dozen divisions from Britain, France, and Serbia each – required a disproportionate amount of shipping. Wilhelm II had once boasted that Salonika was his biggest POW camp. Malaria continued to be a huge problem. There were few opportunity costs to be incurred if the Entente washed their hands of Macedonia, as the Bulgarian Army opposing it was unlikely to be switched to any other front. At the very least, 'the allied army [in Salonika] was too strong for defence and not strong enough for attack'.[26] In 1916, cooperation with Romania had provided a possible *raison d'être* for the Armée d'Orient. But after the Russian collapse, Romanian King Ferdinand had hurried to make his peace with the Central Powers, lest the Germans insist on regime change. Under the terms of the Treaty of Bucharest (7 May 1918) Romania ceded the Dobrudja (on the right bank of the Danube) to the Central Powers, but was rewarded with Russian Bessarabia (present-day Moldavia) in return. German capital played a dominant part in exploiting the oil wells; Austrian diplomats proved adept at pulling strings in Romanian domestic politics.[27]

However, in 1917 the French had finally managed to oust King Constantine of Greece, the Kaiser's brother-in-law. Constantine's nemesis, Prime Minister Eleftherios Venizelos, had declared war on Germany on 28 June 1917 and was busy organizing a Greek army to join the Armée d'Orient. Thus, the Entente felt honour-bound not to throw him to the tender mercies of the Bulgarians. Despite Haig's entreaties, only a few of the French and British troops in Macedonia were replaced by Indians in the spring of 1918. With a growing number of Greeks acting as a reserve, an offensive appeared increasingly possible. Serbians in particular longed to return to their homeland after more than two years in exile. The Allied offensive at Dobro Polje on 15 September, spearheaded by the Serbs who conquered Mount Magla, turned out to be successful beyond expectations. The Bulgarian front was pierced; on 29 September Bulgaria sued for an armistice. Tsar Ferdinand abdicated a few days later. Louis Franchet d'Esperey, the new French commander of the Armée d'Orient, an ultra-royalist who had replaced the left-wing republican Maurice Sarrail, had succeeded in doing what Churchill one war later failed to achieve – penetrate the 'soft under-belly' of Fortress Europe.[28]

It was the news from Bulgaria that led to the collapse and the dismissal of Ludendorff. Austria-Hungary and Germany were suddenly vying with each other over who was going to ask for an armistice first. On 16 October, Kaiser Karl I published his so-called Peoples' Manifesto, which tried to pre-empt Wilsonian ideas of 'autonomous development' by opening the possibility of turning the Habsburg monarchy into a federation of nation states. Britain and France were in two minds as to the best way to exploit the unexpected victory. Britain wanted to concentrate on forcing the Ottoman Empire to surrender; France on pushing towards the Austro-Hungarian border as soon as possible. On 1 November, the Serbs re-entered their capital, Belgrade. The Central Powers were desperately trying to find a few extra divisions (some of them recalled from the Ukraine) to build a make-shift new front somewhere along the Hungarian and Bosnian border.

But before Franchet d'Esperey's multinational army had actually crossed the Hungarian border, the Austro-Hungarian Army had already surrendered – to the Italians. Much as the post-Caporetto Italian Chief of Staff Armando Diaz wanted to avoid his predecessor Cadorna's mistake of launching costly frontal attacks against the Austrian positions, Italian politics put pressure on him to start an offensive as soon as possible, in order to strengthen Italy's position at the peace negotiations. The slogan coined by Pétain: 'Wait for the tanks – and the Americans', would no longer do for a late-comer to the war eager to prove its status as a great power. Italian Prime Minister Vittorio Orlando stated his wishes in no uncertain terms: 'Between inaction and defeat, I prefer defeat. Get moving!'[29]

The resulting battle of Vittorio Veneto has often been derided as a sham victory, unfairly so. Austro-Hungarian morale may have been weakened by the events of the last few months – and by the materiel shortages of the last few years. But Austrian resistance was far from crumbling for the first few days of the offensive that started on 24 October. Actually, it was the remnant of the British support group that first managed to cross the Piave on 26 October: the Gordon Highlanders, rowed by Venetian gondoliers. Following a plan developed by Colonello Ugo Cavallero, the later Italian Chief of Staff in World War II, the Austrian front was split in two. On the evening of 27 October, the newly appointed Austro-Hungarian Foreign Secretary Count Gyula Andrassy – whose father had negotiated the Dual Alliance with Bismarck in 1879 – was forced to appeal for an armistice without waiting for the Germans to follow suit. Technically, Andrassy's note constituted a breach of the alliance that was often held against Karl I later on. Even the Austrian Social Democrats, who had long argued in favour of a compromise peace, voiced their objections to 'Habsburg treachery'.

What gave Vittorio Veneto its bitter taste was the shambles the Austrians made of the negotiations about the truce. The Empire was disintegrating. Andrassy's plea for a ceasefire was widely – and rightly – interpreted as a sign that the Empire was no longer able to defend itself, be it against external or internal threats. The Czechs started the ball rolling by proclaiming their independence on 28 October, quickly followed by the South Slavs. Karl I, following the spirit of his Peoples' Manifesto, did not even resist openly. In fact, on 31 October, he donated the Austro-Hungarian fleet to the emerging South Slav state – the Italians retaliated by sinking the flagship *Viribus Unitis* the next day. None of the successor states wanted to be burdened with losing the war. All of them – even German-Austrians and Hungarians – took care to distance themselves from the old leadership. They took the easy way out: the monarchy had started the war; the monarchy should also bear the responsibility for ending it.

Karl I was looking for a new commander-in-chief willing to shoulder the burden of defeat. On 3 November he appointed Hungarian-born Generalfeldmarschall Baron Hermann Kövess von Kövesshaza, but Kövess was away in the Balkans trying to piece together a line of defence against Franchet d'Esperey. Thus, the Austrian delegation that had travelled to Italian headquarters in Padua's Villa Giusti was frequently left without adequate instructions. On the afternoon of 3 November they signed an armistice that covered the whole of the Austro-Hungarian Army – and was supposed to come into force the next day. The Italians argued that an extra 24 hours were needed to inform all their front-line commands; the Austrians, on the other hand, jumped to the conclusion that the armistice was immediately effective and stopped defending themselves against the advancing Italians. The result was that long columns of retreating Austro-Hungarians were overtaken by Italians in cars and taken prisoner. At the end of the day, the Italians had taken 428,000 POWs, even more than the number the Central Powers had netted after Caporetto. Amidst recriminations of perfidy and treachery, it was often overlooked that the Italian Army – without any overwhelming numerical superiority – had indeed 'inflicted a decisive defeat in the field on its opponent, something its British and French partners were unable to do in the West'. [30]

Conclusion

Naturally, neither the Serbs who stormed Mount Magla nor the Scots who crossed the Piave can be said to have 'won' the war. By June 1918, when the German offensives in the West had run out of steam, Germany had to all intents and purposes lost the war. The Entente offensives in the West suffered a fate almost similar to Vittorio Veneto – they were all too often discounted as an anti-climax. There was safety in numbers. If Germany produced as much steel as the rest of Europe combined, the United States produced as much steel as the rest of the world combined. The Entente could rely on masses of men and money from the United States; the Germans could rely on nothing but visions of future wealth from their newly won Russian hinterland. What the battles of Dobro Polje and Vittorio Veneto did, was to hasten the end. They acted as a catalyst, thus shortening the war by approximately half a year – no more and no less.

Still, the Russian dimension of 1918 needs to be held up to scrutiny a little further. A Russian collapse in 1915 or 1916 would almost certainly have resulted in an outcome of the war favourable to the Central Powers. But after the gamble of unrestricted submarine warfare had brought the United States into the war, their victory in the East was no longer enough to stave off military defeat. It did help to mitigate the long-term strategic and geopolitical effects of that defeat, though. There is a lot to be said for the comment of Czechoslovakia's first Prime Minister, Karel Kramář, who told his French friends that they were kidding themselves if they believed they had won World War I – unless they managed to restore the Tsarist regime. True, immediately following the Armistice, the Western powers had arranged for German forces to stay a little bit longer in the Baltic to prevent a Soviet take-over. A combined German–Latvian–'White' Russian force re-conquered Riga in May 1919. However, the anti-Bolshevik 'White' Russian forces, who enjoyed their high-water mark in August 1919, were only marginally supported by the Western powers. Even worse, the Baltic states that were supposed to serve as their launching-pad were sometimes far more worried about the imperial pretensions of the 'White' generals than about Lenin's revolutionary fervour.[31]

From the point of view of the Entente the result was the worst of both worlds: they had neither won the friendship of the Soviet regime nor managed to do away with it. The pre-1914 balance of powers in Europe had rested on a Franco-Russian combination to offset the industrial might of Germany. The Russian Revolution had severed that link for good and no US guarantee was forthcoming to compensate the French for that loss. That is why in many ways the results of the war were inconclusive. Germany had at one and the same time lost the war in the West but won the war in the East. The results of Brest-Litovsk were far from being annulled by Versailles, except for the Ukraine, and that was no thanks to any design on the part of the 'Big Four'. In the inter-war period, Germany no longer faced the threat of a war on two fronts. It could always play off Poland against Russia, or vice versa. Germany had been defeated. Yet, Russia – as Germany's closest continental competitor in terms of resources – had suffered losses that were far heavier than Germany's. After 1918, the Soviet Union continued to be an international pariah.

Military defeat and the fall of the monarchy, the threat of revolution and the reality of inflation turned the end of World War I into a traumatic experience for the German people. Yet, Germany remained the biggest power in Europe, potentially. Sooner or later, that potential was going to be realized.

CHAPTER 7

THE WAR OUTSIDE OF EUROPE

Dr Rob Johnson

The prevailing view in the British Army's General Headquarters, a view which was supported by Sir William Robertson, the Chief of the Imperial General Staff, was that the centre of gravity of the war was the German Army, and therefore any allocations of men and material to Africa and the Middle East were a waste of critical resources and a distraction from the main theatre in Europe. The attempt to find an alternative, any alternative, to the attritional struggle in France and Flanders in 1915 had led to operations against the Ottoman Empire, but these efforts ended in stalemate in Palestine, an aborted campaign at Gallipoli, and a humiliating defeat at Kut in Mesopotamia. The two commissions to investigate these setbacks, which appeared in 1917, seemed to reinforce the idea that the war would only be decided on the Western Front.

Nevertheless, in 1917, the British forces in the Middle East seized both Baghdad and Jerusalem. The Prime Minister, David Lloyd George, used these victories to argue that General Sir Douglas Haig had wasted the lives of thousands of men in fruitless offensives on the Western Front. He believed that the future of the war, and the security of national interests, lay not in Flanders but east of Suez. With his characteristic eloquence, he answered his critics who argued that Africa and the Middle East were mere 'sideshows':

> The British Empire owes a great deal to 'side-shows'. During the Seven Years' War, which was also a great European War – for practically all the nations now engaged … were then interlocked in a great struggle – the events which are best remembered by every Englishman are not the great battles on the Continent of Europe, but Plassey and the Heights of Abraham; and I have no doubt that, when the history of 1917 comes to be written, and comes to be read ages hence, these events in Mesopotamia and Palestine will hold a much more conspicuous place in the minds and memories of the people than many an event which looms much larger for the moment in our sight.[1]

The division of opinion between government and the army on this issue of priorities would be easy to exaggerate. Robertson had, in fact, given his consent to limited operations in the Middle East, but he was consistent in his judgement that these campaigns must not interfere with the main effort in France. Lloyd George, for his part, was prepared to set aside the rhetoric on his Middle Eastern objectives and gave, for example, consent to the Third Ypres offensive. But the Prime Minister also tried to use the need for close cooperation with the French to subordinate Haig, and then Robertson, with the idea of a Supreme War Council and a supreme command under Maréchal Ferdinand Foch. By early 1918, the differences of opinion had become more acute.

The arguments about the strategic direction of the war were not just based on personalities and priorities: the operational situation in the winter of 1917–18 was a bleak one for the Allies. British shipping losses from U-boat attacks had not yet recovered; Russia had been knocked out of the war by revolution; the French Army was still not able to take the offensive after a series of soldiers' strikes; there was stalemate at Salonika; the Italians were routed at Caporetto; and the Americans were not yet present in great strength in Europe. At home, the public were growing weary of the conflict. On the Western Front, British soldiers expressed their anger at the duration of the war, the filthy conditions, casualties, and tyrannical discipline. Captain J. H.

Dible, RAMC, believed, 'we are living on a [powder] magazine'. Private Archie Surfleet, East Yorkshire Regiment, noted, 'There is nothing but unrest and uncertainty and everyone here is absolutely fed up to the teeth.'[2]

Yet the British capture of Jerusalem had a particularly encouraging effect for Britain and represented, as Lloyd George put it, 'a Christmas present for the nation'.[3] There was also optimism about the coming infusion of American manpower into the conflict. Furthermore, Romania and Greece formally joined the Allies, the Italians broke through in Albania linking the Allied fronts, and, in Africa, most of the German forces in the colonies had been neutralized. Only in East Africa did German resistance continue. On the other hand, there were growing anxieties in that winter of 1917–18 about the prospect of German divisions being released from the Eastern Front, but the government believed that this was a war that was about more than the precarious operational situation on the Western Front. It was, for them, a distinctly global war and the meridian of the struggle ran through Suez and across the oceans, for it concerned Britain's relationship with the Dominions, the Empire, and its share of the world's commerce. After the war, Basil Liddell Hart attributed Allied success to the long-term naval blockade of Germany but praised the 'indirect strategy' pursued by Britain in the Middle East, asserting its utility over the costly and unsuccessful direct strategies which had characterized most of the war. Deflecting the obvious point that the main fronts of Europe had absorbed the bulk of the reserves and prevented their release to the other front, Liddell Hart argued that an opportunity had been missed to exploit the other fronts: 'If the British had used at the outset even a fair proportion of the forces they ultimately expended in driblets, it is clear from the evidence of the opposing commanders that success would probably have crowned the undertaking.'[4]

Strategy and operations in East Africa, 1918

Colonel Paul von Lettow-Vorbeck, the German military commander of East Africa, had defeated two Indian expeditionary forces (Forces C and D) in 1914 and threatened British colonial control in Uganda and Kenya.[5] Obliged, therefore, to conduct a strategic defence of their possessions in the region, the British subsequently established a cordon around German East Africa. With reinforcements, Lieutenant General Jan Smuts, the local British commander, could move over to the offensive, but he knew that the Germans would seek to avoid fixed positions and engagements and use the great depth that eastern Africa offered to manoeuvre and escape the closing jaws of his enveloping forces. Smuts therefore flooded the region with troops from Britain, South Africa, India, and the West Indies, and attempted to coordinate a series of thrusts from every point of the compass that would leave nowhere for the Germans to go.[6] Much to the frustration of the Allies, the terrain and climate added considerable friction to this endeavour, and it was relatively easy to conceal the smaller German contingents and their African partners as they sought to raid and delay Smuts' forces.

Smuts responded by pushing columns into the interior of East Africa on multiple axes. This was still designed to prevent the Germans from being able to use depth to their advantage, but it was also to throw them off balance. While Smuts advanced from the north, paralleled by Major General van Deventer's force, the Nyasaland and Rhodesian Field Force came up from the south, the Belgians drove in from the Congo in the west, and the Portuguese were encouraged to close the southern border. Smuts' operations drove Lettow-Vorbeck away from the northern highlands and prevented any threat of raids on the Uganda Railway. As the columns pressed in on the German territory, a third of Lettow-Vorbeck's forces were cornered in the south-east of the colony and forced to surrender on 28 November 1917. Confusion and communications problems amongst the Portuguese nevertheless allowed Lettow-Vorbeck himself and the remainder of his command to escape into Portuguese East Africa. Regardless of the losses amongst their African porters, the Germans kept moving, and escaped the cordon.

For the next ten months, Lettow-Vorbeck attempted to stay ahead of his pursuers in Portuguese East Africa. He avoided British landings at Porto Amelia in December 1917 and a thrust eastwards from Fort Johnston on Lake Nyasa designed to catch him there in May 1918. He fled south towards the coast, and was pursued first north-eastwards in July, then back north-westwards into the interior. The Germans abandoned the Portuguese colony on 28 September 1918, and moved back into German East Africa at Nagawira. In November, they marched into Northern Rhodesia at Fife, before being chased to Abercorn to the south of Lake Tanganyika. There was a brief skirmish on 12 November with the lead element of the King's African Rifles. Lettow-Vorbeck, when learning of the Armistice in Europe, surrendered on 25 November 1918.

Although some writers have chosen to praise Lettow-Vorbeck for his guerrilla war and ability to tie down Allied forces, up to 70,000 at any one time, he really achieved very little. Isolated, forced into a protracted flight, and increasingly irrelevant to the outcome of the war, there was little of real virtue in his operations. At the end of the war, there were just 175 European and 3,000 African forces left from an original strength of 10,000. Worse, Lettow-Vorbeck's campaign had also led to the deaths of over 250,000 African civilians.[7] If strategy is, to some extent, a balance of cost and benefit, Lettow-Vorbeck's apparent achievements seem even more diminished.[8]

After the war, Germany was considered to have forfeited the European prestige of a civilizing power that would make the possession of colonies acceptable. Consequently, it was stripped of its African and Pacific territories. Smuts, by contrast, had prevented the Central Powers threatening the Allied control of Africa, and especially Sudan, Egypt, and the strategically vital Suez Canal. If any commander was deserving of praise in the East African theatre, then it was surely Smuts and not Lettow-Vorbeck.

Strategy and operations in the Middle East, 1918

At the outbreak of war, Britain had moved an Indian Army expeditionary force to the head of the Gulf to secure the oil refineries in southern Persia, since oil was already emerging as critical to the functioning of the Royal Navy and Britain's war economy. But it was not just a concern to acquire reserves of oil that drove the British into Mesopotamia; it was the far older, pre-war anxieties of regional and Great Power influence that they needed to forestall during the war and after.[9] The 'Great Game', the rivalry for influence in order to create security zones for imperial possessions, had dominated British thinking about the region in the late

19th century. Concerns about German and Ottoman schemes against British interests in Persia, the Gulf, and India also drove the strategy of 1914–18. The subsequent appearance of the Bolshevik threat in 1918 ensured continuity in this policy priority.[10] Sir Henry Wilson, who succeeded Robertson as Chief of the Imperial General Staff in the final year of the war, believed that the Bolshevik threat and Britain's control of the Middle East far outweighed any other consideration. He wrote: 'Europe should be left to stew in its own juice' while 'from the left bank of the Don to India is our preserve'. As the war drew to a close, Wilson noted in his diary: 'All the Cabinet agreed. Our real danger now is not the Boches but Bolshevism.'[11]

In 1915, there had seemed to be an opportunity to seize Baghdad when the Ottomans were defeated in a series of tactical engagements in southern Mesopotamia. The Government of India had encouraged the local commanders to press forward on a tenuous line of communication and the result was that the British division on the Tigris, which was dangerously overextended, was bundled back to Kut where it was besieged. All efforts to relieve them were a costly failure, and, when the garrison capitulated in 1916, the British government stepped in to demand an end to offensive action.

By late 1916, the British and Indian forces in Mesopotamia had made significant improvements. There were steady increases in the manpower available. There was development in combined arms operations (including integration of the Royal Flying Corps), with the import of ideas from the Western Front.[12] There was more artillery, providing a superiority in firepower. There were improvements in logistics and river transport, more efficient staff work, and increased intelligence collection. More proficient in combat, more efficient in supply, and arguably more realistic about its capabilities and limits, the British and Indian forces in Mesopotamia were far more effective as a fighting force.[13]

When in February and March 1916 the Russians advanced south from Persian Azerbaijan to Khanaqin, within the Ottoman borders, there seemed a possibility that the Tsar's forces, rather than the British, might seize Baghdad. General Sir Stanley Maude, who had been building up his forces on the Tigris, was eager to make his long-awaited offensive against

Kut, and the Russian movements might encourage the government at home to let him go forward. Fortunately, the Ottomans played into Maude's hands. As General Halil, commander of the Ottoman Sixth Army, thrust against the Russians on the Persian border and then into the interior of the Shah's domains in July 1916, they were drawn further away from their original positions on the Tigris. The Ottoman forces remaining around Kut were eventually reduced to 20,000. Even so, Robertson, always eager to preserve resources for France and Flanders, argued that, even if it could be taken, Baghdad had no value from a strategic point of view, and therefore he felt no advance could be justified. The War Cabinet initially agreed. For now, the British and Imperial forces on the Tigris remained where they were.

Maude was not prepared to accept the inactivity implied by his appointment to command in Mesopotamia in August 1916. He had fought at Gallipoli, and had seen action in France, where he had been wounded, so he was fully aware of the character of this war. He was no 'Château General' of the popular imagination, and his approach to operations mirrored the practices employed on the Western Front. He knew that taking an entrenched position required overwhelming firepower, close coordination of all arms, and resolution throughout every level of the army. Training and preparation were crucial. He would not be hurried, but would proceed with methodical and relentless calculation towards his objectives in his own time.

The preparations were meticulous. Reinforcements were introduced, acclimatized, and trained, and formations rehearsed. His divisions enjoyed a stronger ratio of artillery to provide crucial fire support. Basra was redeveloped as a port, greatly increasing its capacity to handle large volumes of stores and munitions. A light railway was constructed up to the front lines, while new river boats and hundreds of Ford motor lorries were brought in to speed up the supply system. Depots were opened up along the route to the front, and a precise approach was adopted to the question of logistics.

At the strategic level there was much better synchronization. On 1 October 1916, General Charles Carmichael Monro, the commander-in-chief of the Army in India, assumed overall direction of the Middle

East theatre, integrating it into the strategy of the other theatres, which offered the opportunity for truly coordinated action against the Ottoman Empire. In contrast to the early years of the war, Monro was served by an experienced staff.[14] While the Chief of the Imperial General Staff continued to insist that the theatre commanders make do with what they had, a coalition effort was emerging. The Russian General Staff agreed in principle there should be coordination between the Army of the Caucasus and the British forces in the Middle East.[15]

In December 1916, finally given the go-ahead, Maude deluged the Ottoman positions on the Tigris with artillery fire. Using a methodical series of belts of fire, the barrage proceeded with ruthless mathematical timing. Ottoman front-line trenches were subjected to intensive bombardment, while rear areas were shelled to prevent reinforcements coming up. British and Indian troops advanced as close as they could behind the advancing curtain of fire. Yet, the opening bombardment, intense though it was, could not guarantee success. Some infantry units were pinned down by Ottoman machine-gun fire, and others took heavy losses as they tried to get forward. In some locations, more fortunate bands penetrated the lines and started to consolidate. But this was a battle that would not be decided in one day. As had been found on the Western Front, engagements lasted weeks and even months. Ottoman positions were subjected to 'bite and hold', before reserves came up and developed the lodgements.

Maude had opened his assault with two corps advancing in parallel up both banks of the Tigris, a manoeuvre that made it more difficult for the Ottomans to concentrate their resistance. Heavy rain had impeded progress and the low-lying, marshy ground dissolved into a sea of mud, but it was actually Maude's concern to minimize casualties and proceed methodically from one objective to the next that made this a painstaking process. For two months, he pounded the Ottoman defences, then carefully pushed his units into the gaps.

Maude possessed a skill that made this more than a mere attritional process. While the Ottoman defenders concentrated all their attention on their immediate front, Maude transferred part of his force across the Shumran Bend of the Tigris on a pontoon bridge on 23 February 1917 and assaulted the right of the Ottoman line. Simultaneously, his corps attacked the Ottoman left, opposite the Sanniyat defensive bastion. The crossing of the Shumran Bend, which enabled a force to establish a position some five miles upriver from Kut, threw the Ottomans completely off balance. The bridgehead was expanded quickly and the Ottomans, whose position was unhinged, were in danger of complete encirclement. They withdrew, but Maude now unleashed a pursuit. Having proceeded so slowly hitherto, the sudden and penetrating advance threw the Ottomans into shock. Captain W. Nunn of the Royal Navy led the chase with a flotilla of five British gunboats, seizing Kut and then steaming upriver. The Ottoman rear guard caught Nunn's little fleet in an intense crossfire at point-blank range from the banks, but his crews pressed on regardless, and steaming parallel to the main body of retreating Ottoman troops, they opened up with devastating results. The entire Ottoman force was destroyed or dispersed. Barely 5,000 Ottoman troops escaped Maude's offensive.

Maude regrouped his forces at Aziziyeh, restocking his logistics, resting the troops, and preparing for the next pulse of the offensive. He did not wish to repeat the error of 1915 and advance so far that he risked reaching a culminating point. The Ottomans were meanwhile being forced to completely redesign their defences of Mesopotamia. Their planned advance into Persia had to be abandoned. The priority now was the defence of Baghdad, a prestigious symbol of Ottoman power in the region.

In Britain, the army and the government were divided about the next move. Robertson was adamant that there should be no further advance. While insisting the War Cabinet left the direction of the war to the military, he reasoned that if Baghdad was taken, it was not clear how it would be held and to what purpose.[16] If the Ottomans reinforced the front, there was a risk that the British would merely repeat the siege of Kut but in the more exposed and extended location of Baghdad. He would permit raiding by cavalry, the extension of 'influence' into the province of Baghdad, but he cautioned against any situation that would compel a withdrawal of British forces because of the 'objectionable political effect' that might ensue.[17] He repeated his determination that the war would be won or lost on the Western Front against the main adversary Germany, and continued to regard Mesopotamia as an expensive and wasteful sideshow.

General Monro in India took a diametrically different view. He urged Maude to press on and seize Baghdad while the Ottomans were broken on the Tigris. He argued that taking Baghdad would prevent the Ottomans from reforming and it would provide an important prestige victory for the British amongst their colonial Muslim subjects.[18] Maude concurred with Monro, but the deciding factor for the government was the prospect that the Russians might extend their own area of control from the Caucasus to Mosul and northern Mesopotamia.[19] A renewed Russian offensive toward Baghdad could not be ruled out, particularly with Ottoman troops so significantly reduced. In a post-war settlement this would give Russia enormous influence across the Middle East, and such empowerment left British officials in India concerned. Robertson relented. He permitted an advance if Maude judged it prudent, with all his previous caveats.[20]

Maude therefore resumed his offensive on 5 March 1917 and it took just three days to reach the Diyala River where Halil had prepared defences on the confluence with the Tigris. On 9 March, the initial British probing attacks were repulsed and Maude opted to outflank the river positions and threaten Baghdad directly. The city was 226 miles away but Halil could not protect it if Maude's force moved around his defences. The British manoeuvre forced Halil to readjust his line, and shift the bulk of his force to face the new threat and leave the main defences in the hands of a single regiment. Maude then switched axis again, assaulted the Diyala defences frontally, and overwhelmed them. The Ottomans were defeated decisively. On 11 March, Maude was able to secure Baghdad without resistance. Some 9,000 Ottoman troops were captured in the confusion and their resistance in the area had been broken. It was an enormous encouragement to the British government: with this achievement, they wondered whether similar progress could be made in the Near East.

After the capture of Baghdad, Maude's concern was to prevent the remainder of Halil's force north of the city joining with the 15,000-strong corps led by Ali Ihsan Bey, a formation that was withdrawing from Persia under Russian pressure. Maude's solution was to seize the rail junction at Samarrah, some 80 miles to the north. Marching out with 45,000 men, Maude planned four short attacks and his first objective was to prevent any attempt to flood the Euphrates plain and thus render further British operations impossible. A secondary objective was to secure the western approaches to Baghdad since Ottoman forces still lay out along the Euphrates. The first thrust to the north was resisted strongly but the British drove the Ottomans back 22 miles to the Adhaim River.

Halil was therefore compelled to withdraw to a much stronger series of prepared defences at Istabulat, which lay between the Tigris and the Ali Jali Canal. Maude made a series of attacks along these defensive lines on 21 April, and some positions changed hands several times in close-quarter fighting. The Ottomans were eventually pushed out, and occupied a low ridge some six miles from the Samarrah railway junction. Maude kept up the pressure, and when the Ottomans realized their position could no longer be held, Maude's force secured the town. His offensive had been a complete success.

The Russian war effort had been ebbing just as the British advanced up the Tigris. In the autumn, communist revolutionaries seized power and the Russian Army began to break up and withdraw. Thus the German and Ottoman strategic dilemma in late 1917 was how to make best use of the new reserves that had been released from Europe and the Caucasus following the collapse of the Russian war effort. With the Bolsheviks in power, Russian resistance in the Caucasus and northern Persia was melting away. The divisions now available from South-East Europe and the Caucasus gave Istanbul a strategic reserve, the Yıldırım (Lightning) Army Group, and this could be committed either to the recovery of Baghdad or to bolster the Palestine front against an expected British offensive. The German contribution was the seasoned and well-equipped brigade Pasha II, which was armed with a generous scale of machine guns and field artillery. This force was designed to support an Ottoman offensive to retake Baghdad, although General Falkenhayn, effectively now in command of the Middle Eastern theatre, was conscious that any attack in that direction would first have to ensure the security of Jerusalem and Palestine lest the Allies break through and threaten the Turco-German lines of communications in Syria.

Just as the Central Powers agreed on where the strategic weight of the Ottoman Empire would be committed, namely in Mesopotamia against Maude, General Allenby commenced his operations in Palestine and the Ottoman Yıldırım Group had to be diverted. The strategic situation therefore altered again, and further operational successes for the British in both theatres began to alter the balance irrevocably in their favour.

Meanwhile, to the west of Baghdad, Maude had taken Fallujah on 19 March 1917 and his units fanned out to pacify the area. When operations were resumed here in March 1918, the 15th Indian Division took Hit without resistance, as the Ottoman garrison gave way in its path. The Ottomans adopted delaying tactics, fighting just long enough to inflict casualties, and then pulling out to new positions in the rear. In September, Ramadi was taken in a brilliant British mobile operation that had cavalry, horse artillery, armoured cars, and infantry in motor transport working in close cooperation. Swinging around the Ottoman positions to get into depth, a series of cut-off groups decimated the Ottomans' attempts to make their usual tactical withdrawal. The manoeuvre broke Ottoman resistance, rolled up its reserves and headquarters units, and effectively placed the Euphrates under British control.

To the north, the final phase of the Mesopotamia campaign fell to Maude's successor Sir William Marshall. The strategic direction was the British government's desire that Mosul, and its valuable oil resources, should be in British hands at the end of the war. This was to be a vital diplomatic advantage for London in any peace negotiations, for it was anticipated that Bulgaria would soon be knocked out of the war and this would cut the lines of communications from the Central Powers to Istanbul. The British government was eager to exclude France and Russia from the region, and ensure a strong security zone could be established for the allied independent Arab territories to the south.[21]

The problem was that Marshall's Tigris force had been denuded of some of its transport by the need to convey 'Dunsterforce', a detached contingent, to Baku, where it could provide security against a final Ottoman attempt to control the oil resources of the Caucasus and

Trans-Caspian region.[22] Resources also had to be diverted to Palestine for Allenby's offensive beyond the Judaean Hills, so the final push in Mesopotamia was made by a much smaller force than had been available to Maude.

Marshall was undaunted by the loss of his numerical advantage, defeating the remnants of Halil's Sixth Army, restyled as the *Dicle Grubu* (Tigris Group), in a series of engagements that culminated in the battle of Sharqat. The Ottoman Army in Mesopotamia were at the end of their endurance, with too few horses and mules to move, short of ammunition, in rags of uniforms, and ravaged by disease. Ottoman officers feared a breakdown of discipline as their forces wasted away. Marshall had correctly deduced that he needed to keep up the pressure by advancing into depth. The Armistice was declared when Marshall's force was just a few miles short of Mosul, but the city was taken in anticipation of the peace settlement that would follow.

The British and Indian troops in Mesopotamia had achieved a significant victory. Supported by modern aircraft and motor transport, they had fought their way over 600 miles up the Tigris and Euphrates, against determined resistance and in demanding climatic conditions. They had endured floods, sandstorms, choking dust, and deep mud. They had broiled under the sun, and frozen in the exposed plains in the winter. Sicknesses had taken their toll, and it is worth remembering that more lives were lost through disease than combat in this campaign.[23] The Ottomans had fought for virtually every mile, hurling at the British forces every available weapon of war. Maude's and Marshall's forces had fought with endurance and imagination, combining material advantages and efficient organization with skilful manoeuvre. Yet an even more stunning campaign had unfolded in Palestine to the west, and it was here that the Ottoman armies were finally broken.

Palestine and Syria, 1918

Although they were in strong positions and had repulsed two British offensives in 1917, severe supply problems affected the Ottoman troops dug in at Gaza. But the relative weaknesses of the Ottoman forces on the

Palestine front were not the immediate concern of the British War Cabinet or of the Chief of the Imperial General Staff. Robertson informed the headquarters at Cairo that their request for two divisions would be denied and that, while 'every opportunity should be taken' to defeat the forces to their front, the Egyptian Expeditionary Force (EEF) in southern Palestine would simply not be required to conduct major offensive operations.[24] Nevertheless, the Prime Minister, given the grave situation in Russia and on the Western Front in late 1917, could not permit inactivity, and more mounted troops were dispatched. The whole mobile contingent of the EEF was then reorganized as three distinct divisions, with supporting artillery.[25] Eventually, despite Robertson's objections, the two infantry divisions that had been requested were also dispatched. Rail and water supply lines were extended to support the EEF's lines and the troops were subjected to intensive training, incorporating lessons derived from operations on the Western Front.

The British EEF therefore had the 'means' to break through at Gaza and drive the Ottomans out of the Near East. The force had been expanded to ten infantry divisions and four mounted divisions, and possessed 116 heavy guns. The EEF was supported by new aircraft, particularly the Bristol Fighter plane, which gave a technological advantage over the Central Powers' air forces on their front. With numerical superiority, the British and Indian troops were grouped into three corps. The XXI Corps of three infantry divisions, facing Gaza and its south-eastern approaches, was commanded by Lieutenant General Edward Bulfin. Opposite Beersheba, Lieutenant General Chetwode commanded the XX Corps, with three infantry divisions with an attached Yeomanry division, while Lieutenant General Harry Chauvel's Desert Mounted Corps, on the right flank of the EEF, faced Beersheba's south-eastern approaches.

What the EEF needed was the 'ways'. The arrival of the new commander, General Edmund Allenby, seemed to herald the end of the stalemate that had prevailed for months. The appointment of a new commander, the soldiers believed, increased the likelihood of an advance into the more temperate landscape of Palestine out of the exhausting desert conditions of southern Palestine. Allenby's confidence, his physical

The Middle East and Palestine, 1918

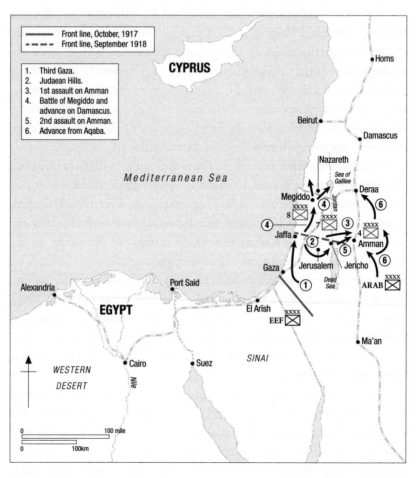

presence, his experience from the Western Front, his willingness to talk to soldiers, and his intolerance of oversights amongst his officers had a positive and energizing effect across the army.[26]

The strategic situation was becoming more urgent by the day. There was growing concern that, with the situation in Russia deteriorating, more Ottoman troops might be released from the Caucasus front and deployed against the EEF. According to Lloyd George, Allenby was expected to defeat and then pursue the enemy to the limit of his resources. Robertson was more cautious. He wrote to Allenby that 'it will be a good thing to give the Turk in front of you a sound beating, but that the extent to which we shall be justified in following him by an advance into Northern and Central Palestine is a matter which for the moment must be left open'.[27] Referring to the Clausewitzian problem of a culminating point, he added: 'The further we go north the more Turks we shall meet; and the greater will be the strain upon our resources.' He added a 'PS', in which he pointed out it was not so much going forward that he opposed, but how to 'maintain ourselves after going forward and to a useful purpose'.

Allenby therefore devised a plan with his corps commanders to unhinge the Ottoman defences. The Third Battle of Gaza (31 October–8 November 1917) opened with a sustained artillery bombardment on the defences of the town lying on the extreme left, and was then extended by Chetwode's XX Corps against Beersheba on the extreme right flank. Along the line in the centre, the infantry of the 60th and 74th divisions approached methodically from the south-west, the troops following just 30 yards behind a curtain of explosions, suffering some casualties from Ottoman retaliatory fire. Significant features such as Hill 1070 were captured, but progress was slow because of the resistance shown by Ottoman units.[28] It was not until the evening that all their objectives were secured.

Then, in an unexpected manoeuvre, the Desert Mounted Corps used the cover of darkness overnight on 30–31 October to ride around to the east of Beersheba. As planned, the XX Corps' attack from the south-west and west had compelled the Ottoman III Corps commander, Colonel Ismet Bey, to push his reserves against Chetwode's infantry. As a result, Chauvel's Desert Mounted Corps outnumbered the Ottomans on the extreme right. The Australian 7th and 5th Light Horse regiments drove back the 3rd Ottoman Cavalry Division north of Beersheba, while the 6th Light Horse acted as a reserve in support of the New Zealanders' attack on the hill at Tel es Sabe. An Ottoman battalion was dug in on this high ground, and their commanding position gave them wide fields of fire across Beersheba's eastern approaches. It took the New Zealand Mounted Rifles brigade most of the day to assault and capture this tactically vital position.[29]

Clearing this feature made it possible for the Australian 4th and 12th Light Horse regiments that evening to charge through the twilight, 800 strong, towards the town. Under machine-gun and small-arms fire, the leading squadrons dismounted when they reached the Ottoman trenches and engaged in a close-quarter battle, mostly with bayonets.[30] The squadrons behind them continued to fight their way into the town on horseback. The result was the capture of Beersheba and a haul of Ottoman prisoners. The Ottomans' attention was fixed on their extreme flank, but before reserves could be committed, they had to consider that Beersheba was a feint as the British attacks were now developing near the coast.

The attack on Gaza itself began on 1 November with Bulfin's XXI Corps artillery hammering the Ottoman defences, before mounting an infantry assault with the advancing troops keeping just behind the belt of exploding shells. Attacks were made on the advanced strongpoints, and raids made against others, but what the Ottomans did not realize was that the full weight of the offensive had not yet come.[31] This was understandable since Bulfin's artillery barrage was the largest outside Europe to date in the war, with 15,000 rounds smashing into the ground around the settlement before the infantry reached the position. Despite the staggering volume of fire, the Ottoman garrison defended their blasted and collapsing trenches with courage and determination.[32] Believing that the British would press home the attack, more Ottoman units were rushed into these defences, while the line beyond Hebron was stripped of available manpower. Allenby had also succeeded in weakening his enemy's positions in the centre, at the 'hinge' of Hareira and Tel el Sheria, two settlements at the heart of the Ottoman defences. On 6 November, the main attack went in against this section, and the Ottoman line was cut.[33] A gap seven miles wide was opened up, through which his reserves now advanced, and kept moving, right into the Judean Hills.

After Third Gaza there was continuing debate between Robertson and Lloyd George over the ends and means of the Palestine operations, and how the campaign fitted into the overall strategy of the war. Impatient with the Chief of the Imperial General Staff, the Prime Minister forced Robertson out in February 1918. In December 1917, Robertson had stated, 'it is for serious consideration whether the advantages to be gained by an advance [in Palestine] are worth the cost and risk involved'. He added, 'The answer depends to some extent upon whether the conquest of Palestine would put Turkey out of the war.'[34]

Nevertheless, on 9 December 1917, it was Allenby's entry into Jerusalem that mattered to the Prime Minister. It was strategically important, not least for Britain's prestige and its bargaining position in the post-war world. Lloyd George told the House of Commons: 'The capture of Jerusalem has made a most profound impression throughout the whole civilised world … the name of every hamlet and hill occupied by the British Army … thrills with sacred memories.'[35] Allenby, conscious of the sensitivities in the city and globally, chose to walk in on foot in simple khaki service dress. After a brief ceremony lasting 15 minutes, he returned to the soldiers' business of finishing the Ottomans in the Near East.

Allenby had been instructed to resume his offensive in February 1918 but he could not progress north into Syria until he had neutralized the 20,000 Ottoman troops on his eastern flank in Amman. His first manoeuvre, to take Jericho, was successful, with the town falling to Allied troops on 21 February. Next, Allenby seized the hills above Wadi Auja, which put Jericho and its line of communications beyond the reach of Ottoman artillery. In March, an attempt to raid towards Amman met with defeat, largely because of the weather and topography. Heavy rains made all movement arduous and prevented the deployment of field artillery. A second attempt was then delayed because divisions were being withdrawn for service in France to face the massive German offensive of the spring.

The second raid, when it came in May, also met with failure. General Liman von Sanders, now the commander of the Yıldırım Group of Ottoman reserves, had called in his more-exposed posts in order to concentrate his forces around the city. He knew that Amman represented the last rail link with the garrison in Medina, and therefore was a vital junction for the entire campaign theatre.[36] He called for further reinforcements from the north and dispatched Ottoman cavalry to threaten the British lines of communication astride the Jordan River. Meanwhile, Allenby's force was struggling with the rain and mud, and a decision was made to transfer as much arms, equipment, and baggage as possible to camels and mules because of the difficulty in moving wheeled transport. Such were the conditions that men and animals died of exposure on the wind-swept slopes of the valley. Consequently, the British force that arrived in front of the Ottoman positions was exhausted before the fighting had even begun.[37] The EEF's brigade, with the ammunition and guns they could carry, launched four days of assaults against strong positions. Some 2,000 defenders were dug in, armed with 70 machine guns and supported by field artillery which had been zeroed in on prearranged targets and beaten zones. Further Ottoman reinforcements arrived during the fighting. Yet Liman von Sanders was so concerned about the mounting casualties and wavering resolve of the defenders that he ordered their positions to be held regardless of the cost. The British and Imperial forces could not, however, continue the attacks indefinitely. On 30 March 1918, they commenced their withdrawal, accompanied by large numbers of refugees from Es Salt who feared Ottoman retribution.[38]

Nevertheless, Allenby's aborted attack convinced the German and Ottoman commanders that more reinforcements must be sent to this city that commanded the British right flank. If the British could not secure Amman, it was reasoned, they would not be able to press on into Syria.

In fact, Allenby went to great lengths to conceal the direction of his intended offensive. Some 15,000 wooden and canvas horses were built and dummy camps erected to persuade intrusive reconnaissance pilots that the EEF intended to attack from the Jordan valley towards Amman. Units were moved at night, and camouflaged by day. Air patrols did their best to deny access over Allenby's formations. Bridges were built across the Jordan to give the impression of an impending thrust against the city, and false wireless traffic was generated to support the idea of intense preparations.

The Arab Northern Army played their part in creating the deception. With the bulk of the Arab force laying siege to Ma'an, a detached contingent advanced to within 50 miles of Amman. On 16 September, covered by aircraft of the Royal Air Force, Colonel T. E. Lawrence's Arab irregulars conducted a series of guerrilla actions on the railway line either side of the junction of Daraa. Lawrence reported that he 'burnt a lot of rolling stock and two lorries, broke the points, and planted a fair assortment of "tulip [mine]s" down the line'.[39] Despite considerable harassment from German and Ottoman aircraft, and the resistance of the local garrisons, the Arabs repeatedly cut the line and succeeded in generating a rout in some of the Ottoman Fourth Army troops. Some of the Ottoman troops exacted a terrible retribution against the civilian population of the village of Turaa. This inspired more local Arab tribes to join the revolt and drew in Ottoman reinforcements to defend the area. The Arab Northern Army caught the Ottoman forces trying to evacuate Daraa and exacted revenge by taking no prisoners.[40] This overwhelming Arab victory was possible because Allenby had unleashed his long-awaited final offensive, not against Amman as the Ottomans had anticipated, but right along the line, 50 miles wide, between Jericho and the sea.

The battle of Megiddo, which opened at 0400hrs on 19 September 1918 with a tremendous artillery barrage, was fought between the three corps of the EEF and the remnants of the Ottoman Fourth (near Amman) and the Seventh and Eighth armies of Yıldırım. Allenby had deployed 35,000 infantry, 9,000 cavalry, and 400 heavy guns, the bulk of which were concentrated on a 15-mile front close to the Mediterranean coast, north of Jaffa. The shelling was the most intense delivered outside a European theatre, with 1,000 rounds a minute detonating on the Ottoman positions in this sector.

The engagement developed as Allenby had planned. The infantry assault of the XXI Corps carried the first two Ottoman lines and overcame the resistance of the third and fourth lines soon after. In just two and a half hours, they had penetrated 7,000 yards into the Ottoman positions, and broken open a wide gap in their defences. Chauvel's cavalry exploited the gap perfectly, chasing the routed Ottoman troops up to Tulkarm, which was captured. The cavalry pressed on with aircraft above them, seizing depots, rounding up prisoners, and destroying the telephone communications' nodes on which the Yıldırım depended to allocate its reserves. Megiddo, the Biblical site alleged to mark the end of times, was reached soon after, more than 30 miles beyond the front line. The speed of the advance seemed to exceed all expectations: the British 4th Cavalry Division covered 70 miles on 20 September, while the Australian Mounted Division in one bound advanced 11 miles in just 60 minutes. The Ottoman forces began to disintegrate in the confusion: entire Turkish battalions found themselves encircled or under relentless air attack. A key manoeuvre was the decision of the cavalry to switch to a new axis to the south-east, from Nazareth and Beth Shean, which cut off the retreat of the Ottoman Seventh Army. On 23 September, British and Indian cavalry took Acre and Haifa. Resistance from Ottoman forces in Palestine was ebbing away.

British and Indian cavalry circled round to cut off Ottoman forces making for Beirut and Homs. Deraa was taken on 27 September and the race was on to drive northwards into Syria before the Ottomans could create any new defensive line. But the rout of the Ottomans was complete. By 30 September, the combined British and Arab force was on the edge of Damascus. A ceremonial entry was arranged for the Arab Northern Army, accompanied by T. E. Lawrence 'of Arabia'. The British entry was more prosaic, but Emir Feisal was accorded the honours of a conqueror for a short time before being informed, by Allenby, that, according to standard procedure, the city was under British military occupation. It had been a whirlwind campaign which had driven the Ottomans pell-mell out of the Near East. The pursuit continued and Aleppo was taken on 26 October, but resistance had almost ceased altogether by that stage. Just four days after Aleppo was captured, on 30 October, the Ottomans concluded an armistice, agreeing to all the Allied terms.

Robertson's successor as Chief of the Imperial General Staff, Sir Henry Wilson, wrote to Allenby soon after the victory and he concluded that the German strategic plan had been 'command of the sea [and] the Near and Middle East'. Wilson believed Britain had prevented German command of the sea and 'I was always casting about in my mind how this second objective [German domination of the Middle East] could be frustrated'.[41] He concluded: 'You [Allenby] and Franchet[42] did that. The collapse of the main theatres followed almost automatically.' In 1918, in Mesopotamia, East Africa, and the Near East, the Central Powers had been defeated. Despite their determined resistance, both Germany and the Ottoman Empire were stripped of their territorial possessions. The Allies had won decisive operational and strategic victories, achieved all their objectives, and acquired new security responsibilities in the process.

CHAPTER 8

THE GREAT WAR AT SEA IN 1918

The role of sea power in achieving victory

Professor Dr Michael Epkenhans

On 24 November 1918, the Great War at sea was eventually over. Having moored all ships under his command – those of the Grand Fleet and those of the beaten enemy, the High Seas Fleet – at Scapa Flow, the commander-in-chief of the Grand Fleet, Admiral Sir David Beatty, delivered an address to his officers and men on board the battle-cruiser HMS *Lion*: 'England owes the Grand Fleet a great, great debt. The world owes the Grand Fleet great debt. It has been said before, and it will be said many times again, that the war, which is now on the threshold of coming to an end, has been won by sea-power.'[1]

The pride visible in Beatty's words is understandable, because the victory which had been achieved and which was celebrated here had been no easy one. There had been, of course, no more battles of Jutland in which all the big ships had clashed in the last two years of the war. However, many minor encounters at sea, the hardships of convoying, and the war under water, mercilessly waged by Germany until almost the eve of the Armistice on 11 November, had been great challenges for Beatty, his officers, and his men.

When war broke out in August 1914 all naval officers as well as the public hoped that a great Trafalgar-like battle would soon decide the war, at least at sea. Instead, almost all fleets remained in their homeports. The Grand Fleet, the most powerful navy of the time, had no interest in offensive action. Following plans developed in the last years before the war, the Royal Navy established a distant blockade to keep the Germans at bay. Though many British admirals and sailors wanted to fight, this strategy seemed fully apt to achieve Britain's main aim: to successfully prevent the enemy from using the great common – as Alfred T. Mahan had called the oceans of the world – and thus cut off Germany from its lines of communications. This strategy did not exclude occasional sweeps into the North Sea as in 1914, when British battle-cruisers attacked and sank three German light cruisers on patrol off Heligoland. However, a battle was no aim in itself, due to the risks it entailed against the background of this overarching strategic aim.

This strategy also applied to the Mediterranean. After the German Mediterranean Squadron, consisting of the battle-cruiser SMS *Goeben* and the light cruiser SMS *Breslau*, had fled into Turkish waters, and, moreover, after Italy had joined the Entente in 1915, all the Allies wanted to achieve was to prevent the Austro-Hungarian Navy from coming out into the open sea and trying to attack Allied shipping or from supporting the Austrian Army in its bloody battles against the Italians in the North. Successes and failures had kept the balance throughout the war until the end of 1917.

The Russian Navy was still suffering from the traumatic experiences of the Russo-Japanese War in 1904–05. So it decided to remain on the defensive and to concentrate on the defence of the Finnish Gulf – the entry to St Petersburg – and the long Russian coastline against German attacks. By and large this strategy proved successful, though parts of the Russian coast had to be surrendered after the Russian Army had been pushed back by German troops in 1915–16. In the Black Sea the Russian Navy played a more offensive role. Whereas attacks on Turkish convoys proved very successful, attempts to attack and break the Turkish Straits had no chance of success despite Russian naval superiority in these waters.

And the Central Powers? Due to their geographic positions and their numerical inferiority big battles made no sense, neither for the High Seas Fleet nor for the Austro-Hungarian Navy. As a result both navies remained on the defensive. Nevertheless they hoped to diminish the superiority of their respective enemies in the North Sea, in the Baltic, and in the Adriatic by laying mines, through submarine attacks, or by attacking only parts of their fleets. The German sorties against the British East Coast and the Dogger-Bank in 1914–15, the battle of Jutland in 1916, or the Austrian sorties against the Italian East Coast and the barrage of the Otranto Straits in 1917 had been remarkable events at sea, but they had not changed the strategic situation. Rather, both navies had risked valuable ships and even incurred considerable losses without achieving any real strategic gains.

Though the strategy of fleet-in-being did not match with the great expectations of the naval leaderships in Germany and in Austria, it proved successful, because it helped protect the respective coasts from invasion and secure the lines of communication in parts of the North Sea, in the Baltic, and in the Adriatic. The only really offensive strategy was the introduction of submarine warfare in 1914. Directed first only against warships, this new weapon had inflicted heavy losses upon the Allies, when both the German and Austrian navies began to attack merchant ships in the North Sea, the Atlantic Ocean, and the Mediterranean in 1915.

And the oceans of the world? In 1918 these were free from German warships apart from submarines. The German East Asian Squadron had disappeared in the battle of the Falkland Islands on 8 December 1914 after a successful battle against an inferior British force at Coronel only four weeks before. Similarly all German light cruisers waging commerce warfare had also either been sunk like SMS *Emden*, SMS *Königsberg*, and SMS *Dresden* or disappeared after an internal explosion like SMS *Karlsruhe*. Most German auxiliary cruisers had suffered the same fate. The only exceptions were SMS *Möve* and SMS *Wolf* and the famous

SMS *Seeadler*, a sailing vessel. Sent out in 1915–16, their attacks on Allied supply and trade lines had caused a lot of confusion and damage to British shipping in waters as far away as the South Seas, and had been regarded with great concern by the Royal Navy. Attempts to hunt them down like the big ships of the German Fleet had failed, however. When the German raiders had eventually returned to Germany after long months away from home, their captains and crews had, of course, been welcomed as heroes. Though they had tied down many warships and had inflicted painful losses on the enemy at a time of worldwide shipping shortage, their importance should not be overestimated.

The North Sea and the Atlantic Ocean

The North Sea and the waters around Great Britain were still the most important theatres of the war at sea at the beginning of 1918. For the British Grand Fleet the year 1917 had been a year of great disappointments. Though the Grand Fleet had, like her enemy, decided to avoid bigger actions, it had nevertheless tried to inflict losses upon the enemy's surface ships. However, it was the German High Seas Fleet with its energetic commander-in-chief, Admiral Reinhard Scheer, which had tried to strike again in the North Sea in late 1917. After the Kaiser had forbidden a major attack planned by Scheer into the Hoofden in early 1917, two sorties by light cruisers against Allied convoys in the North Sea had proved very successful. In mid-October two German light cruisers, SMS *Brummer* and SMS *Bremse*, had attacked a westbound Scandinavian convoy 70 miles east of Lerwick, and in mid-December the Germans had struck again. Two torpedo-boat flotillas accompanied by the light cruiser SMS *Emden* attacked Allied convoys in the war channel along the east coast and on the Bergen–Lerwick route. Each time they sank not only many of the merchant vessels, but also most of the convoy escorts. Last but not least, a British attempt to retaliate had failed in mid-November. Hampered by mist, incomplete intelligence, and ill-prepared charts, an attack on the German minesweepers and their covering forces in the waters around Heligoland had to be broken off when superior enemy forces opened fire on the British ships.

Admiral Sir John Jellicoe, who had already lost his command of the Grand Fleet because he was blamed for the escape of the High Seas Fleet at Jutland and who – in order to save face – had been appointed First Sea Lord in 1916, again became the scapegoat of these losses and failures and was forced to resign from his position on Christmas Day 1917. This change went hand-in-hand with a new strategy, developed by the commander-in-chief of the Grand Fleet, Admiral Sir David Beatty. For Beatty a great battle was no option, at least for the time being. Despite superiority in numbers, the risks were too high in his eyes. The High Seas Fleet could always 'dictate' the place of the battle, he argued, and thus try to ambush his ships and whittle down his strength. Moreover, British numerical superiority, which was enlarged by the arrival of a US battle squadron at Scapa Flow in December 1917, to some extent existed only on paper, because many ships were bound by escort duties and therefore not available for a great battle. Most importantly, however, despite some technical improvements, Beatty was not convinced of the quality of his ships. The battle of Jutland had made clear that his own as well as Jellicoe's apprehensions at the beginning of the war that British warships were 'inferior in construction and protection' to the German vessels had been justified. Under present conditions, Beatty wrote to the First Sea Lord in December 1917, a battle between the High Seas Fleet and the Grand Fleet might result in a 'rude awakening for the Country'.[2]

Contrary to Beatty the Admiralty expected an improvement of the general situation and more offensive action after the arrival of urgently needed US destroyers for escort and other duties. Nevertheless, they approved Beatty's decision to concentrate on the protection of the convoys and the fight against the U-boats. In addition to the already existing minefields in the German Bight, thousands of mines were laid in spring and summer in the northern North Sea as well as in the Channel. The so-called Northern Barrage eventually consisted of more than 70,000 mines. Its effectiveness was, however, more than doubtful, because the American mines very often exploded prematurely. Only six U-boats became victims of the barrage; another two may have been damaged. The convoy system, which had been much improved in the meantime, proved much more effective and also much cheaper than this undertaking.

In addition depth charges, Q-ships, and aerial bombing also proved increasingly effective weapons against the U-boat threat.

In contrast to the almost useless Northern Barrage, the mine-offensive in the Channel war was far more successful. From the early months of 1918 British warships effectively blocked the Channel for the U-boats with mines, anti-U-boat nets, and drifters backed by monitors and destroyers. The result was that the U-boats were forced to take the much longer route around the British Isles or face grave danger in the Channel. Some U-boats tried to find a way through the minefield and 14 U-boats were lost. The Royal Navy also tried to block Germany's U-boat bases in Flanders by sinking blockships and destroying the locks of the sea-canals. Attacks on Zeebrugge and Ostend in April and May 1918, however, failed utterly. Despite attacks from the air all U-boat bases therefore remained open until the end of October, when the Germans withdrew from Flanders after the Allied success in the 'Hundred Days' campaign. German attempts to break the Dover Barrage and to attack Allied positions on land with torpedo boats in mid-February, in March, and in April proved unsuccessful and costly, for several torpedo boats were sunk or severely damaged.

And what did the Germans plan for and do in 1918? Scheer was fully aware of his weaknesses. Since U-boat warfare had become his priority, the sweeping of minefields in the German Bight kept the fleet occupied to a steadily increasing degree. Without the support of big ships, minesweepers had no chance of fulfilling this dangerous and difficult task. Moreover, German operations in the Baltic against Finland in spring 1918 required further support from the fleet. As a result all ideas to support the army's great offensive in the West in March 1918, which was supposed to crush the Allies by attacking Allied transport in the Channel, were put aside. Economic pressure exerted by submarines remained the only contribution of the High Seas Fleet in these months. The risks of an operation against the French coast as far as Calais seemed too high compared with the gains such an attack might bring about.[3] Nevertheless, this did not mean that the High Seas Fleet wanted to remain idle. In late April the High Seas Fleet left port again, though not for the French coast but for Scandinavian waters as in the year before. 'Our U-Boats,' Scheer argued in his memoirs, had learnt that the steamers were assembled there [between Britain and Norway] in large convoys, strongly protected by first-class battleships, cruisers and destroyers. A successful attack on such a convoy would not only result in the sinking of much tonnage, but would be a great military success, and would bring about welcome relief to the U-boats operating in the Channel and round England, for it would force the English to send more warships to the northern waters.[4]

The rationale behind this strategy seemed sound; reality, however, proved much more difficult. Though the High Seas Fleet left Schillig Roads – the Jade bay and the approach to the main naval base of Wilhelmshaven – without being detected and reached the envisaged position off the Scandinavian coast safely, the convoy they wanted to intercept and attack had already left due to a change in departure times. To make things even worse, on the way back the battle-cruiser SMS *Moltke* not only lost its starboard screw, but was eventually also torpedoed by a British submarine on patrol in the German Bight. Though the Grand Fleet had put to sea after receiving news of the sortie of the High Seas Fleet, it was unable to intercept it before Scheer's vessels reached Wilhelmshaven again. For the High Seas Fleet it proved to be the last sortie for the remainder of the war.

With only 22 operational capital ships left compared to the Grand Fleet's 43, a new attempt would have been suicidal, especially after Beatty's decision to transfer the Grand Fleet closer to the German bases and seek a battle at the same time. Scheer therefore again fully concentrated on submarine warfare. After long discussions on this strategy between the Kaiser, the Chancellor, and the navy, the Empire had eventually put all its stakes upon this weapon in early 1917 with the declaration of unrestricted submarine warfare. The admirals had promised that Britain would be forced to its knees within six months. Victory would thus be won before the United States with all her resources could turn the scales in the Allies' favour. The first months seemed to justify this all-or-nothing strategy. Allied losses had jumped from 335,106[5] tons in January 1917 to 841,118 tons in April. From then on, they had, however, continued to fall. Whereas the U-boats had sunk another 669,218 tons in June, numbers had slowly gone down to 285,593 tons in January 1918. For the navy this had been a disaster – politically and military. Instead of supporting the Empire in winning the war quickly and decisively, it had helped to enlarge the numbers of enemies. Apart from the United States of America, other neutrals had also declared war on Germany. Most important in this respect was the enormous weight the United States could throw onto the scales with their economic power and the men they could mobilize for the Allied war effort. Militarily, the entry of the United States meant for the navy that the number of Allied ships in the North Sea as well as in the Mediterranean increased, and made naval operations even more difficult than they already were. It was not the big ships that mattered in this case, but the number of destroyers, which were so important for convoy services and hunting for U-boats in the North Sea as well as in the Mediterranean, and, last but not least, the huge amount of mines they could and did drop in the German Bight.

Scheer was, however, determined to put all his stakes upon the continuation and, if possible, the intensification of submarine warfare. Eventually appointed chief of the *Seekriegsleitung* (Naval Command) in August 1918 and thus the most powerful naval officer within in the German High Command, he developed a so-called Scheer Programme to greatly increase the number of U-boats built.

Eventually Scheer failed not only because the war was lost only a few months later, but because the obstacles to square the circle proved too high to overcome. Though the U-boats continued to sink many ships in 1918 – figures varied from 250,000 to 343,000 tons – these successes had little impact upon the course of the war. First, after many difficulties in the early months the Allied convoy system had proved a very effective scheme to protect ships from U-boat attacks. Second, even more important were the increasing problems in building and manning the U-boats urgently required to replace losses, which continued to rise. In September 1917 the High Seas Fleet lost 13 U-boats, and in the following months until the end of the war numbers varied from three – the lowest figure – in February 1918 to an incredible 20 in October. On average nine U-boats were lost after the beginning of the U-boat offensive. The decision to try to win the war in a final land offensive meant that all men available were either sent to the Western Front or – if they were skilled workers – had to work in arms and ammunitions factories. Scheer's appeals to the army to make more men available for Germany's shipyards in order to repair and maintain the ships the navy had under commission and, moreover, to build as many U-boats as possible – he envisaged increasing the monthly output from 12 to 36 in 1919 – accordingly fell on deaf ears. As a result the Imperial Navy had great problems to keep up the level of U-boats available for operations in the North Sea. Losses and new commissions just kept the balance in 1917 and 1918. In 1917, for example, the navy lost 75 U-boats, in 1918 another 102. In the same period only 87 and 88, respectively, entered the service. With only roughly 120 U-boats available on average in all theatres of war, victory in the tonnage war was not achievable. Especially in the North Sea and in Flanders the number of U-boats amounted to only 55 to 60 and 25 to 30 U-boats, respectively, on average.[6] The main reason for this was that, in contrast to the decreasing shipbuilding capacities of the Germans, the Allies were able not only to replace those sunk by the U-boats but to build even more to support the Allied war effort on the Western Front – not to speak of the steadily increasing amount of food, war materiel, and men that crossed the Atlantic successfully and without being detected by U-boats. Attempts to increase Allied losses by concentrating several U-boats – like the 'wolf packs' that would be used in World War II – on convoy routes in the Western approaches, sending U-boat cruisers far into the Atlantic and even to the US coast, did not bring about the expected results. Obviously, as in World War II, the Allies had begun to intercept U-boat signals and were thus able to take precautionary measures. Though the U-boat war was eventually given up following US demands in the negotiations about an armistice on 24 October 1918, it had been lost long before. The mines in the German Bight and the inability of the German minesweepers to sweep the routes fast enough to allow safe passage into the North Sea had effectively stopped the U-boat war. In September only seven U-boats could get through; the only exception was the passage through the Baltic, but this cost time and fuel, thus diminishing the time left for operations against Allied ships.

The Baltic

Compared to other theatres of war, the German Navy was in a very favourable situation in the Baltic. After severe losses in 1915 and 1916, the Russian revolutions in 1917 had changed the situation completely. The Russian Baltic Fleet was severely weakened by revolutionary turmoil right from the outbreak of the revolution. Dozens of officers and petty officers were murdered by revolutionary sailors at Kronstadt and in Helsinki, Russia's main naval bases in the Baltic. Among them were the harbour admiral at Kronstadt, Vice Admiral Robert N. Viren, and the commander-in-chief of the Baltic Fleet, Vice Admiral Adrian Nepenin. Even before the Bolsheviks took over in November, revolutionary committees, so-called soviets, were elected and played an increasingly important part in planning and conducting naval operations. The result was idleness. The German Navy watched these events carefully, hoping that the collapse of the Russian Empire would only be a matter of time. However, the decision of the OHL to accelerate Russia's downfall by attacking Riga eventually resulted in Germany's first amphibious operation. After successful operations on the land-front, the army and navy attacked the Baltic Islands of Ösel, Dagö, and Moon in mid-October 1917 in order to remove the threat of an attack on the army from the costal flank and pave the way for a further advance on Petrograd. Despite heavy resistance by the remaining Russian ships, the islands were quickly conquered. Only a few weeks later the Bolshevik revolution effectively ended all naval operations in the Baltic.

However, for the German Navy this was not the end of the war in this area. Though Russia had been beaten and had to sign a harsh peace treaty in early March 1918, German intervention in the Finnish War of Independence led to a final naval operation in March 1918. A task force including several battleships convoyed 10,000 German troops to Finland in early April. Following the wishes of the German High Command the German task force had occupied the Aaland Islands, which after diplomatic negotiations with Sweden were divided between the two countries. The unmolested retreat of the rest of the Russian Baltic Fleet from Helsinki to Kronstadt at the same time, however, ended the war in the Baltic. Plans of the German High Command to attack Kronstadt and Petrograd in late 1918 in order to crush the Bolshevik movement came to nothing. Neither the army nor the navy had enough men and ships available for such an operation.

The Black Sea

In the Black Sea the situation was very similar to that in the Baltic. Here, the revolutionary movement had also hampered naval operations, but contrary to the Baltic, the commander of the Russian Black Sea Fleet, Vice Admiral Aleksandr Kolchak, was at least able to conduct convoy operations between the Crimea and the Caucasus front in the first four months of 1917. Revolutionary soviets, however, forced him to resign in June. His successor, Rear Admiral Aleksandr Nemits, left port again for a mining operation against the Bosphorus. Discovered by the light cruiser *Medilli*, the former SMS *Breslau*, the ensuing short exchange of fire was in fact the last clash of the Turkish and Russian fleets in three years of war in the Black Sea. Later Russian attempts to attack Turkish positions were thwarted by protests from the soviets whose influence had increased enormously in the meantime.

The Bolshevik revolution and the peace treaties dictated by Germany to Russia and Romania in 1918 opened the Black Sea for the Germans and their allies, the Ottomans. Though Sevastopol, formerly the main Russian naval base, now belonged to the Ukraine, which had emerged from the ruins of the Tsarist Empire, the Germans were keen to get their hands on the rest of the Russian Fleet. The German High Command, as well as leading admirals, even dreamed of using these ships together with the *Yavuz Sultan Selim*, the former SMS *Goeben*, for a sudden attack on Allied forces in the Mediterranean and a junction with the Austrians to mop up Allied forces in the region. The effect upon the Allied positions in the Middle East and in the Balkans might – in theory – have been disastrous.[7] In the event, these plans – or better dreams – came to nothing, although they had also occupied the Allies for some time. While all modern Russian ships managed to escape, those left were not only old pre-dreadnoughts, but also proved difficult to repair and man for the Germans. Political disputes between the Germans and the Ottomans, who also wanted their share of this precious booty, caused further delays. As a result, the Black Sea remained quiet apart from the increasing unrest between revolutionary and counter-revolutionary troops in the area. The Germans viewed these with increasing suspicion, concerned that these developments might hamper their own expansionist plans in the East. In order to emphasize Germany's claim Ludendorff ordered the transportation of a German submarine to the Caspian Sea in mid-September 1918, deeply convinced that the imperial ensign would strengthen Germany's position there and help pave the way to even farther Asian countries such as India.

The Mediterranean

Apart from both German and Austrian submarine attacks on Allied shipping, the eastern Mediterranean had seen no action for a long time. The only exception was a sortie of the Turkish battle-cruiser *Yavuz Sultan Selim* and the light cruiser *Medilli* into the Aegean Sea on 20 January 1918. This surprise attack on Allied ships guarding the entrance into the Dardanelles proved successful. Two British monitors were sunk off the Greek island of Mudros. On the way back, however, the *Medilli* ran into a minefield and sank. To make things worse, the *Yavuz Sultan Selim* also hit a mine, when it tried to tow the listing *Medilli* back into the Dardanelles. With great luck it limped back into the Dardanelles, where it ran onto a sandbank. Towed back to Constantinople, it proved so badly damaged that it could not be repaired there. The only dry-dock in this area was in Russian Sevastopol, which had been taken over by the Germans in mid-March. There the *Yavuz Sultan Selim* was repaired in the following months. When it returned to Constantinople at the end of October the Ottoman Empire was on the verge of collapse. The German naval mission, which had run the ship, accordingly left only a few days later, thus ending the war in the Middle East even before the Armistice in the West.

As in the North Sea, only German and Austrian submarines proved successful. The introduction of the convoy system had caused problems for the U-boats in this part of the world as well, and so had the increased numbers of US, Australian, and eventually even Brazilian destroyers employed both to protect convoys and to hunt submarines. Yet, the U-boats were still able to inflict losses upon the Allies. These losses, however, steadily decreased from 103,738 tons in January to 28,007 tons in October. Apart from Allied countermeasures, maintenance problems and the fact that the bigger U-boats, which had achieved remarkable successes in the years before, were not replaced were also responsible for this development. Eventually only less effective small U-boats were available to wage the tonnage war in the Mediterranean.

The Adriatic

In the Adriatic the situation had been very similar to the one in the North Sea right from the beginning of the war. Only occasional sorties from either side against major or minor targets or in the support of operations on land from the sea had broken the stalemate that had existed since Italy's entry into the war in 1915. Successes had always been very limited, though both sides had suffered losses. From the Austrian point of view, however, the situation began to change dramatically in 1918 with the arrival of more Allied destroyers in the Adriatic to support the defence of the Otranto Barrage and thus prevent German as well as Austrian submarines from entering the Mediterranean. To make things worse for the Austrians, the navy was severely hampered by unrest in the early months of 1918. This unrest coincided with a wave of workers' strikes in Austria as well as in Germany. Political discontent, war-weariness, and hunger were the main motives of those who went onto the streets or mutinied as at Cattaro. For the first time, red flags were hoisted indicating the impact of the Russian Revolution on soldiers, sailors, and the people on the home fronts. Eventually the Austrian Navy managed to solve the problem. Some of the ringleaders were executed, hundreds imprisoned. In contrast to the German naval mutiny in 1917, however, the Austrian Navy, tried to solve some of its problems by relieving incompetent officers from their command. Nevertheless, the Cattaro mutiny remained a warning that the situation was on the verge of getting out of control and that the war had to come to an end – the sooner the better. In early June 1918, the new and more-energetic commander-in-chief of the Austro-Hungarian Navy, Rear Admiral Niklas Horthy, planned a new sortie to destroy the Otranto Barrage and open it for the submarines of the Austrian and German navies as in the year before. His formidable task force, which consisted not only of light cruisers and destroyers but also of seven battleships, returned after the dreadnought *Szent István* had been sunk by an Italian motorboat which had found it by chance and torpedoed it. Whether this attack on the Otranto Barrage would have changed anything if it had been successful is a matter of speculation. It did, however, prove that the change from the strategy of a fleet-in-being to a more offensive fleet was a disaster. It was the last time that the Austrian Navy went out to sea. Following this unexpected success, the Allies increased their pressure upon the Austrian Navy by attacking Austrian ports as well as sending submarines to patrol off Austrian naval bases, though with no success. When two Italian officers secretly entered the Austrian naval base at Pola on 1 November 1918 and succeeded in putting charges to the battleship *Viribus Unitis* and the steamer *Wien* – which exploded, although they had been detected already – the Dual Monarchy was, like its allies, on the verge of collapse.

The end of the Great War

Though fighting against the Bolsheviks continued in the East until 1919 and though the Middle East remained an area of unrest until 1923 for the Allies, the Great War came to an end in late 1918. The end of this war at sea is, strangely enough, closely connected not only with the 'Hundred Days' campaign of the Allies in the West as well as the collapse of Germany's allies in the East and in the South-east, but also with the plans for a final sortie of the High Seas Fleet. Somehow an irony of history, Scheer's decision to launch a final and suicidal offensive against the Grand Fleet into the Hoofden in October 1918, when the war was virtually over and when the new and more democratic German government had already begun to negotiate the terms of an armistice with the Allies, was the spark to the powder-keg that blew up the whole Empire. Scheer's idea that a final battle was necessary to save the honour of the naval officer corps and help to justify the requirement for a huge navy after the war was a clear sign that the navy's leadership had still not understood the signs of the times. Unwilling to die for their officers who had mistreated them in many ways throughout the war, unwilling to defend a political order which they had experienced as unjust and undemocratic, and simply wanting to go home as soon as possible, the sailors put out the fires in the big ships and mutinied. Now the naval leadership had to pay the price for its mishandling of the unrest on many ships in the year before. Instead of introducing reforms and improving the situation on board, they had reacted with harsh punishments. Within days this mutiny spread all over Germany with Red sailors often marching at the front of the demonstrations against the old authorities. On 9 November 1918 Germany became a republic, and on 11 November representatives of the new government signed the Armistice at Compiègne in France.

The stipulations of the Armistice were harsh, but the great majority of Germans were simply glad that the war was over. The High Seas Fleet had to disarm under the supervision of Allied officers and to sail into internment in Britain. All preparations finished, 21 November 1918 was eventually '*Der Tag*' – the day of victory many officers of the Royal Navy had allegedly longed for for almost a decade. A long line of German ships, led by the light cruiser HMS *Cardiff*, steamed through the North Sea towards Britain. This time, however, the High Seas Fleet had not left Schillig Roads to attack its most dangerous enemy, as Grand Admiral Alfred von Tirpitz, the father of the German battle-fleet, had called Britain 20 years before, but to surrender. Some 40 miles east of the Firth of Forth, which was one of Britain's major naval bases, the German vessels were met by the combined British, American, and French fleets. In two columns with the German ships between them, the commander-in-chief of the Grand Fleet, Admiral Sir David Beatty, led the beaten enemy to the place of his internment, Britain's naval base at distant Scapa Flow in the Orkneys. Before he left his flagship, the battleship *Queen Elizabeth*, Admiral Beatty gave the signal: 'The German flag will be hauled down at sunset today, Thursday, and will not be hoisted again without permission.'[8] Finally the naval war was over. Somehow, it was an irony of history that the Germans were nevertheless able to retaliate and triumph. When Rear Admiral Ludwig von Reuter, commander of the German ships lying at anchor in Scapa Flow, was informed that the German ships would not be allowed to return home after the signing of the peace treaty, as many officers had hoped, but be distributed among the victors, he ordered the scuttling of the ships under his command. Within a few hours, most ships disappeared in the water; only a few could be saved at the last moment by British guards. For many Germans the scuttling of the once-proud fleet was a symbol of justified defiance. To some extent it foreshadowed the eventual outcome that most naval officers would be unwilling to learn their lessons from what had happened before, but instead look for the right moment to take revenge.

Aftermath

Due to the restrictions imposed by the Treaty of Versailles, the German Navy would pose no threat in the future. Nevertheless, the Allies soon tried to take measures to prevent a renewal of the naval race which had contributed so much to the deterioration of international relations before the war. This time it was the US naval programme of 1916, which had demanded the build-up of a fleet second to none, that was the trigger to come to some kind of international agreement. In 1921–22 delegates from the United States, Great Britain, Italy, France, and Japan assembled in Washington DC to negotiate an agreement. Though a naval race between Britain and the United States was politically very unlikely, such an agreement was also a good opportunity in particular to curb Japanese ambitions in the Far East. Apart from Japan, which only grudgingly entered into these negotiations, all powers had a great interest in an agreement because their financial resources had been depleted by the war. Moreover, political and social unrest were a warning that governments had to meet the wishes of the people, instead of wasting money on new armament programmes. In all countries people also wanted nothing but peace for the future after the horrors of the war they had experienced. After long discussions the delegates signed an agreement limiting the strengths of navies for a ten-year period. In capital ships the agreement stipulated a quota of 525,000 tons for the United States and Britain, of 315,000 tons for Japan, and of 175,000 tons for both France and Italy. Separate provisions along the same lines included tonnage limits for aircraft carriers. The tonnage of cruisers was also limited to 10,000 tons, but their numbers were not. Submarines, the new deadly weapon of the war, were completely left out. In the public these results were welcomed almost enthusiastically as a first step to worldwide disarmament and peace. In the navies the view was more ambiguous, though most admirals had realized that they simply could not afford more ships than they already possessed. Rather, they had to scrap many, which also eased their financial burden. Whether this system of arms control would work was, however, a question of the future. In 1930, at the London naval conference, it did, despite a severe quarrel between the United States and Great Britain about the inclusion of cruisers into the agreement; six years later it collapsed because Japan proved unwilling to renounce its ambitious aims.

Conclusion

As Arthur J. Marder has rightly claimed in his magnificent account on the role of the Royal Navy in World War I, French Maréchal Foch was never able to understand the role of sea power in this seminal struggle, whatever arguments were put forward by politicians and admirals alike. He always asked: 'What have the Navy done? Have they done any fighting?' These questions were typical for army officers in all nations, but not for them alone, because most of the fighting took place on land and the great majority of soldiers of all nations had lost their lives in the trenches and not on the rough seas. And it is true. The navies, especially the Royal Navy, the former mistress of the sea, displayed deficiencies during the war. The great challenges of the revolution of naval warfare during the war were sometimes difficult to overcome for officers who had been trained in the era of the last sailing ships. Nevertheless without sea power the Allies would not have been able to secure their life-lines all over the world. In this respect, the Great War was indeed a proof of the teachings of the naval prophet, Alfred T. Mahan, who believed that the great power status of a nation was inextricably associated with the sea, with its commercial use in peace and its control in war. Vice versa this meant that the Germans eventually had no chance of winning the war, unless they were powerful enough to improve their strategic position by either occupying the doors into the open Atlantic – Brest and Bergen –

or (following one of Mahan's critics, Halford J. Mackinder) by enlarging their continental basis. A generation later, they tried to achieve both aims. They failed again, not least because of the importance of sea power in this even-greater struggle for world dominance.

CHAPTER 9

THE AIR CAMPAIGN OF 1918

Dr James S. Corum

Breaking the stalemate

From 1914 to 1917 the Germans and the Western Allies were stalemated by their inability to make a decisive break in the array of trenches and fortifications that ran the length of the Western Front. Since early 1915 the combatant powers had mounted repeated major offensives at places like Verdun, the Somme, Champagne, and Flanders; these were an attempt to make a decisive breakthrough, but instead resulted in massive casualties for minor gains. Although the defence had an advantage in this style of warfare, the casualties in these campaigns were almost as high for the defenders as for the attackers. Yet, by early 1918 both sides had developed some revolutionary tactics that would again enable offensive warfare and manoeuvre without incurring high losses for the attacker – and airpower had a central role in this revolution.

This chapter on the air war in 1918 focuses on two issues that determined the conduct of the campaign: how the small air services of

1914 had become large air forces involved in all aspects of operations; and the role played by aviation in the tactical revolution that broke the trench deadlock and enabled offensive warfare.

The tactical revolution

The most lethal weapon of the war, and the key to success on the battlefield, was artillery. Over 80 per cent of all casualties of World War I were inflicted by artillery. Troops in deep entrenchments were relatively safe from artillery, but when forces massed for the attack and counter-attack and moved out of the trenches, artillery inflicted massive casualties. However, in late 1917, in a series of parallel developments, the French, German, and British armies came to a highly effective solution to overcome the firepower of the defenders and enable the infantry forces to advance through the enemy trenches without excessive casualties.

Indeed, airpower was linked to the artillery from the start of the war and it was the air arm that made the artillery so effective. The primary role of the air services was reconnaissance and observation and almost half of the German, British, and French air services was composed of squadrons assigned to reconnaissance and artillery spotting. The rapid evolution of aircraft and observation techniques, as well as radios and aerial photography, allowed the combatants a clear picture of enemy defences and forces from the front lines to deep in the rear areas. Reconnaissance aircraft mapped not only the enemy front lines, but reserve positions, artillery batteries, and support units far to the rear. By the mid-point of the war the air services had large intelligence branches capable of processing thousands of aerial photos every week. Major operational plans were based primarily on aerial intelligence, which provided the targets for the artillery. The artillery relied heavily on two-seater observation aircraft equipped with radios and specially trained to work with the gun batteries. Radio sets of World War I were bulky affairs, but by 1916 both sides made radio transmitters small enough to fit in an aeroplane and able to transmit messages in Morse code directly to radios located with the artillery. The basic procedures were highly effective. Artillery fliers would spot a target such as a troop concentration or an enemy artillery battery. They used a simple code key in which grid references were letter and number coded, with typical targets assigned Morse code letters, and the aircraft observer could tap out a brief message directly to the artillery units.[1] This enabled the artillery to fire immediately and the observing aircraft could adjust the artillery's fire, again with messages of just a few letters. Thanks to aircraft, artillery could be used with an accuracy unimaginable before World War I.

Aerial observation and aerial artillery spotting was so essential to defence and offence that controlling the air over the battlefront became a top priority for the Germans and Western Allies. Control of the air enabled the air service to provide accurate intelligence and artillery fire and, at the same time, deny these advantages to the enemy. By 1916 British, French, and German air services were fielding aircraft squadrons specifically equipped and trained to shoot down the enemy's aircraft and win air superiority. The fighter forces, equipped with fast and manoeuvrable single-seat aircraft, quickly grew in size and sophistication and garnered the attention of the press, which featured the exploits of the 'ace' fighter pilots who lent a touch of individualism to a war dominated by mass operations. Yet it should not be forgotten that the primary mission of the fighter pilots was to serve as support forces to escort observation planes over enemy territory and to intercept the enemy observers.

In earlier campaigns the attacking artillery had concentrated mainly on destroying the enemy front defences. But this approach invariably failed when the defender employed artillery against the attack. The prolonged British bombardment of enemy defences at the Somme clearly signalled an attack and enabled the Germans to bring up reserves and prepare for the onslaught. In 1916–17 the normal way to strike a target was to fire a ranging shot, observe the fall of the round, and adjust fire by plane or balloon observation post. Yet ranging shots also alerted the defender. So in 1917 leaders on both sides developed a system by which the defending artillery could be neutralized without ranging shots and firing solely from map references. First of all, guns could fire more accurately if each gun was taken to a firing range and test fired to determine the precise characteristics of the gun. Intensive research created meteorological tables that determined how weather conditions would affect the course of each shot. Finally, aerial reconnaissance could provide aerial maps with the exact positions of enemy artillery, headquarters, and strongpoints. These new tactics were based on surprise and massed and centrally controlled artillery fire. Troops and guns were moved up to the front line at the last minute with all care taken to ensure cover and secrecy. No ranging shots were fired or any other actions taken that would alert the defender. A few hours before the attack the artillery, all under one command and firing according to a single plan, would initiate a massive bombardment with the primary target not the enemy trenches but the enemy artillery, whose positions had been plotted by aerial reconnaissance before the battle. The new method of gun calibration and meteorological tables enabled the artillery to fire fairly accurately to destroy, or at least suppress, the enemy artillery. Only in the last hour of the barrage would much of the artillery fire shift to striking the enemy trenches.

When the barrage lifted, the infantry, armed with plenty of firepower in the form of light cannons and mortars, and light machine guns, would overrun the enemy trenches, isolating and reducing strongpoints while maintaining an advance as rapidly as possible. During the attack air units would fly support, spotting surviving enemy artillery for counter-battery fire and using fighters and light bombers to bomb and strafe enemy artillery. Other fighter units flew high overhead to protect the observation craft. If the enemy artillery could be neutralized, then the attacker could break through the defender lines with acceptable losses.[2] The ability of the air services to accurately photograph and map large areas of the front at this time was made possible by major advances in aerial photography technology, including automatic cameras.[3]

This new doctrine was first tried by the Germans when their Eighth Army attacked the Russian Twelfth Army south of Riga on 1 September 1917. The Germans had centralized more than 800 guns and mortars under a single carefully orchestrated fire plan. The onslaught took the Russians, dug into deep defences along the wide Duna River, completely by surprise. Having identified all the Russian artillery positions and infantry strongpoints by aerial photography, the German artillery managed to destroy or suppress the Russian artillery in a short, but very violent, bombardment.[4] Six German infantry divisions crossed the river and quickly drove through the Russian defences. The Russian Twelfth Army collapsed and began a hasty retreat, abandoning its artillery, supplies, and heavy equipment to the Germans. The Germans took Riga and inflicted 25,000 Russian casualties with only 4,000 casualties of their own. The German High Command was so impressed by these new methods that it sent the authors of the plan, army commander Oskar von Hutier and artillery colonel Georg Bruchmüller, to the Western Front to employ the same methods for the 1918 attack. The German Western Front generals were initially reluctant to adopt the new tactics, but Ludendorff pushed them on his army commanders and in January and February 1918 the German High Command issued directives that the great Spring Offensive would use the methods of surprise, artillery centralization, short but very heavy preparatory fires, barrages using map coordinates, and priority of fire on enemy artillery.[5]

Air doctrine of the major powers in 1918

Because the primary mission of the air services was to win control of the air, and thereby to provide effective support to the ground armies, in 1917 and 1918 the Western Allies and the Germans developed an extensive body of doctrine for air operations. The air doctrine centred on the mass employment of the main elements of the air service – reconnaissance, artillery spotting, bombers, and fighters – all to be closely coordinated to support the ground battle.[6] The German, French, and British doctrines made control of the air over the battlefield the first priority of the air services. By 1917 the air services had organized their air squadrons into large operational organizations with the British Royal Flying Corps organizing their squadrons (each 15 to 20 aircraft) into wings (three to four squadrons) and the wings into air brigades. The Germans in 1917 had organized their fighter squadrons into wings (*Geschwader*: four to five squadrons) and their specialized ground attack force into groups of three squadrons. The French also formed their fighter and bomber squadrons into groups.

Behind the fighting units each air service (the Royal Air Force would only be born as an independent air force in April 1918) had created a vast infrastructure of training units, specialist schools, air intelligence units, depots and repair units, and specialized signals units. Each air service had its own general staff and headquarters, churning out plans and doctrine for the fighting units. To ensure swift movement from one part of the front to another the German, French, and British air services became highly mobile. Air squadrons could quickly set up airfields (usually any fairly dry and flat piece of ground near the front) complete with temporary canvas-covered hangars for the aircraft. Each air service comprised a large organization in 1918, with the Luftstreitkräfte and the Aéronautique Militaire each having approximately 100,000 personnel in the army and naval air arms. By the end of the war the RAF had grown to 291,000 men and the US Air Service had 195,000.[7] Every squadron required a large support force of ground personnel and motor vehicles. In short, by 1918 one can easily talk of fully fledged air forces despite their status in France, Germany, and America as being officially part of the army or navy.

The fighter forces were one of the keys to success in 1918 and the fighters had several responsibilities. As well as winning air superiority, fighters provided escort for the vital artillery and reconnaissance aircraft over the battlefield. The Royal Flying Corps also emphasized the mission of ground attack. Fighters were to attack German troop columns, artillery, and supply columns ahead of the attacking divisions. Finally, fighters and reconnaissance planes were tasked to fly 'contact patrols', to fly low and observe the location of friendly troops and report to the division and corps headquarters on the progress of the ground forces. Getting an accurate picture of the ground battle was essential for the ground armies and, given the lack of mobile radios in 1918, aircraft were the best means of informing the ground commanders of the battle. This low-level work was especially dangerous as the unarmoured aircraft were particularly vulnerable to machine-gun fire from the ground and anti-aircraft guns, with which the Germans were amply supplied. The Germans also relied upon contact patrols called 'Infantry Fliers' and in 1918 were able to field some flights of all-metal and armoured aircraft for the task. But given the small number of these planes available, contact work also fell to the fighter and observer units. This also meant that the infantry had to be trained to work with the air service. Various signals, including setting out ground panels and use of coloured flares, were used.

In 1917 the Luftstreitkräfte issued new doctrine manuals that outlined the role of the air service in major operations (*Instructions on the Mission and Utilization of Flying Units within an Army*) and the Germans updated their doctrine to include the use of close air support of the infantry.[8] The operational manuals emphasized the need for surprise in supporting army attacks by quietly moving air units to the sector to be attacked at night, and then camouflaging and dispersing them. The infantry advance would be made under cover of ground attack squadrons, which would seek out the enemy reserves and artillery as well as carry out planned attacks on selected front-line strongpoints. Ground attack squadrons were attached to divisions based on the army aviation commanders' assessment. The German High Command believed the morale effect of low-level bombing and strafing attacks upon enemy infantry and artillery was especially important: 'the object of the battle flights is to shatter the enemy's nerve by repeated attacks in close formation'.[9] General Hugh Trenchard, chief of the Royal Flying Corps in France, was also a firm believer in using fighter aircraft in ground attack role and British operations orders assigned a large part of the fighter force to this duty. The French Army operations doctrine of October 1917 laid out the principles of air operations in some detail and placed a heavy emphasis on close cooperation of air and ground units through all phases of the battle and on gaining air superiority and using aircraft to provide targets for the artillery. French operations orders also assigned air squadrons to support each division in the assault.[10]

In the latter half of 1917 and early 1918 the Germans, French, and British pulled divisions behind the lines and trained their armies in the new offensive doctrine. One major part of the training programme was to ensure that the artillery and the supporting aircraft learned to plan and work together. In preparation for the 1918 Spring Offensive the Germans pulled their best infantry divisions to the rear for intensive training which included live-fire exercises with ground attack squadrons against mock trench lines.[11] Tactical experience was assimilated by the air staff and guidance was issued in a series of 'Tactical Guidelines' issued by the

Luftstreitkräfte which advised air unit commanders on formations, tactics, and task organization of their forces.[12] While providing a highly effective training programme and detailed doctrine for the fliers cooperating with the army artillery, the Royal Flying Corps failed to create specialized aircraft or training programmes for the ground attack role – it was just another duty of a fighter pilot.[13] In contrast, the German Air Service set up a special training programme for the ground attack pilots behind the front and practised group attacks upon simulated targets.[14]

One of the most important organizational developments for airpower came in May 1918 when Général de Division Pétain, commander of the French front armies, ordered the creation of the 1st Air Division, under Général de Brigade Maurice Duval, commander of the Aéronautique Militaire at the front. The French concentrated groups of their elite fighter, bomber, and reconnaissance squadrons into a well-balanced 600-plane division, which was highly mobile and to be deployed to support the main effort of the army, either in defence or offence. While each ground army had a complement of reconnaissance and fighter aircraft to support its operations, the 1st Air Division came under the direction of the French High Command and served as the special aerial reserve. The 1st Air Division provided a massive reinforcement capable of all air missions and designed to ensure French air superiority over the front. The 1st Air Division played a prominent role in all the French offensives and also supported the American attack at St Mihiel in September as well as the British attack at Amiens in August.[15]

The aircraft of 1918

Winning the air superiority battle, and being able to effectively support the ground armies through bombing and reconnaissance, depended on having superior aircraft in large quantities. Aircraft design had come a long way since the start of the war and sophisticated aircraft were fielded by the British, French, and German air forces. In early 1917 the British aircraft had been outclassed by the new German Albatros and Pfalz D III fighters. But by the autumn of 1917 the Royal Flying Corps had been re-equipped with the SE 5A, the Sopwith Triplane, and the Bristol two-seat fighter and these planes made the fight equal in terms of quality. The French also fielded the Nieuport XVII and SPAD VII fighter in 1917, easily equal to anything the Germans flew, and these would soon be superseded by the fast, manoeuvrable, and sturdy SPAD XIII, which became the main fighter of the French and American Air Service in 1918. The German fighter force at the start of 1918 consisted of the Albatros D V, a slight improvement over the D III model, and a few hundred new Fokker Triplanes, which, despite their popular fame, were mediocre fighters and much slower than the Allied models. In the spring of 1918 the German fighter force was generally outclassed.

Knowing that their fighters were inferior, the German High Command tested several new fighter designs in January 1918, with the famous Rittmeister Baron Manfred von Richthofen personally test-flying the prototypes and giving his strongest recommendation to the Fokker D7 design by Anthony Fokker. Von Richthofen, in one of his last acts before being shot down three months later, had chosen wisely. The Fokker D7 used a revolutionary wing design of a thick, internally supported wing. Contrary to expectations, a thicker wing proved superior in reducing drag and improving lift, and the internally supported wing, combined with a fuselage frame of welded steel tubes, made for a very strong and sturdy aeroplane. Equipped with the 185hp BMW engine, it proved to be a superb fighter plane. The Fokker D7 was put into mass production and began arriving at the front units in late May 1918, and through the summer much of the German fighter force was re-equipped with the D7. The new Fokker quickly put the German fighter force back in the running in the air superiority battle. It was fast, highly manoeuvrable and had the fastest rate of climb (a very important part of fighter combat) of any fighter in 1918. It was said that the D7 handled so well that it turned an average pilot into a very good one. The memoirs of the Allied fighter pilots show the D7 great respect as an opponent. Although a well-handled SE 5 or SPAD XIII could readily knock down a Fokker D7 (both the SE 5 and SPAD were faster), airmen such as US Air Service commander General Billy Mitchell called the Fokker D7 the best all-round fighter of the war.[16]

The fighters, which comprised 40 to 50 per cent of the aircraft in all the air services on the Western Front, receive most of the attention in literature and film. But a major portion of all the air services, and operationally the most important part, were the ubiquitous two-seater observation and artillery aircraft employed in large numbers by all combatants. After all, reconnaissance and artillery spotting was the essential mission of the air services. To fulfil this mission in 1918 the British fielded the DH 9 and DH 4, the Germans a variety of two-seater models, and the French relied mainly on the Salmson A2. The newly arrived American Air Service employed mainly the DH 4, but some observer squadrons had the Salmson A2 which French and Americans regarded as the best plane of its type. The two-seater planes were heavier than the fighters but powered by much larger engines (the Salmson had a 400hp engine) which made them as fast as many fighters. The observation planes normally carried forward-firing and rear-mounted machine guns, the latter operated by the observer. With speed and firepower fore and back, the two-seat observation planes were no easy prey for the fighters, yet destroying them was the fighter's main mission. All the air services fielded light and heavy bombers in 1918. Often the two-seater observation planes doubled as light bombers, although many two-seat bombers were built specifically for that purpose. The main French light bomber of 1918 was the Breguet XIV, one of the best bombers produced in the war, which carried 300kg (660 pounds) of bombs.

Some of the specialized aircraft of 1918 bear mentioning. One of the most important of the German aircraft was the Rumpler C7 high-altitude reconnaissance plane. It was designed to fly at 20,000 feet with the pilots and observers using bottled oxygen and electronically heated flying suits to combat the extreme altitude and cold. At 20,000 feet the Rumplers flew well above the top ceiling of Allied fighters, so they could photograph Allied rear areas with relative impunity.[17] Another major German innovation in aircraft development was a series of aircraft specifically designed for ground attack. In 1917 the Germans introduced purpose-built ground attack planes which were organized into squadrons and groups. The rugged Halbertstadt and Hannover two-seaters were modified with armour plate around the pilot and engine and equipped to drop small bombs. With three machine guns (two forward and one operated by the observer) these planes were used in mass to strike targets just behind the front lines, especially troop columns and artillery positions. The armour plating and the relatively fast speed of these planes made them far less vulnerable to ground fire, which caused high losses among unarmoured fighter planes that attempted this mission. In late 1917 the Germans introduced an all-metal armoured ground attack plane – the Junkers J1. In 1918 other all-metal attack planes and fighters were introduced, but only saw action in small numbers in the last months of the war.

Producing all these aircraft and engines required a large and sophisticated aircraft and engine industry and these industries quickly evolved from small operations building aircraft by hand in 1914 to large aircraft factories often using mass-production techniques. Despite the much larger size of the German economy and Germany's ability to produce some revolutionary aircraft designs, the German aircraft industry consistently failed to produce aircraft in the numbers the General Staff had planned for, and would consequently lose the attrition battle in the air. The German High Command's aircraft mass-production plan, called the 'Amerika Plan', required production of more than 2,000 aircraft a month in 1918, a number that the German aviation companies consistently failed to meet. Germany produced 48,000 aircraft during the war and 43,486 engines, but these numbers were not enough to keep the Luftstreitkräfte at full strength through the 1918 battles.[18] In contrast, the Allied aviation industries outperformed the German in every respect. The Allies' winning advantage in the air war was the French aviation industry, which produced 52,000 aircraft during the war as well as 88,000 aircraft engines.[19] Indeed, from 1914 to 1917 the British were heavily reliant on French-made aircraft and engines. The French supplied 24,000 aircraft engines to their allies and 9,500 aircraft. The American Air Service was only able to enter combat because it received 4,800 aircraft (SPAD and Nieuport fighters, Breguet XIV bombers, and Salmson observation planes) from French industry.[20]

The French managed to master the techniques of mass production of aircraft and engines before the other powers. The French efficiently managed their aircraft industry and ruthlessly standardized their aircraft for large production runs. In 1918 the French aircraft industry had standardized with 13 aircraft models. The Germans were at the other extreme. Germany's 30 aircraft companies produced some wonderful advanced designs, but suffered from poor management decisions by the high command and air service staffs. In the last year of the war Germany's aircraft manufacturers were producing a dozen different fighter models, usually in small production runs. The Fokker D7 was the only German fighter to see a production run of more than 2,000. This stands in contrast to the British and French manufacturers that produced the Sopwith Camel, SE 5A, and SPAD XIII by the thousands.[21]

But as the aircraft industries (especially the French) managed to master the methods of mass production of aircraft, none of the powers applied any principles of quality control in manufacturing aircraft and engines. Many aircraft and engines were quickly designed and put into production without proper testing or consideration for ease of mass production. This process resulted in some rapid advances in aircraft technology, but also the production of a lot of bad aeroplanes. Pilots of 1918 had almost as much to fear from their own aircraft as from the enemy, and 15 years after the invention of the aeroplane flying was still intrinsically dangerous. The air service reports and pilot memoirs are filled with accounts of propellers breaking in the middle of combat, engines failing at critical moments, and the upper wing fabric simply shredding away in mid-flight (the German Fokker Triplane and French Nieuport 17 were notorious for this). Deaths from operational accidents ran almost as high as deaths from combat in 1918, and some of the top aces from each air service died due to mechanical or aircraft structural failure far from combat. For example, one of the RAF's top aces, Captain James McCudden, died when his engine failed on take-off. But these are the deadly accidents that are well recorded. In most cases pilots whose aircraft failed them managed to crash-land their crippled aircraft and walk away from the wreck. Landing accidents on wet and muddy airfields were almost a daily event, especially as none of the World War I aircraft had brakes on their landing wheels. The fragile aircraft of the era were often not worth the trouble to repair, although efforts would be made to salvage engines.

What this all meant for the air war is an enormous weekly wastage of aircraft, mostly from non-combat causes. This also explains why, despite production of aircraft reaching over 3,000 a month for the French and British in 1918, it still took a long time to increase the air forces at the front as large-scale production mainly went to replacing the constant aircraft wastage.[22] As for the Germans, their aircraft production of 1918 (the best production year of the war) failed to keep up with aircraft losses during the 1918 battles even though the Germans began the 1918 Spring Offensive with a reserve of 1,600 replacement aircraft in depots behind the front.

The great offensives – March to November 1918

In an interesting example of parallel development British artillery commanders by mid-1917 had developed a new artillery doctrine that was basically the same as the one von Hutier and Bruchmüller had developed on the Eastern Front. The British artillery doctrine relied on surprise, calibrating each gun, firing from map coordinates, massive but short preparations, and targeting the enemy artillery.[23] The German success at Riga provided ample proof that these methods worked, so on 30 November 1917 the British Army launched a surprise attack on the Germans at Cambrai. The British added 400 tanks to the plan to break through the Germans on a nine-mile front. The initial attack was very successful, much more than the British High Command had expected, and gaps smashed open in the German lines were not fully exploited. The German counter-attacks a week later drove back the British Army, but the Cambrai attack proved that even a well-prepared defence line could be readily broken by the new methods. As with the Germans at Riga, aircraft at Cambrai played a major role, not just in obtaining detailed information on the German defences, but in supporting the lead tank and infantry with squadrons assigned to ground attack roles. Observer aircraft were assigned to support the artillery and identify German artillery and German reserves after the attack started. The Royal Flying Corps massed 400 aircraft to support the attack and ensure British air superiority.

While Cambrai made the British believers in the new artillery and infantry tactics, the French took some time to accept these views. The French Army's new operational doctrine was issued in October 1917 and, while emphasizing air/ground cooperation, it still supported an extensive artillery preparation. However, when the French saw the new artillery and surprise tactics used against the British and themselves, they dramatically changed their views. In June 1918, in preparation for a series of major Allied offensives, the French High Command wholeheartedly adopted the tactical and artillery support system now commonly used by the Germans and British and based the plans for their upcoming offensives on attaining surprise, using a short and violent artillery preparation, and firing without prior registration. In their offensives from July onwards the French would prove to be quite proficient in the new tactics and would train the Americans in their use (the Americans simply adopted the French doctrine as the best solution for employing their inexperienced army).[24]

The great Spring Offensive

The Germans saw an attack in the spring of 1918 as their best chance to win the war. Through the winter the Germans trained and prepared their army and air service for the offensive operations to come. Airpower would play a key role in the German plans. By March, the Luftstreitkräfte had massed 3,668 front-line aircraft on the Western Front. The Germans had created 40 new fighter squadrons and 17 new observation detachments to support the Spring Offensive.[25] The Germans had about 1,000 combat aircraft fewer than the Allies but, in order to gain air superiority for the offensive, the Luftstreitkräfte concentrated a powerful force of 35 fighter squadrons, 22 ground attack squadrons, 49 observation detachments, and four bomber wings to support the three ground armies mounting the attack on the British Fifth and Second Army fronts.[26] When the offensive opened the Germans had 730 aircraft concentrated on the offensive front versus 579 British aircraft.[27]

The Germans strove to keep their point of attack secret and quietly moved up troops and air squadrons at the last moment. The attack by the

German Army on 21 March again demonstrated the effectiveness of the new offensive doctrine. The attack by three German armies took the British by surprise as 6,000 German guns, in a short and intensive bombardment based on careful aerial reconnaissance, efficiently neutralized the British artillery. Aeroplanes played an important role in the German attack plans and the assault divisions were supported by masses of fighters and ground attack planes. The offensive plan detailed the ground attack units to attack British front-line positions and then to concentrate efforts on the British troop reserves and artillery. Some fighter squadrons were detailed to fly top cover for the observation and ground attack craft and to aggressively engage Allied fighters. The German bombers were tasked to carry out night attacks on Allied headquarters and airfields. In the first days of the offensive the ground attack units successfully pounded the British reserves strung out on the open roads and caused considerable British casualties.[28] The Germans kept some ground attack squadrons in reserve to support the ground troops and could attack enemy positions 30 minutes after receiving a call for air support.[29]

The preparatory aerial reconnaissance was just as important for the infantry as for the artillery in ensuring success in the initial breakthrough. The first wave infantry units in 1918 counted on suppressing and outflanking the enemy strongpoints and aerial photography provided the attacking infantry with precise information about the defences they faced.

The violence of the attack and the accurate artillery fire dislocated and disorganized the British forces. Royal Flying Corps airfields came under fire from German long-range guns and the British squadrons evacuated airfields close to the front. They would also have to evacuate and relocate to the rear, major depots, and repair installations. Yet many British aircraft got into the battle immediately and British artillery aircraft located lucrative targets for the British guns as the Germans moved vast columns of reinforcements and supplies behind the first wave divisions. However, the British artillery could not be used effectively as the British Fifth Army guns that survived the German opening barrage retreated swiftly, often leaving the 30-foot tall radio masts (a cumbersome piece of equipment that took time to set up) behind and putting the British artillery out of radio contact with their supporting aircraft. The carefully prepared German plan came close to success in its early stages.

However, German air superiority over the attack front did not last for long. The Allied air services were far better prepared to fight an air campaign in 1918 than in 1917. The Royal Flying Corps had reorganized its training programme in late 1917 and the new British pilots were better-trained than before.[30] The Allied fighters were of high quality and the Allies had far greater reserves of aircraft as the air war became an attrition war. Even as the British Army retreated, the Royal Flying Corps rushed additional units to the Fifth Army front and the French deployed ground and air reinforcements to support the British flank. Even if the British artillery could not effectively respond in the first days of the Spring Offensive, French and British fighters flying in large formations aggressively struck the advancing German columns and artillery positions. In the first five days of the German offensive the Royal Flying Corps and the Aéronautique Militaire lost 189 aircraft, but the relentless air attacks helped blunt the German advance.[31] By 28 March the German advance was halted before Amiens as the French and British had managed to put together a defensive line. In places the German advance had reached a depth of 40 miles. But the main chance for a decisive victory was lost.

During the Spring Offensive and subsequent campaigns the Germans and Allies used their airpower in similar manner in some cases and in others took divergent paths. Both the Germans and the British set aside most of their heavy bomber forces in 1918 to provide support to the ground campaigns. In early 1918 the Germans had eight wings of heavy bombers on the Western Front and the British had created a special long-range bomber force. Both the British and Germans used strategic heavy bomber forces to attack the enemy homeland in 1918 – the Germans bombed London and French industrial cities while the British Independent Air Force (the British strategic bombers) struck cities in Western Germany. However, once the major ground offensive began most of the bomber missions of both sides were allocated to attacking enemy airfields and key rail yards behind the front.[32] With only rare exceptions, these missions had little effect as the accuracy of 1918 bombers at a few thousand feet was abysmal. Even if a target was hit the small size of most bombs (50kg, or 110 pounds, was normal) ensured no major damage.

However, the Germans and British took different approaches to using the aircraft in close support of the ground battle. The Germans preferred to use their ground attack planes and fighters at low level to support their most forward units in the attack. This use of aircraft as 'flying artillery' was effective and also important for the morale of the assault troops. The British preferred to send their fighters and light bombers to carry out low-level attacks well behind the German lines to strike at the artillery and infantry columns reinforcing the offensive. Strung out for miles on the roads, they made excellent targets for low-level attacks with machine guns and light 25-pound (11kg) bombs. The British tactics had more operational effect and the German accounts constantly refer to damaging low-level attacks by British fighters in the German rear. The German Air Service missed the chance to seriously damage the British in the first days of the March offensives by not sending most of their battle planes and fighters deep into the British rear while the Royal Flying Corps was still in some disarray. The roads behind the British front were packed with units being rushed to set up a new defensive line and would have been easy prey for massed low-level air attacks.

In March 1918, the British could draw a considerable air reinforcement from other sectors of the front and, after quickly reorganizing their forces, were able to restore communications for their artillery aircraft and get the artillery back into the fight. Royal Flying Corps fighter and light bomber aircraft rushed to reinforce the threatened sector and carried out low-level attacks with bombs and machine guns on the advancing Germans. However, it was also very costly in men and aeroplanes. The Royal Flying Corps lost 245 aircrew dead or missing before the end of the month.[33]

The Germans attacked again in April and May in different sectors of the front, but never again with the same number of divisions and artillery firepower, never with the frontage as in March. But the Allies managed to counter these smaller offensives and create sound defensive lines after yielding ground. Throughout these weeks the air forces were in the thick of combat and taking heavy losses. But the British and French could readily replace lost aircraft and men and the Germans could not.

The Allied offensives – July–November 1918

The time had come for the Allies to mount major offensives of their own using all the techniques of offensive warfare with the addition of a large tank force – an advantage the Germans lacked. The first major Allied counter-offensive was the French attack at Soissons on 18 July. Intensive aerial reconnaissance gave the French an accurate picture of German positions and defences and the French planned the attack carefully and chose the ground well. The French ensured full surprise by moving the attacking divisions up to the front under cover of darkness and more than 1,000 aircraft supported the French attack while the French artillery efficiently suppressed the German guns. The French Tenth Army, with two US divisions playing a key role, quickly eliminated the salient along the Marne that the Germans had won in May.

By now, the Germans had lost air superiority and the Luftstreitkräfte was now fighting a desperate defensive battle. By the summer of 1918 the aerial attrition war moved sharply in the Allies' favour. Where the Germans had 3,668 combat aircraft on the Western Front in March, by November 1918 the Luftstreitkräfte had 2,709 aircraft available.[34] In the summer of 1918 the Allied air forces, despite heavy losses, had a total of more than 6,000 combat aircraft on the Western Front and the Allied airpower was steadily increasing.[35]

One of the great moments for airpower in World War I was the British offensive at Amiens on 8 August. RAF aerial reconnaissance had been thorough and before the battle the British fliers had located 504 of the 530 artillery pieces supporting the German Second Army.[36] To ensure complete surprise the British opened the attack without any preparatory bombardment and instead began the battle with an infantry advance behind a rolling barrage. At that moment the British heavy guns unleashed massive suppressive fires against all the German gun batteries previously identified by the RAF.

Amiens was a masterpiece of camouflage and deception before the battle. Detailed staff plans required the British and French forces to maintain cover to ensure that German aerial reconnaissance would not spot the massive build-up of the assault forces. The 1,000 extra British guns and seven additional British divisions with nine tank battalions were moved at night in order to arrive at the front just in time to attack. The plan included some imaginative new methods of using airpower to gain surprise. RAF heavy bombers flew over the German front lines all night before the attack, dropping the occasional bomb to harass the Germans – but their real mission was to have the aircraft engines drown out the noise of the tanks arriving in the forward positions.

The army and RAF plans ensured air superiority for the Amiens attack. The RAF deployed two brigades – 800 aircraft of all types – to support the attack, while the Germans had only 300 aircraft in the sector. The squadrons deployed were all given specific missions in the detailed operational plan. Eight squadrons (150 planes) were to do close support on the front line. A squadron of two-seater observation planes was assigned to work with the tanks and specifically tasked to look for German anti-tank guns. Two squadrons of light bombers were used to drop smoke bombs to cover the first wave's advance and later in the day these squadrons would drop machine-gun ammunition to the most forward units. Heavy bombers attacked the German airfields and major rail yards behind the front. Artillery observation squadrons flew patrols up to ten miles behind the German lines and half the fighter force flew escort for the bombers and observers. However, squadrons were also available to fly into the German rear to carry out low-level attacks against German reserves.[37]

The first response of the Germans was to rush air units to the threatened sector to contest the Allied air superiority. The elite Jagdgeschwader 1 (von Richthofen's old unit) arrived the first afternoon of the battle and began attacking the RAF fighters. During the next three days the Germans sent in hundreds of aircraft, but still could not match Allied numbers. They took a heavy toll of British and French planes, though.[38] The German armoured ground attack planes also played a notable role in slowing the British advance on the third day of the Amiens offensive.[39] As the German records indicate, the RAF's support work in attacking the German troops had generally been very effective and had caused considerable casualties and disorder in the German rear. But the low-level attacks had also been costly. The RAF on 8 August lost 45 planes and another 52 were so badly damaged as to be written off – almost 13 per cent of the RAF planes engaged that day with 23 per cent of the bombers lost or damaged.[40] One reason for the heavy losses was the effectiveness of the German anti-aircraft force. The Germans had put more emphasis on developing anti-aircraft guns than the Allies and by 1918 the Luftstreitkräfte fielded a force of 2,558 anti-aircraft guns, ranging from 37mm automatic cannon to motorized 77mm and 88mm heavy guns. Major improvements in mechanical time fuses in 1918 greatly increased the lethality of the German Flak and the Allied air forces would lose 748 aircraft to German Flak gunners in 1918, mostly in the last four months of the war.[41]

The Amiens offensive stopped after four days and had been remarkably effective. Ground, air, tank, and artillery had worked as an efficient team and the German front had been quickly cracked open. Over three days the Germans lost more than 48,000 men, with 30,000 taken prisoner.[42] The Amiens breakthrough, which convinced the German High Command that its only option was to make peace soon, was followed by further British attacks in late August. On 12 September the American First Army made its debut in the first major American operation of the war. A set-piece attack to take the St Mihiel salient saw most of its objectives fall to the American and supporting French divisions by the second day of the attack. The attack was supported by more than 1,400 aircraft and included the French 1st Air Division (600 aircraft) and 700 aircraft of the American Air Service. By 13 September the Americans had captured 16,000 Germans and killed or wounded as many while also capturing 450 German guns. American losses were 7,000 men.[43]

The final three months of the war saw the British, French, and American armies striking hard, simultaneous blows against the German lines. On 26 September the Americans began their second major offensive of the war with a massive attack in the Meuse–Argonne region. The American attack quickly bogged down and the American Air Service was largely ineffective in the early stages of a campaign that lasted to November. The problem was the state of American training. A few squadrons of the American Air Service had been flying since April and were experienced, but most of the squadrons going into battle were newly formed and had not had time to train with the infantry divisions and artillery units they were assigned to support.[44] At the start of the offensive communications largely broke down. Confusion reigned when the ground units repeatedly failed to display the correct ground panels and signals for the air contact patrols. The inexperienced American artillery observers also dropped messages to the wrong headquarters. Coupled with a lack of training was the poor weather which kept the artillery spotting planes on the ground for much of the battle.[45] After a poor start the Americans finally broke through the German defences in November, but only after heavy casualties.

The Meuse–Argonne campaign shows the complexity of conducting effective air/ground operations in 1918. The French, British, and German armies had only mastered joint operations techniques with a considerable training effort. The staff planning for each offensive in 1918 was very extensive and was beyond the competence of most of the inexperienced American division and corps staffs in the Meuse–Argonne. A German Air Service report from the period gives their view of the air war over St Mihiel and the Meuse–Argonne battles. The Germans rated the Americans as being aggressive and well-trained pilots on the individual level (the Americans had been well trained by the French). They also rated the French-supplied American aircraft as being very capable. However, the American Air Service had not had time to conduct training as larger units – a strength of the Germans – and this clearly showed in combat. Although outnumbered, German units such as the elite Jagdgeschwader 1 inflicted heavy losses on the American fliers, because they could coordinate the operations of three or four squadrons against the Americans, who barely understood squadron tactics.[46]

The final weeks of the war saw the Luftstreitkräfte fighting a losing battle but still able to inflict heavy casualties on the Allied air forces. In the last months of the war the outnumbered Germans shot down their Allied opponents at a two or three to one ratio. In August 1918 the

Germans shot down 487 Allied aircraft for a loss of 150 of their own planes.[47] Jagdgeschwader Nr II, one of Germany's top fighter wings, shot down 81 Allied aircraft in September 1918, with only two losses of their own.[48] The Luftstreitkräfte inflicted an especially high toll upon the inexperienced American air units. For example, the 80th US Aero Squadron averaged a 75 per cent monthly loss of their aircrew from March to November 1918.[49] The Allied air doctrine of relentless offensive action paid off very well in gains on the ground and the incalculable advantage gained of being able to observe the enemy and use artillery effectively. But the Allied air doctrine was also very costly.

Effective air/ground operations was the key to the early German successes of 1918 and one of the main reasons for the final Allied victory in November. The tactical revolution in the use of artillery that broke the trench deadlock was only possible through aerial reconnaissance and artillery spotting. The use of aircraft to support ground attacks was a major part of the breakthrough concepts of both the Germans and the Allies and has been largely overlooked in World War I literature. The documents of the ground and air operations of 1918 show highly sophisticated armies and air forces whose senior leaders managed these forces in an effective manner to bring operational success. Indeed, the role of aircraft in ground operations was also just as vital in the defence as in the offence. When the Germans broke the British lines on 21 March the first effective counter-attacks came from the Royal Flying Corps and the Aéronautique Militaire, which threw themselves at the attacking German columns. In the critical first days the Allied aviators played an important role in slowing the German advance and preventing the loss of Amiens. In a similar manner the German Air Service counter-attacked the British breakthrough at Amiens and their actions at least allowed some of the German units to retreat in good order.

CHAPTER 10

LEARNING FROM 1918 ON THE WESTERN FRONT

Major General (Ret'd) Mungo Melvin CB OBE

Introduction*

Over the last two decades, the current generation of NATO's serving sailors, soldiers, and airmen has gained much hard-won experience in countering insurgencies (formerly known as 'Small Wars'), fighting cunning, resolute, and at times very deadly opponents. Yet no one in uniform today, let alone civilian politicians or policy-makers, has any memory of 'Big Wars' against equally well-equipped and well-led 'peer'

---

*   The author wishes to acknowledge the kind advice and assistance he has received from
     Dr Tim Gale, Dr Matthias Strohn, and Major General (Ret.) David T. Zabecki PhD in
     researching and writing this chapter; and from Mr Bob Evans of the British Army Historical
     Branch in providing access to a number of important British Army publications of World
     War I and the inter-war period.

enemies, in which the margin of success over failure is often paper-thin. Indeed, so slim that prolonged and costly campaigns in multiple theatres may occur, as in the two world wars of the 20th century.

As described in the preceding chapters, 1918 saw the German Army coming tantalizingly close to victory on the Western Front in the early summer, only then to be decisively defeated by the Allies in under four months, ultimately leading to the Armistice of 11 November. While nations continue to honour the sacrifice of their fallen in the Great War, other than in specialist historical teaching and writing, far less attention is given as to how this rapid, if not remarkable, change in military fortunes came about. Curiously, perhaps for fear of offending present-day allies, the words 'defeat' and 'victory' have been exorcized from the British commemorations of World War I, notwithstanding the official histories and a wealth of more recent academic work that incorporates such terminology.[1]

The learning experiences of the four principal armies fighting in Belgium and France – German, French, British, and United States – during the final year of World War I are highly instructive on a number of counts, whether in campaign design, tactical development, or in coalition command.[2] Most strikingly, static trench warfare turned into a war of movement. Thus operational manoeuvre returned to the battlefield. Perhaps as significantly, how the armies concerned applied their battlefield experience thereafter in the inter-war years tells us much about military force development process. Such vicarious understanding remains evermore important when memories lengthen and resources shorten.

This chapter seeks not only to explore how armies learned at the time, but also attempts to show how we might draw appropriate lessons from the Western Front of 1918 today. As the political, economic, social, and technological contexts are vastly different a century on, it would be futile to draw directly applicable 'hard lessons' in terms of doctrine or organization. Therefore a 'softer' approach, which identifies a number of enduring aspects of learning from 1918 and its aftermath, has been adopted.

One important caveat must be added. National biases and historical distortions have bedevilled the historiography of World War I, not least accounts of 1918 on the Western Front. Large doses of selective hindsight have also been administered, such as asserting that the German Army had absolutely no chance of winning on the Western Front in 1918. That was not how the Allied leaders felt or saw it at the time. Ludendorff may have gambled for the highest stakes, but in the short term the odds were not all against him. Some British authors have also tended to underestimate the pivotal French contribution in halting the German offensives of that year, often fighting alongside hard-pressed British troops or taking up the main strain of battle while the BEF recuperated following Operations *Michael* and *Georgette* in March and April respectively. Furthermore, while a reinvigorated BEF assumed a leading role in the series of Allied counter-offensives that led to the Armistice, the war could not have been concluded without the French Army, together with the two-million-strong American Expeditionary Forces (AEF), by 11 November 1918. It was thus an Allied victory *par excellence*.

Interdependence

Interdependence – unlike interoperability – is a term rarely seen in military lexicons. Yet an understanding of the multiple interdependencies in war is essential in differentiating between cause and effect, in considering the linkages between first- and second-order effects, and in appreciating the impact of unintended or unforeseen consequences of political and military actions. Whereas in the realm of strategy, interdependences can be geographical, industrial, or multinational in character, at the lower operational and tactical levels they can be found in the cooperation of armed services (now termed joint business) and of combined arms on the battlefield.

All armies are critically dependent on both direction and support from the domestic base, the latter not only in terms of the supply of men and materiel, but also in the moral sphere. Mutual understanding and trust between home and battle fronts is essential to success, not least in political–military relations. Where these break down, the consequences can be dire. Such a situation affected the BEF in early 1918, which laboured under a severe manpower crisis, largely political in origin. Apart from absorbing the losses incurred at Third Ypres (31 July–20 November

1917) and Cambrai (20 November–6 December 1917), the BEF had to dispatch valuable forces to Italy in order to bolster up the Italian Army in the wake of its crushing defeat at Caporetto (24 October–19 November 1917). In early November, Allied leaders, including British Prime Minister Lloyd George, had agreed to send 12 divisions to Italy's aid. In the event, six French and five British divisions were deployed, together with significant air, artillery, and engineer support.[3] General Sir Herbert Plumer assumed overall command of British forces in Italy. As a result, Haig had lost not only one of his most talented commanders on the Western Front, but also a considerable part of his ability to form a general reserve in France.[4] The British Army's presence in Italy, which peaked at 113,759 men in January 1918, was subsequently reduced when two divisions were returned to France, along with four French, in February and March.[5]

In January 1918, the British GHQ on the Western Front, backed by the War Office, had requested 650,000 men in order to sustain the BEF in France and Belgium, but had received from the War Cabinet only a promise of 100,000 replacements. Nominally, the rationale for this decision rested on higher priorities for manpower being allocated elsewhere. Apart from the mines and munitions production, men were required for: shipbuilding; the Royal Navy; air units to defend London from air attack (one of the reasons for the creation of the RAF on 1 April 1918); and agriculture and forestry (in an effort to boost home production so reducing imports, still vulnerable to German U-Boat attack).[6] Yet behind this official reasoning also lay Lloyd George's lack of trust in Haig's ability to win future battles economically, based on the disappointments on the Western Front in 1917, and his preference for seeking decisive results elsewhere. In so doing, according to the British Official History, the Prime Minister 'placed the Allied cause in jeopardy in 1918'.[7]

In consequence of this lack of fresh manpower, excepting the ten Australian, Canadian, and New Zealand Divisions, the remaining 46 British infantry divisions in the BEF were restructured from 12 to nine battalions, with each brigade losing one of its four battalions. This turmoil of reorganization involved the disbandment of 141 battalions. In an operational emergency, however, the necessary reinforcements could, and would, be found to bolster the ranks. Between 21 March and 31 August 1918, no fewer than 544,005 men were shipped to France from the United Kingdom, with a further 100,000 redeployed from Italy, Salonika, and Palestine.[8] Yet the loss of fighting power and flexibility at both divisional and brigade levels was to be sorely felt during the course of 1918 in both defensive and offensive operations. As the bitter battles of 1918 proceeded, with the supply of replacements struggling to match mounting losses, there were never sufficient men available to restore the former formation structure. The Dominion divisions, however, retained 12 battalions to the war's end.

Following the collapse of the Russian Empire in the wake of the two revolutions of 1917 and the cessation of major operations, as many German divisions as possible – some 40 – were transferred from East to West over the winter of 1917/18. Although the Germans now held the strategic initiative in early 1918, by 21 March the OHL could only muster a limited advantage in forces over the Allies on the Western Front: 191 to 175 divisions. As each month passed, however, increasing numbers of American divisions (of about 28,000 men apiece and hence double the size of an equivalent Allied or German formation) would augment exhausted British and French forces. The Eastern Front, however, could not remain unguarded as the new Bolshevik regime in Russia had yet to sign a peace. Thus while OHL prepared to attack in the West, German forces in the East launched on 18 February 1918 a major offensive called Operation *Faustschlag* (Punch). Its ostensible purpose was to 'topple the Bolshevik government' and to support that of the newly independent Ukraine.[9] There was a further justification: as a result of the unrelenting Allied blockade, the populations of both Germany and Austria-Hungary were going increasingly hungry. As Ludendorff recorded in his memoirs, 'The Ukraine had asked [for] our help. We ourselves, and Austria and her army even more so, needed corn; the country could not therefore be allowed to become a prey, and a source of strength, to Bolshevism.'[10] Within three weeks, the German campaign, in which Austro-Hungarian forces also took part, achieved its first political goal. As Kiev was being occupied, on 3 March 1918 the Bolshevik government was forced to sign the harsh and humiliating Treaty of Brest-Litovsk.

Strategic mission creep then occurred in the East: the German Army was drawn ever eastwards into the Donbas industrial region and southwards into the Crimean peninsula until the main base of the Russian Black Sea Fleet at Sevastopol fell unopposed on 1 May 1918.[11] Although the forces employed in the East (47 divisions) were about a quarter of those employed in the West, and many, but by no means all, comprised lower-grade *Landwehr* (i.e. reserve) formations of older age classes, the considerable effort in occupying Ukraine might have been better expended in supporting the campaign to achieve decisive victory on the Western Front. Political, economic, and coalition considerations, however, had made it imperative to act offensively in the East. Whereas Austria was saved from starvation, Germany did not obtain the large quantities of foodstuffs it expected. It did receive, however, 'horses in great numbers'. Without them, as Ludendorff declared, continuation of the war 'would have been altogether impossible, for if Germany had been obliged to raise these horses our own agriculture would have been hard hit'.[12] While all armies on the Western Front relied on horsepower to move field guns and to bring up supplies, the most heavily dependent was the German Army, which lacked the increasing numbers of motor vehicles employed by the Allies. This scarcity of motorized support would impair Germany's ability to sustain her offensive operations in the West in 1918. Thus, as in Britain, Germany was forced to distribute its manpower in order to sustain its war economy, to support its allies, and to conduct campaigns on several fronts. Such were the demands of a modern, industrial, and global war.

Meanwhile, as Ludendorff prepared to launch Operation *Michael*, Haig's problems were far from over. Following War Cabinet direction, he had agreed that the BEF would take over the French front as far as the Oise River near Barisis-aux-Bois. This involved a southwards extension of the British line by some 25 miles, with no additional troops forthcoming either to man, let alone improve, the neglected former French positions. In return, in the event of a major German attack, Pétain had promised French reinforcements (five infantry divisions and a cavalry corps) under command of Général de Division Georges Louis Humbert's Third Army. Compounding the BEF's difficulties of simultaneous restructuring while absorbing a new stretch of front was the self-imposed imposition of a new concept for the defensive battle, as explained by Jonathan Boff in Chapter 4. These factors compounded the challenge in meeting the coming German offensive. It all made for a perfect storm that would be experienced by the Third and Fifth British armies between Arras and St Quentin on Thursday, 21 March 1918.

David Zabecki and Jonathan Boff have described the course of Operation *Michael* in some detail in chapters 4 and 5. The extent of the French intervention in this battle in support of the BEF, and of the Fifth Army in particular, is worth highlighting here. Although the Gallic assistance appeared slow to the British, it not only met the timescale originally agreed before the German offensive, but also vastly exceeded it in scale. On his own initiative, on 21 March 1918 Pétain had ordered the move of French reserves before Haig requested them. The fate of Fifth Army's III Corps (58th, 18th, and 14th divisions) on the extreme right of the British line is indicative of how much Allied formations were intermeshed in a common fight. The first French reinforcement, the 125th Division from the neighbouring Sixth Army, came into action during the early hours of Sunday 23 March, followed during the course of the day by the 9th Infantry and the 1st Dismounted Cavalry Division (both from Third Army). 'Before nightfall', as the British Official History narrates,

> French troops had taken over the whole front of the III. Corps, with the exception of Condren, south of the Oise canal, which was still held by a garrison of 58th Divn troops. North of the Oise, on the right, the French 125th Division held from Viry Noureuil to Villequier Aumont (exclusive); in the centre … stood the French 1st Dismounted Cavalry Division; and on the left … were the French 9th Division and the British 14th Divn, mixed together.[13]

By this time, the battered remnants of the 18th Division, having been forced to abandon the Crozat Canal line at midday, were concentrated in reserve positions further to the west. The more unfortunate 14th Division, having obtained no relief through a rearward passage of lines, was left in the line. III Corps, now separated from the remainder of Fifth Army, was subordinated to Humbert's Third French Army.

Over the course of Operation *Michael*, the French Army fed a steady stream of divisions into the fray in first slowing down, then blocking the German offensive. The British Official History lists 12 infantry divisions and a cavalry division, which had been deployed to assist Fifth Army up to and including 26 March 1918. By 1 April, no fewer than 32 French divisions had been brought up.[14] In his biography of Foch, Liddell Hart claimed that a total of 34 infantry and six cavalry divisions were 'assembled on or behind the 50-odd miles of new front north of the Oise'.[15] To put this final French figure into perspective, it exceeds the combined total of 26 infantry and three cavalry divisions in the Third and Fifth British armies at the start of the German offensive, including reserves.

Of all the threats posed by Operation *Michael*, none was more dangerous to the survival of the BEF than the German advance towards Amiens, the vital British communications centre and logistics hub, although Ludendorff had failed to recognize it as such. The German offensive culminated on 4/5 April 1918 in the desperate fight for the small town of Villers-Bretonneux, lying ten miles to the east–south-east of Amiens, and for nearby Hangard village, the latter at the junction of the British and French armies.[16] By this final stage of the battle, Général de Division Marie-Eugène Debeney's French First Army, as well as the Third, was fully engaged. Without this Allied support, it is clear that the British Fifth Army (which came under the command of General Sir Herbert Rawlinson, and was renamed the Fourth on 28 March), would have fared far worse, and the German Army might even have taken Amiens. The German seizure of Montdidier on 27 March, a town of far less operational significance, provided no consolation. During Operation *Michael*, French and British forces had fought together, not as parallel armies as at the Somme in 1916, but closely interwoven with British formations coming under French command for limited periods. While the German offensive had failed strategically, it brought home the interdependence of Allied forces, leading directly to Foch's historic appointment at Doullens on 26 March 1918 as overall Commander-in-Chief. Hence Operation *Michael* achieved a perverse outcome: Allied unity of command.[17]

It is true that many of the French divisions, such as the 125th, were rushed into battle in March 1918 and hence may have appeared to the British as disorganized. But operational needs must. In his memoirs, however, Gough criticized the staff work of his ally as being 'not particularly good', and observed their divisions arriving 'extremely ill-equipped, short of even ball ammunition, as well as their transport and artillery'.[18] Bearing in mind the substantive French contribution to holding the Allied front in the first, and arguably most dangerous, German offensive of 1918, his remarks appear somewhat ungenerous. Perhaps Gough's poor view of Foch, who visited Fifth Army's headquarters on 26 March, may have coloured his thinking. Their antipathy was mutual, for Foch formed an equally dim opinion of the British general. In turn, Foch, as the freshly appointed Allied generalissimo, welcomed the arrival of Rawlinson as 'an able and energetic commander who restored [Fifth Army's] confidence' in Gough's place on 28 March.[19]

Innovation

Each of the major armies involved in the fighting of 1918 demonstrated considerable technical and tactical innovation. Yet we must go back to 1917, if not earlier, to witness the dawn of a modern style of warfare – a development so profound that it has been termed a revolution in military affairs (RMA). It rested on a combination of near-simultaneous advances in indirect fire, fire planning, intelligence, survey, and logistics, closely synchronized with air operations and ground manoeuvre (and on the Allied side, increasingly supported by tanks). As Jonathan Bailey describes it, the 'First World War was probably the period of most radical and rapid innovation in military history'.[20] From a British perspective, it achieved its first demonstration at Cambrai in 1917, and reached its apogee during the war at Amiens in 1918. The former battle is best remembered in the United Kingdom for the first *en masse* employment of tanks in the attack launched on 20 November. But it also featured a largely forgotten German counter-attack on 30 November 1917 that recovered most of the ground lost. Both operations were equally significant.

A comparison between the British and German tactics and techniques at Cambrai helps us understand how the fighting developed during the following year. In many ways, their respective operations at Cambrai provided rehearsals of (a) what the German Army demonstrated on a much larger scale during Operation *Michael* on 21 March 1918 (and subsequent offensives to mid-July); and (b) what the BEF undertook at Amiens on 8 August 1918 and attempted thereafter. Common to both armies' approaches, however, were critical advances in the science of artillery and the synchronization of 'all' arms making them more truly 'combined'. Similar developments were also taking place in the French Army. At the same time, airpower came of age and began to have a direct impact on the conduct of war, not least during Operation *Michael* and the battle of Amiens.[21]

Taking British innovation first, it rested on parallel advances in artillery and armour, which converged effectively for the first time on the Cambrai battlefield. Together, they generated tactical surprise and shock effect. The artillery's efforts were redirected from the *destruction* of the enemy's positions, the attempt at which typically had taken several days before a major offensive, thereby compromising it (such as at the Somme prior to 1 July 1916), to much shorter *neutralizing* bombardments. These were launched immediately before, or at, zero hour – aimed as much at the enemy's artillery as his defences. Based on many technological and procedural leaps in meteorology, air reconnaissance and photographic interpretation, sound-ranging, and cartography, *predicted fire* could now be achieved accurately and reliably without tell-tale prior registration. This new capability proved particularly important in conducting effective counter-battery fire.

Meanwhile, breaking through the enemy's obstacle zone (mainly of thick belts of wire) and eliminating his machine-gun posts became the prime task of the tanks, which carried their own firepower (either six-pounder guns or machine guns) for direct support of the infantry. At Cambrai, no fewer than 476 tanks were assembled, a far cry from their first employment at the Somme on 15 September 1916, when only 49 Mk Is were involved and 32 made it into action. Now nine battalions of tanks were massed, numbering 378 'fighting' Mk IVs, a model first employed at Messines on 7 June 1917, with an additional 98 machines used on supply and other tasks. Experience gained at Third Ypres in the autumn had showed that tanks should not be employed on heavily shelled wet ground, should be massed in depth, and not be dispersed into 'penny packets'. As the British Official History observed:

> A strong reserve should be retained intact for the purpose of turning battle opportunities to account. Close co-operation between tanks and infantry was essential: each arm must understand perfectly what the other could and could not do. And tanks, as much as infantry, were dependent upon efficient counter-battery work until the enemy guns were either captured or withdrawn ...[22]

In the event, such learning was not fully applied at Cambrai. Although the terrain was firm and not heavily cratered – hence good 'tank country' – the tanks were primarily employed in the initial assault (the break-in battle) in order to allow the infantry to pass through the wire. As a result, 'no reserve echelons were spared for special employment in the exploitation of success'.[23] Thus the conditions were never set for a break-out by the tanks. The only arm available for this task was the Cavalry Corps, which was given the role of surrounding and isolating Cambrai and then pushing further on to the north. Such ambitious objectives were never realized.

Cambrai, in both planning and execution, represented a nascent 'combined arms' battle, in which the various arms were integrated and reliant on each other for mutual support. If fully practised, such innovation promised great results. Yet Cambrai, and later battles such as Amiens in August 1918, demonstrated that it would take much further development to perfect the orchestration of combined arms on the battlefield. Once tanks and infantry crossed the line of departure it proved difficult to maintain communication, and to call on artillery to provide timely close support. Cavalry and tanks never made an ideal combination during World War I since the latter could not keep up with the former. Even the introduction of the faster (eight miles per hour) Medium Mk A Whippet tanks in addition to the five miles per hour

Mk Vs (the direct successor to the Mk IVs) in 1918 did not provide a balanced solution of firepower, mobility, protection, and mobile communications – this only appeared in World War II.

The British were not alone in developing tanks. The French Army employed 125 Schneider tanks in their assault on the Chemin des Dames on 16 April 1917, which was followed up by the introduction of a heavier model, the St Chamond, the following month. Neither machine of limited cross-country capability proved a battle-winning design. The most ubiquitous French type, which first saw action on 31 May 1918, was the smaller Renault model FT-17, the first turreted tank, many of which were also used by the US Army.

Artillery, meanwhile, had numerous tasks on the battlefield. In addition to high explosive, British artillery units now employed copious quantities of gas and smoke munitions in closely integrated fire plans. By way of example, on 20 November 1917 at Cambrai:

> Seventy 60pdrs fired 16,000 rounds of tear gas to force enemy gunners into respirators, to reduce their efficiency, and a smoke screen was planned to cover the advance. 18pdrs spaced every 25 metres fired smoke 300 metres ahead of the tanks, lifting from trench to trench along a 10,500-metre long front firing 93,000 rounds. At the same time the 6-inch howitzers fired 500 metres ahead of the tanks and the 'heavies' [eight-inch and above] fired 15-minute concentrations on selected targets.[24]

Apart from the extreme discomfort of their machines, one of the biggest problems British tank crews faced was the danger posed by German artillery, particularly if no suppressive counter-battery fire could be called in support. The loss in tanks sustained on 20 November 1917 through German field guns at Flesquières Ridge in the centre of the Cambrai battlefield is a case in point.

Neither the BEF nor the French Army, which had experimented with neutralizing fire plans at the battle of Malmaison (17–25 October 1917), had its own way in revolutionizing the battlefield. Although the Germans had yet to develop an effective tank, and were never able to field more than a handful of their own A7Vs or captured Allied machines at any time in 1918, they were able to make equally significant advances elsewhere. David Zabecki has already stressed the importance of Colonel Georg Bruchmüller in developing the effectiveness of the German artillery, and thus making major contributions to the initial successes scored by the German offensives in 1918. Much of Bruchmüller's method rested on the predicted fire and counter-battery techniques practised by the Allies. Yet in many ways his approach was more sophisticated. In intense 'hurricane' bombardments he targeted not only defending troops, fortifications, and guns, but also the enemy's command and control system, including observation posts, headquarters, and communications.

Apart from the First and Second Battles of Ypres in late 1914 and early 1915 respectively, the BEF had been offensively minded on the Western Front for three years. Although it shared this outlook with the French Army, unlike its ally, it had not been through the ordeal of a defensive battle such as Verdun in 1916. In 1918, however, *both* the British and French armies would face a major revolutionary type of German combined arms offensive, based on the generation of surprise, shock effect, and high tempo of attack, which would demand a new defensive approach. In the absence of any extant British Army doctrine on the subject other than that contained in the pre-war Field Service Regulations (FSR) of 1909, on 14 December 1917, GHQ issued a memorandum to the BEF on defensive measures.[25] It stated, rather gratuitously, that 'the general situation on the Russian and Italian Fronts may enable the enemy to release a considerable number of effectives both as formed units and as reinforcements to the Western Front'. More ominously, the document conceded that manpower pressures would 'make it impossible for our units to be brought up to establishments'. Hence GHQ anticipated the BEF adopting a 'defensive attitude for some time to come'. While too early to reflect specifically on recent German operations (such as those at Riga, Caporetto or Cambrai), the new instructions stated more generally:

> We must accept the possibility of a strong attack being delivered against any part of our line, supported by a large concentration of artillery ... [and] accept an attack by masses of infantry, offering a very vulnerable target,

but preceded by an intense bombardment which may be of either long or short duration according to whether the enemy aims at success by surprise or not.[26]

Such assessment would hardly have helped subordinate formations in forming a practical understanding of the type of attack they would face and in preparing for it in the best possible way. GHQ offered no real guidance on how the battle was to be fought as a whole – not least on what forces should be allocated to defence and counter-attack.

At the same time, as previously mentioned, the BEF was reorganizing, losing an infantry battalion per 'square' brigade and so shedding precisely the element of flexibility and resilience required at that level. While the French, German, and American armies all trained and fought with three-battalion regiments of infantry, the British Army was forced to adopt an unfamiliar and untested 'triangular' brigade structure. As there was precious little time to prepare, let alone rehearse, an innovative scheme of defence carried considerable risk. Official doctrine on the matter was sadly lacking. Although issued in January 1918, *Instructions for the Training and Employment of Divisions* (SS 135) represented for the most part an update of *Instructions for the Training of Divisions for Offensive Action*, first published in December 1916.[27] More comprehensive guidance, *The Division in Defence* (SS 120), was not issued until May 1918, by which time the BEF had taken the full brunt of two major German offensives, operations *Michael* and *Georgette*. In the meantime, all GHQ could offer in guidance in December 1917 were translations of German defensive doctrine: certainly better than nothing, but surely not the best way to adapt and learn on the battlefield.[28] The final wartime edition of SS 135, *The Division in Attack*, although not published until November 1918, embodied much of what had been learnt since July following the battles of Hamel, Amiens, and the Hindenburg Line. Against this background, historian Williamson Murray's criticism that the British 'never established a coherent doctrine in 1918', while containing an element of truth, is also misleading.[29]

Initiative

Looking back a hundred years and more, it may at first sight seem difficult to identify much personal initiative amongst the senior generals of World War I. If the 'butchers and bunglers', responsible for so many losses, had demonstrated greater ability, surely the war could have been fought and won more economically?[30] Mistakes seem to have been repeated time and time again, whether at Verdun, the Somme, or Third Ypres.

Each of the armies of World War I learned through a bitter cumulative experience. Although not demonstrating a steady progression (perhaps more a sine-wave than a curve), the learning process in the BEF is well documented, not least through the SS series of publications.[31] The associated training regime reached its apogee during 1918 following the appointment of an Inspector General of Training, Lieutenant General Sir Ivor Maxse, in July. Doctrine and training, however, can only provide a framework of understanding. Furthermore, preparation and rehearsal provide no guarantee of success in battle, which depends on taking purposeful decisions once contact is made. Germans describe the priceless ability to assess the situation quickly and to amend plans expeditiously either to maintain or to grasp the initiative as *Fingerspitzengefühl* (intuitive feeling). Such intuitive decision-making, however, is the product of innate ability combined with experiential learning.

Initiative is not necessarily rewarded. General Sir Hubert Gough gets a poor press for his performance in command of Fifth Army in March 1918, notwithstanding controversies pertaining to his earlier decisions at the Somme and Third Ypres. With his removal from command, Gough was made a convenient scapegoat for the reverse suffered by his army, and for that suffered by the BEF as a whole. Yet given the unfavourable local force ratios he dealt with, typically 1:4, Gough had handled his army competently enough during the first week of the German offensive in one of the most taxing operations of war – the withdrawal. In particular, he had surely made the correct decision on 21 March 1918 in pulling back III Corps to the Crozat Canal. Indeed, on that fateful day Haig had recorded that 'with my approval, Gough decided to withdraw from the sector between La Fère and the Somme to the St Quentin Canal'.[32] By initiating a delaying battle rather than maintaining a futile forward defence, Gough probably saved III Corps, if not a larger part of his army, from destruction.

Général de Division Charles Emmanuel Marie Mangin, although *limogéd* (sacked) as the commander-in-chief of the French Sixth Army following the abortive Nivelle offensive of April–May 1917, was luckier than Gough. Unlike the British Fifth Army commander who remained on half pay for the rest of the war, Mangin was given a further chance that restored, if not made, his reputation in the summer of 1918.[33] A highly controversial figure in the French Army, nicknamed the 'Butcher' for his alleged disregard for casualties, Mangin was appointed commander-in-chief of the French Tenth Army prior to the Second Battle of the Marne.[34] His army defended the western side of the 'Marne' salient (also known as the Château-Thierry pocket) some 25 miles deep and 37 miles wide achieved by German forces during Operations *Blücher* and *Gneisenau* in May–June. Mangin is given much credit for his personal initiative and organizational agility during the planning and mounting of the French counter-attack of 18 July 1918, which can be regarded as a decisive turning point of World War I.[35]

On 15 July 1918, Ludendorff opened what turned out to be his last great offensive on the Western Front. Although its aim was to capture the city of Reims, it was in fact designed to draw in as many Allied reserves as possible, and so set the conditions for a subsequent attempt to defeat the BEF (Operation *Hagen*) in Flanders, much further to the north. Operation *Marneschutz-Reims*, having achieved only a limited penetration across the Marne River to the west of Reims, culminated after three days of hard fighting. Yet both Foch and Mangin had already started thinking about attacking the Germans' weakly defended western flank *well before* the Germans mounted their own offensive.

On 14 June Foch had written to Pétain suggesting that 'there would be advantages, as soon as circumstances permit, in mounting an offensive action aimed at giving us mastery of the plateau dominating Soissons to the west'. On receipt of this direction via his army group commander (Général de Divison Émile Fayolle), Mangin submitted proposals to seize a tract of open ground immediately to the east of the Forest of Villers-Cottérêts (part of the larger Forêt de Retz). Gaining approval, he launched a series of small-scale attacks between 15 June and 3 July to secure this area as a suitable line of departure for his counterstroke. Believing that the situation was now ripe for an even larger-scale operation, perhaps leading to the 'elimination of the Marne salient', Mangin advised on 5 July:

> [Achieving] surprise is perfectly possible. On the one hand the forest provides the means of concealing the concentration of the infantry until the last moment; on the other, the constant redeployment of artillery along the front of 10th Army during the last three weeks will in all likelihood hinder the enemy in detecting the installation of fresh batteries in the area of Villers-Cottérêts.[36]

While Pétain favoured an immediate launch of the operation, Foch demurred, considering that it should be conducted in conjunction with one mounted by the French Fifth Army in the opposite direction from the south of Reims – but only when the timing was right. He sensed that the counter-blow should follow once the German offensive operations had culminated. After further planning, it was determined that both arms of the attack would be directed towards the high ground in the centre of the salient at Fère-en-Tardenois.

Although Mangin had already much of his preparation and planning for his counterstroke well in hand, at Foch's urging, on 12 July Pétain issued new instructions concerning offensive operations. His Directive No. 5 emphasized the importance of 'simple, audacious and rapid attacks'. It set out conditions for their success including: the 'training of commanders, staffs and troops'; 'secrecy of preparations'; an 'initial surprise attack'; the 'rapid execution and development in depth of the attack' and its 'immediate exploitation'. Notably, the Directive required simple and concise orders, stressing:

> It will be left for the most part to the initiative and the temperament of each [commander] for the accomplishment of their mission; better a simple plan of manoeuvre, executed by those who understand it, than a better plan, which is less adapted to the temperament of those undertaking it.[37]

On 13 July, two days before the launch of *Marneschutz-Reims*, Pétain ordered that the twin French counter-strokes should begin on 18 July. Keys to the success of the operation, as Mangin had stressed, would be strictest operations security, concealment, deception, and the achievement of surprise. To ensure tactical overmatch, the French Army assembled very significant forces for the Tenth Army, which would be supported by the Sixth Army to its south.[38] Fortunately for the Allied cause, in response to *Marneschutz-Reims*, Foch countermanded Pétain's attempt to delay Mangin's attack and to strip him of resources.[39]

The Tenth Army's counter-stroke (also termed the battle of Soissons), spearheaded by XX Corps (the Moroccan Division with the 1st and 2nd US divisions), achieved the desired tactical surprise and penetrated about four miles on 18 July. However, this gain was about half that expected despite the heavy air and artillery support, and the impressive employment of tanks. Furthermore, at the end of the first day Pétain denied Mangin the additional forces required for immediate exploitation, thereby negating an important condition for success enunciated in Directive No. 5.

Under pressure on both their flanks, the Germans reorganized their defences in depth over the next few days and so prevented the link-up of French forces at Fère-en-Tardenois. In what then became a gruelling attritional battle of nearly three weeks' duration, rather than one of grand manoeuvre, the Germans were forced to withdraw progressively from the Marne salient. Apart from the physical damage inflicted on the German Army (ten divisions had to be broken up), one result of the Allied counter-blow was the psychological effect on Ludendorff. Correlli Barnett highlights his 'three days of virtual mental paralysis following the news of 18 July 1918'.[40] Unsurprisingly, Ludendorff makes no mention of any such trauma in his memoirs, only glibly conceding that the 'attempt to make the nations of the Entente inclined to peace before the arrival of the American reinforcements by means of German victories had failed'.[41] And so it had.

The enduring value in this case study lies not in the tactical method employed by Mangin, but rather in how he recognized the opportunity for a decisive counter-blow and 'sold' his plan to his superiors, Général de Divisions Fayolle, Pétain, and Foch; and in how they expanded his proposals into a winning design for battle. Hence the counter-stroke of 18 July 1918 represents a good example of collective operational-level design and initiative, albeit one based on Foch's and Mangin's original ideas. Mangin excelled in preparing his multinational army for battle: his operation confirmed the age-old benefits of surprise, and associated deception measures. Furthermore, the resulting victory at the battle of the Second Marne was an Allied one: French-led, but with significant American, British, and Italian forces involved. Germany's military locker was now laid bare. As a result, Ludendorff had to abandon his plans for Operation *Hagen* and the strategic initiative now passed irretrievably to the Allies. The Franco-British battle of Amiens-Montdidier, which opened on 8 August (the 'black day' of the German Army), followed – initiating the 'Hundred Days' campaign of the 'advance to victory'.[42]

Conclusion

In his memoir of the 1944–45 campaign in North-west Europe, Eisenhower famously observed that a 'professional sequel' to war is 'the study and evaluation of its lessons'.[43] Thus it behoves all militaries to thoroughly analyse past operations. Despite the passage of a hundred years, there is still much to learn from World War I generally, and from the Western Front in 1918 specifically. This chapter has described the various interdependencies that affected the German and Allied armies alike, whether across or within theatres of war. Many of these, such as the requirement for trust and mutual support between coalition partners, have an enduring quality. Likewise, the Western Front remains a rich source of useful examples of innovation and initiative, be they technical or tactical, or a combination thereof.

The lessons of war reflected both continuities and changes, reflecting national perspectives and traditions – as in the exercise of command. In the British case, the Kirke Report of 1932 rested its observations on previously published official histories. Although the *Reichswehr* under von Seeckt was quicker off the mark with its detailed studies of the early 1920s, both the British and German armies addressed to varying degrees the requirements of mobile war – rather than institutionalizing the lessons of trench warfare. For the British, that was perhaps the greatest doctrinal legacy of the fighting of 1918. While the Germans always anticipated recreating a mass army from the cadre of the *Reichswehr*, in practice the British Army reverted to its pre-1914 type – one of colonial policing. As a result, very quickly it lost both its feel and taste for large-scale operations, let alone manoeuvre at echelons above division, as seen in the 'Hundred Days' campaign. Never again would a British general officer command as large a force as Haig did.[44]

Meanwhile, during the inter-war period the French derived their concept of a methodical battle (*la bataille conduit*) under the tutelage of Debeney and other like-minded officers. With their preference for firepower over manoeuvre, centralized command, and a step-by-step, strictly phased approach to battle, the French drew more inspiration from the First Army's action at Montdidier of 8–11 August 1918 than they did from the Tenth Army's counter-stroke at the Marne during the previous month. Close tactical control of the battlefield, designed to minimize casualties and to guarantee limited success, was preferred over embracing larger risk for bigger potential operational gains. Had Mangin rather than Debeney been the father of French doctrine following World War I, then perhaps a different conceptual path might have emerged. It could have included, for instance, an emphasis on generating a fluid, mobile battle, which required decentralized command. It remains an intriguing thought.

So how far should one attempt to learn lessons from past wars if the conditions of the next may prove startlingly different to those presently predicted? While no army can hope to anticipate these precisely, it may nonetheless take an informed view as to the character of future conflict. Again, history may guide us. Bearing in mind that World War II would break out within seven years of its publication, the Kirke Report concluded presciently:

> In looking back at the war and all its lessons we must not overlook the most important lesson of all, viz, all wars produce new methods and fresh problems. The last war was full of surprises – the next one is likely to be no less prolific in unexpected developments. Hence we must study the

past in the light of the probabilities of the future, which is what really matters. No matter how prophetically we may be, the next war will take a shape far different to our peace-time conceptions.

With specific regard to training, the Report added, 'In order to cope with this upset to our preconceived ideas our leaders must be versatile, mentally robust and full of common sense and self-reliance. To produce this sort of mentality must be the object of our training.'[45]

Engendering this sort of adaptability and initiative institutionally, perhaps, represents the greatest teaching lesson of all from World War I. But such an approach must also rest on sound, *forward-looking*, doctrine and training, and not one derived from a particular perspective of previous warfare, potentially based on faulty historical analysis. The differences between French and German doctrinal development in the inter-war period, and not least the outcome of the battle of France in 1940, surely highlight this point. As Doughty has sagely noted,

> By over-reliance on the historical example as the correct model of operations, the French doctrine for the methodical battle was moulded more by past experiences than by technological or conceptual advances, or by careful analysis of more recent wars.[46]

In this light, the broader lessons of interdependence, innovation, and initiative from the Western Front in 1918 surely remain worthy of study, as is its doctrinal legacy.

ENDNOTES

Foreword

1 A staff ride is an instructional military exercise involving the study of a military problem on a particular piece of ground (often an historical battle studied at its site) as a means to teach doctrine or rehearse operational plans. It was a method developed by Generalfeldmarschall Helmuth von Moltke the Elder as Chief of the Prussian Großer Generalstab from 1855–88 and remains an effective, efficient, and frequent mechanism for military instruction today.

2 In several instances this diversity reveals aspects of historical controversy; as ever there is no universal version of historical truth.

3 The British Army's Leadership Code requires our leaders to: lead by example; encourage thinking; apply reward and discipline; demand high performance; encourage confidence; recognize strengths and weaknesses; and strive for team goals.

4 Although of course the global war did not end neatly in November 1918 and the British Army had to fight on in Russia, Turkey, and Iraq.

Chapter 1

1 The other defeated nations had to sign similar treaties: Austria at St Germain on 10 September 1919, Bulgaria at Neuilly on 27 November 1919, Hungary at Trianon on 4 June 1920, and the Ottoman Empire at Sèvres on 10 August 1920. On the treaties and the immediate criticism of them, see Carole Fink, 'The Peace Settlement, 1919–1939', in John Horne (ed.), *A Companion to World War I* (Oxford: Blackwell, 2012), pp. 543–557, here p. 546. For an in-depth description of the Treaty of Versailles negotiations, see H. W. V. Temperley (ed.), *A History of the Peace Conference of Paris, published under the auspices of the British Institute of*

International Affairs, 6 vols, (London: Frowde and Hodder and Stoughton, 1920–1924).

2   Quoted in Georg Alexander von Müller, *The Kaiser and his Court* (London: Macdonald, 1961), p. 344.

3   Sönke Neitzel, *Weltkrieg und Revolution 1914–1918/19* (Berlin: be.bra verlag, 2008), p. 75. On the battle, see John and Eileen Wilks, *Rommel and Caporetto* (Barnsley: Pen & Sword, 2001)

4   See Alan Palmer, *The Gardeners of Salonika. The Macedonian Campaign 1915–1918* (London: Faber and Faber, 2009).

5   For the war in the Levant see Rob Johnson, *The Great War & the Middle East* (Oxford: Oxford University Press, 2016).

6   Named after Alexander Kerensky, first Minister of War and then Prime Minister of the new regime until he was toppled by the Bolsheviks in the October Revolution.

7   Peter Lieb, 'The German Occupation of the Ukraine, 1918: Blitzkrieg and Insurgencies', in Matthias Strohn (ed.), *World War I Companion* (Oxford: Osprey, 2013), pp. 210–225.

8   Stéphane Audoin-Rouzeau and Annette Becker, *14–18. Understanding the Great War* (New York, Hill and Wang, 2002), p. 22. For a general discussion of these figures, see Jennifer D. Keene, 'The United States' in: Horne, *A Companion to World War I*, pp. 508–523, here p. 517.

9   Stephen Broadberry and Mark Harrison, *The Economics of World War I* (Cambridge: Cambridge University Press, 2005), pp. 7 and 10. For a discussion of the US economic figures, also see David Stevenson, *With our Backs to the Wall: Victory and Defeat in 1918* (London: Penguin, 2012), pp. 350–370.

10 Paul Kennedy, *The Rise and Fall of the Great Powers: Economic Change and Military Conflict from 1500–2000* (London: Random House, 1987), p. 557.

11 Charles Gilbert, *American Financing of World War I* (Westport: Praeger, 1970), p. 221.

12 For a discussion of this, see Dieter Storz, '"Aber was hätte anders geschehen sollen?" Die deutschen Offensiven an der Westfront 1918', in: Jörg Duppler and Gerhard P. Groß (eds), *Kriegsende 1918: Ereignis, Wirkung, Nachwirkung* (Munich: Oldenbourg, 1999), pp. 51–96.

13 Martin Kitchen, *The German Offensives of 1918* (Stroud: Tempus, 2001), p. 16. This book offers a good introduction to all of the German offensives in the West in 1918. Short overviews of the individual battles (not only the German offensives) on the Western Front are also provided in Mungo Melvin (ed.), *The First World War Battlefield Guide*, vol. I, *The Western Front* (Andover: [British] Army Headquarters, second edition 2015). The German official history provides an in-depth narrative of the offensives:

Reichsarchiv, *Der Weltkrieg 1914–18*, vol. XIV, *Die Kriegführung an der Westfront im Jahre 1918* (Berlin: Mittler und Sohn, 1944).

14 Even in 1932, Generalleutnant Gerhard Tappen, former head of the operations section of the OHL, stated in an interview conducted by members of the Reichsarchiv that the French soldiers had been 'morally inferior' to the Germans; see *Besprechung mit dem Generalleutnant a.D. Tappen im Reichsarchiv am 6. IX. 1932*, BA-MA, RH 61/1674.

15 Paul Greenwood, *The Second Battle of the Marne 1918* (Shrewsbury: Airlife, 1998).

16 Erich Ludendorff, *My War Memories 1914–1918*, vol. II, (London: Hutchinson, 1920), p. 679.

17 *History of the Great War Based on Official Documents by Direction of the Historical Section of the Committee of Imperial Defence. Military Operations: France and Belgium, 1918*, vol. III: *May–July: The German Diversion Offensives and the First Allied Counter-Offensive*, compiled by James E. Edmonds (London: Macmillan, 1939). Between March and September 1918 the German Army lost 536,000 killed and missing and 808,300 wounded; see David Stone, *The Kaiser's Army: The German Army in World War One* (London: Bloomsbury, 2015), p. 134.

18 Holger Herwig, *The First World War: Germany and Austria-Hungary 1914-1918* (London: Bloomsbury, second edition 2014), p. 407.

19 Quoted in Klaus-Jürgen Müller, *Generaloberst Ludwig Beck: Eine Biographie* (Paderborn: Schöningh, 2008), p. 57.

20 Bundesarchiv- Militärarchiv BA-MA PH3/3, *Chef des Generalstabes II Nr. 10162*, 4 September 1918. Also see Wilhelm Solger, *Vorarbeit u Band XIV: Die Oberste Heeresleitung in der Abwehr (ab dem 15. Juli 1918)*, BA-MA W10/51844, p. 109.

21 A good case study of this can be found in Jonathan Boff, *Winning and Losing on the Western Front: The British Third Army and the Defeat of Germany in 1918* (Cambridge: Cambridge University Press, 2012). See also Chapter 4 in this book.

22 Bayerisches Hauptstaatsarchiv, Abteilung IV, Kriegsarchiv, HKR Band 99/11, *OHL Nr. 10552*, 30 September 1918.

23 Carl Groos and Werner von Rudolf, *Infanterie Regiment Herwarth von Bittenfeld (1. Westfälisches) Nr. 13 im Weltkriege 1914–1918* (Oldenburg: Stalling, 1927), pp. 330–331.

24 Adolf Hitler, *Mein Kampf. Zwei Bände in einem Band. Ungekürzte Ausgabe*, 395th–399th edition (Munich: Zentralverlag der NSDAP, 1939), pp. 223–225.

25 For this, see Thomas Weber, *Hitler's First War: Adolf Hitler, the Men of the List Regiment, and the First World War* (Oxford: Oxford University Press, 2010); and idem, *Hitler: The Making of a Nazi* (New York: Basic Books, 2017).

26 For a short overview of this, see Hagen Schulze, 'Versailles', in Etienne François and Hagen Schulze (eds), *Deutsche Erinnerungsorte*, vol. I, (Munich: C.H. Beck, 2003), pp. 407–421.

27 Eberhard Kolb, *Der Frieden von Versailles*, 2nd Edition (Munich: C.H. Beck, 2011), p. 76.

28 For the discussion of the stab-in-the back myth, see Friedrich Freiherr Hiller von Gaetringen, '"Dolchstoß"-Diskussion und "Dolchstoß-Legende" im Wandel von vier Jahrzehnten', in Waldemar Besson (ed.), *Geschichte und Gegenwartsbewußtsein: Festschrift für Hans Rothfels zum 70. Geburtstag* (Göttingen: Vandenhoek und Ruprecht, 1963).

29 Gesundheitsamt, *Schädigung der deutschen Volkskraft durch die feindliche Blockade. Denkschrift des Reichsgesundheitsamtes, Dezember 1918.*

30 Leo Grebler, *The Cost of the World War to Germany and Austria-Hungary* (Yale: Yale University Press, 1940), p. 78. For a discussion of the blockade and its impact see C. Paul Vincent, *The Politics of Hunger: the Allied Blockade of Germany, 1915–1919* (Athens, OH and London: Ohio University Press, 1985); and Avner Offer, 'The Blockade of Germany and the Strategy of Starvation, 1914–1918. An Agency Perspective', in: Roger Chickering and Stig Förster (eds), *Great War, Total War: Combat and Mobilization on the Western Front, 1914–1918* (Cambridge: Cambridge University Press, 2000), pp. 169–188.

31 For the issues surrounding the US decision, see Ralph A. Stone, *The Irreconcilables: The Fight Against the League of Nations* (Lexington: University Press of Kentucky, 1970).

32 Niall Ferguson, *Civilization: The Six Killer Apps of Western Power* (London: Penguin, 2012), p. 309.

33 Michel Hubert, *La Population de la France pendant la Guerre. Avec une appendice sur les revenus avant er après la guerre* (Paris: Les Presses U. de France, 1931), p. 420.

34 On this topic see Robert Gerwarth, *The Vanquished: Why the First World War Failed to End, 1917–1923* (London: Allan Lane, 2016). Also see Timothy Snyder, *Bloodlands: Europe Between Hitler and Stalin* (London: Penguin, 2010).

35 Ernst Jünger, *Der Krieg als inneres Erlebnis*, edited by Helmuth Kiesel (Stuttgart: Klett-Cotta, 2016), pp. 35–36.

Chapter 2

1 Douglas Haig, *Dispatches: General Douglas Haig's Official Reports to the British Government* (New York: J. M. Dent & Sons, 1919), p. 320.

2 For an in-depth study of the 1918 Ludendorff Offensives see David T. Zabecki, *The German 1918 Offensives: A Case Study in the Operational Level of War* (London: Routledge, 2006).

3   War Office General Staff Great Britain, *Handbook of the German Army in the War, April 1918* (reprint) (London: Arms & Armour Press, 1977), pp. 36–9.

4   David T. Zabecki, *Chief of Staff: The Principal Officers Behind History's Great Commanders*, vol. I, *Napoleonic Wars to World War I* (Annapolis: US Naval Institute Press, 2008), pp. 5–9.

5   General Erich Ludendorff, *My War Memories, 1914–1918* (London: Hutchinson, 1920), vol. 1, p. 239.

6   Christian O. E. Millotat, *Understanding the Prussian-German General Staff System* (Carlisle, PA: US Army War College, 1992), pp. 23–4.

7   Bruce I. Gudmundsson, *Stormtroop Tactics: Innovation in the German Army, 1914–1918* (New York: Praeger, 1989), pp. 151–2.

8   Oberkommando des Heeres, *Der Weltkrieg 1914 bis 1918*, vol. 12, *Die Kriegsführung im Frühjahr 1917* (Berlin: Mittler und Sohn, 1939), pp. 53–4.

9   William Balck, *Development of Tactics: World War* (Ft. Leavenworth: General Service Schools Press, 1922), pp. 153–60.

10 General Erich Ludendorff, 'Der Angriff im Stellungskrieg', in *Urkunden der Obersten Heeresleitung über ihre Tätigkeit 1916/18* (Berlin: Mittler und Sohn, 1921), pp. 641–66.

11 Balck, *Development of Tactics*, p. 266.

12 Ibid., pp. 62, 81, 91.

13 Max Hoffmann, *The War of Lost Opportunities* (Nashville: The Battery Press, 1995), p. 135.

14 Ludendorff, *War Memories*, vol. 2, p. 606.

15 For a comprehensive examination of Bruchmüller and his tactical innovations see David T. Zabecki, *Steel Wind: Colonel Georg Bruchmüller and the Birth of Modern Artillery* (Westport: Praeger, 1994).

16 Georg Bruchmüller, *Die Deutsche Artillerie in den Durchbruchschlachten des Weltkriegs*, 2nd ed. (Berlin: Mittler und Sohn, 1922), p. 80.

17 Zabecki, *Steel Wind*, pp. 48–50

18 Gerhard Gross, *The Myth and Reality of German Warfare: Operational Thinking from Moltke the Elder to Heusinger* (Lexington: University Press of Kentucky, 2016), p. 131.

19 A. M. Henniker, *Transportation on the Western Front, 1914–1918* (London: Macmillan & Co. Ltd., 1937), pp. 398–411.

20 David T. Zabecki and Dieter Biedekarken (eds and trans.), *Lossberg's War: The Memoirs of a World War I German Chief of Staff* (Lexington: University Press of Kentucky, 2017), p. 312.

21 Oberkommando des Heeres, *Der Weltkrieg 1914 bis 1918*, vol. 13, *Die Kriegsführung im Sommer und Herbst 1917* (Berlin: Mittler und Sohn, 1942), pp. 323–6.

22 Oberkommando des Heeres, *Der Weltkrieg 1914 bis 1918*, vol. 14, *Die Kriegsführung an der Westfront im Jahre 1918* (Berlin: Mittler und Sohn, 1944), pp. 51–5.

23 Ibid., pp. 68–9.

24 Ibid., pp. 76–7.

25 Quoted in Kronprinz Rupprecht von Bayern, *In Treue Fest: Mein Kriegstagebuch*, vol. 2 (Munich: Deutscher National Verlag, 1929), p. 372.

26 Oberkommando des Heeres, *Der Weltkrieg*, vol. 14, p. 278.

27 Zabecki, *1918 Offensives*, pp. 280–310.

28 Oberkommando des Heeres, *Der Weltkrieg*, vol. 14, pp. 393–8.

29 Ludendorff, *War Memories*, vol. 2, pp. 638–40.

30 Hermann von Kuhl, *Personal War Diary of General von Kuhl*, in Bundesarchiv/Militärarchiv, File: W-10/50652, entry of 18 July 1918.

31 Zabecki and Biedekarken, *Lossberg's War*, pp. 345–9.

32 Ibid., p. 350.

33 'General Foch Memorandum from the Commanders-in-Chief Conference No. 2,375', 24 July 1918, in United Kingdom National Archives, Kew, Great Britain. Record Group WO 158/105 358219.

34 Hew Strachan, *The First World War* (London: Simon & Schuster, 2014), p. 178. Henniker, *Transportation*, p. 438.

35 Elizabeth Greenhalgh, *Foch in Command: The Forging of a First World War General* (Cambridge: Cambridge University Press, 2014), p. 443.

36 Colonel T. Bentley Mott (trans.), *The Memoirs of Marshall Foch* (Garden City: Doubleday, 1931), pp. 408–9.

37 Richard Holmes, *Tommy: The British Soldier on the Western Front 1914–1918* (London: Harper Collins, 2004), p. 69.

38 David Stevenson, *With Our Backs to the Wall: Victory and Defeat in 1918* (London: Allen Lane, 2011), pp. 160–1.

39 Wilhelm II, *The Kaiser's Memoirs 1888–1918* (London: Harper Brothers, 1922), pp. 273–4.

40 Rupprecht, *Mein Kriegstagebuch*, vol. 2, p. 178.

41 Walter Görlitz, *History of the German General Staff, 1657–1945* (New York: Praeger, 1953), p. 183.

42 Ludendorff, *War Memories*, p. 550.

43 Gerald D. Feldman, *Army, Industry, and Labor in Germany, 1914–1918* (Princeton: Princeton University Press, 1966), pp. 154, 301.

44 Görlitz, *German General Staff*, p. 184.

45 Feldman, *Army, Industry, and Labor*, pp. 190–6.

46 John W. Wheeler-Bennett, *Hindenburg: The Wooden Titan* (New York: St. Martin's Press, 1967), pp. 190–5.

47 Wheeler-Bennett, *Hindenburg*, p. 205.

48 Ibid., p. 200.

Chapter 3

1 For a comprehensive history of the French Army during World War I,
   see Elizabeth Greenhalgh, *The French Army and the First World War*
   (Cambridge: Cambridge University Press, 2014). See also Robert
   Doughty, *Pyrrhic Victory: French Strategy and Operations in the Great War*
   (Harvard: Harvard University Press, 2005).

2 David Murphy, *Breaking Point of the French Army: the Nivelle Offensive
   of 1917* (Pen & Sword, 2015), p.139.

3 Doughty, *Pyrrhic Victory*, pp. 416–417.

4 Grand Quartier Général, 'Note sur l'entretien des armées françaises,
   14 décembre 1917', *Les Armées Françaises dans la Grande Guerre*, 611-183,
   pp. 307–308.

5 Anthony Clayton, *Paths of Glory: The French Army, 1914–18* (London:
   Cassell, 2003), pp. 180–181. See also Doughty, *Pyrrhic Victory*,
   pp. 416–417.

6 The best modern study of Foch is Elizabeth Greenhalgh's *Foch in Command:
   The Forging of a First World War General* (Cambridge: Cambridge
   University Press, 2011).

7 See Doughty, *Pyrrhic Victory*. See also Charles Williams, *Pétain* (London:
   Little, Brown, 2005).

8 See Greenhalgh, *Foch in Command*.

9 David Murphy, *Breaking Point of the French Army: The Nivelle Offensive
   of 1917* (Barnsley: Pen & Sword, 2015), p.159.

10 Jean de Pierrefeu, *French headquarters, 1915–1918* (Paris, n.d.[1923?],
   General Books reprint, London)

11 Douglas Porch, *The French Intelligence Services: a History of French
   Intelligence From the Dreyfus Affair to the Gulf War* (New York: Farrar,
   Straus & Giroux, 1995), pp. 78–114.

12 Doughty, *Pyrrhic Victory*, p. 407.

13 Ibid., p. 405.

14 Ibid., p. 408.

15 Robin Neilland's *The Great War Generals on the Western Front, 1914–1918*
   (London: Robinson, 1999) is an excellent account of the interplay between
   the Allied generals.

16 Ian Sumner, *They Shall Not Pass: The French Army on the Western Front,
   1914–1918* (Barnsley: Pen & Sword, 2012), pp. 184–185.

17 Clayton, *Paths of Glory*, pp. 182–187.

18 See Steven Zaloga, *French Tanks of World War I* (Oxford: Osprey, 2010). See also Bruno Jurkiewicz, *Les Chars Français Au Combat, 1917–1918* (Louviers: Ysec, 2008).

19 Zaloga, *French Tanks of World War I*, pp. 20–40.

20 Elizabeth Greenhalgh, 'Myth and Memory: Sir Douglas Haig and the Imposition of Allied Unified Command in March 1918' in *The Journal of Military History*, 63 (July, 2004), pp. 771–820.

21 Doughty, *Pyrrhic Victory*, p. 429.

22 Clayton, *Paths of Glory*, p. 166.

23 Jean Hallade, 'Big Bertha bombards Paris', in Bernard Fitzsimmons (ed.), *Tanks & Weapons of World War 1* (London: Smith, 1973), pp. 141–147.

24 René Fonck, *Mes Combats* (Paris: Flammarion, 1920), quoted in Sumner, *They Shall Not Pass*, p.190.

25 Greenhalgh, *The French Army and the First World War*, pp. 283–287. The nearby ossuary contains over 5,000 French dead, denoting the intense fighting that took place here.

26 David Bonk, *Château-Thierry & Belleau Wood 1918: America's baptism of fire on the Marne* (Oxford: Osprey, 2007).

27 See Douglas Porch, *The French Secret Services: a History of French Intelligence From the Dreyfus Affair to the Gulf War* (New York: Ferrar, Straus & Giroux, 1995)

28 For Mangin's own thoughts on his career during World War I, see Charles Mangin, *Lettres de guerre, 1914–1918* (Paris: Fayard, 1950).

29 See Randal Gray, *Kaiserschlacht 1918: The final German offensive* (Oxford: Osprey, 1991).

30 For a comprehensive account of this series of actions, see Paul Greenwood, *The Second Battle of the Marne 1918* (Shrewsbury: Airlife, 1998). See also Greenhalgh, *The French Army and the First World War*, pp. 312–344.

31 Alastair McCluskey, *Amiens 1918: The Black Day of the German Army* (Oxford: Osprey, 2008).

32 David Bonk, *St Mihiel 1918: The American Expeditionary Forces' trial by fire* (Oxford: Osprey, 2011).

33 Bullitt Lowry, *Armistice 1918* (Kent, OH: Kent State University Press, 1996).

34 Joseph E. Persico, *Eleventh Month, Eleventh Day, Eleventh Hour: Armistice Day – World War I and its Violent Climax* (New York: Random House, 2005).

35 David Murphy, *Breaking Point of the French Army*, p. 161.

36 Greenhalgh, *Foch in Command*, pp. 508–521.

Chapter 4

1 The 'British Army' here includes forces from the dominions and colonies of the Empire, including Australia, Canada, India, New Zealand, and South Africa, amongst others.

2 War Office, *Statistics of the Military Effort of the British Empire during the Great War, 1914–1920* (London: HMSO, 1922), pp. 260–5.

3 Bryn Hammond, *Cambrai 1917: The Myth of the First Great Tank Battle* (London: Weidenfeld & Nicolson, 2008).

4 The account here closely follows that of Jim Beach, *Haig's Intelligence: GHQ and the German Army, 1916–1918* (Cambridge: Cambridge University Press, 2013), pp. 273–88.

5 Martin Samuels estimates 84 per cent: Samuels, *Command or Control? Command, Training and Tactics in the British and German Armies, 1888–1918* (London: Frank Cass, 1995), p. 217.

6 Ingo Wolfgang Trauschweizer, 'Learning with an Ally: The U.S. Army and the *Bundeswehr* in the Cold War', *Journal of Military History* 72:2 (April 2008), pp. 477–508.

7 Matthias Strohn, *The German Army and the Defence of the Reich: Military Doctrine and the Conduct of the Defensive Battle 1918–1939* (Cambridge: Cambridge University Press, 2011).

8 Jim Beach, 'Issued by the General Staff: Doctrine Writing at British GHQ, 1917–1918', *War in History* 19:4 (November 2012), pp. 464–91, p. 473.

9 'Fighting troops' includes all personnel in France and Flanders who were not employed on the lines of communication. On 31 January 1918 they numbered 1,584,100: GHQ Adjutant-General War Diary, The National Archives (TNA) WO 95/26; 'Statistical Abstract of Information Regarding the Armies at Home and Abroad', No. 25, 1 October 1918, TNA WO 394/10; War Office, *Statistics*, pp. 253–71.

10 General Erich Ludendorff, *My War Memories, 1914–1918* (London: Hutchinson, 1920), vol. 1, pp. 679, 683–4.

11 Ian Beckett, Timothy Bowman and Mark Connelly, *The British Army and the First World War* (Cambridge: Cambridge University Press, 2017), p. 369.

12 David Fraser (ed.), *In Good Company: The First World War Letters and Diaries of the Hon. William Fraser, Gordon Highlanders* (Salisbury: Michael Russell, 1990), p. 306.

13 David Jordan, 'The Royal Air Force and Air/Land Integration in the 100 Days, August–November 1918', *Air Power Review* 11:2 (Summer 2008), pp. 12–29.

14 See Aimée Fox, *Learning to Fight: Military Innovation and Change in the British Army, 1914–1918* (Cambridge: Cambridge University Press, 2017).

15 Alexander Watson, *Enduring the Great War: Combat, Morale and Collapse in the German and British Armies, 1914–1918* (Cambridge: Cambridge University Press, 2008), chapters 5 and 6.

16 Albrecht von Thaer, *Generalstabsdienst an der Front und in der O.H.L.*, edited by Siegfried A. Kaehler (Göttingen: Vandenhoeck & Ruprecht, 1958), pp. 187–8.

17 Nick Lloyd, *Hundred Days: The End of the Great War* (London: Viking, 2013), pp. 242–3.

18 J. F. C. Fuller, *Tanks in the Great War: 1914–1918* (London: John Murray, 1920); B. H. Liddell Hart, *The Remaking of Modern Armies* (London: John Murray, 1927); J. E. Edmonds and R. Maxwell-Hyslop, *Military Operations France and Belgium 1918*, vol. V, *26th September–11th November The Advance to Victory* (London: HMSO, 1947), p. 609; J. P. Harris, *Men, Ideas and Tanks: British Military Thought and Armoured Forces, 1903–1939* (Manchester: Manchester University Press, 1995), p. 178.

19 J. P. Harris with Niall Barr, *Amiens to the Armistice: The BEF in the Hundred Days' Campaign 8 August–11 November 1918* (London: Brassey's, 1998), p. 296.

20 Robin Prior and Trevor Wilson, *Command on the Western Front: The Military Career of Sir Henry Rawlinson 1914–18* (Oxford: Blackwell, 1992), pp. 300, 342, 397.

21 Andy Simpson, *Directing Operations: British Corps Command on the Western Front 1914–18* (Stroud: Spellmount, 2006), pp. xvi, 161–75.

22 Mark Connelly, *Steady the Buffs! A Regiment, a Region, and the Great War* (Oxford: Oxford University Press, 2006), pp. 225–6; David French, 'Doctrine and Organization in the British Army, 1919–1932', *Historical Journal* 44:2 (June 2001), pp. 497–515: p. 514.

23 The author is deeply indebted to Dr John Bourne for the biographical detail on the officers and men involved in 46th Division's attack and to Dr John Lee for the loan of his notes on the battle. This section could not have been written without their help. The account here also draws heavily on R. E. Priestley, *Breaking the Hindenburg Line: The Story of the 46th (North Midland) Division* (London: T. Fisher Unwin, 1919).

24 John Milne, *Footprints of the 1/4th Leicestershire Regiment, August 1914 to November 1918* (Leicester: Edgar Backus, 1935), quoted in Christopher Moore, *Trench Fever* (London: Little Brown, 1998), p. 187.

25 Priestley, *Breaking the Hindenburg Line*, p. 143.

26 Ibid., p. 74.

27 A. Montgomery-Massingberd papers, Joint Services Command and Staff College library, Shrivenham, quoted in Gary Sheffield, *The Chief: Douglas Haig and the British Army* (London: Aurum, 2011), p. 323.

28 The author is grateful to Alistair McCluskey for pointing this out.

29 Edmonds and Maxwell-Hyslop, *1918*, vol. V, p. 557.

30 Of the over five million men who made up the British Army in 1918, nearly two million (36 per cent) were fighting in France and Belgium but another one and a quarter million (24 per cent) were serving in expeditionary forces elsewhere: War Office, *Statistics*, pp. 29, 62–3.

Chapter 5

1 Mitchell Yockelson, *Forty-Seven Days: How Pershing's Warriors Came of Age to Defeat the German Army in World War I* (New York: New American Library, 2016).

2 Leonard Ayres, *The War With Germany: A Statistical Summary* (Washington: Government Printing Office, 1919), pp. 17–25.

3 Robert B. Bruce, *A Fraternity of Arms: America and France in the Great War* (Lawrence: University Press of Kansas, 2003), p. 151.

4 Baker to Pershing, 24 December 1917, File #14903-19, Entry 11, RG 120, NARA.

5 General Pershing to Chief of Staff, 1 January 1918, File #14903-20, Entry 11, RG 120, NARA.

6 Ibid.

7 Reports of Commander-in-Chief to the Chief of Staff, AEF, 1 January and 3 January 1918, Folder #21, Entry 22, RG 120, NARA.

8 'Agreement between the Commanders-in-Chief of the American and British Forces in France regarding the training of the American troops with British troops', 31 January 1918, File #14903, Entry 11, RG 120, NARA. (Hereafter cited as File #14903).

9 William B. Fowler, *British-American Relations, 1917–1918: the Role of Sir William Wiseman* (Princeton: Princeton University Press, 1969), pp. 130–5 and 145–53.

10 File #14903.

11 Bruce, *A Fraternity of Arms*, pp. 159–61.

12 John J. Pershing, *My Experiences in the World War* (New York: Frederick A. Stokes Company, 1937), vol. 1, p. 153.

13 See Terrence J. Finnegan, *Delicate Affair on the Western Front: America Learns How to Fight a Modern War in the Woëvre Trenches* (Stroud: The History Press, 2015).

14 Matthew Davenport, *First Over There: The Attack On Cantigny: America's First Battle of World War I* (New York: Thomas Dunne Books, 2015) and Peter Pederson, *Hamel: Battleground Europe* (Barnsley: Pen and Sword, 2003).

15 See Edward G. Lengel, *Thunder and Flames: Americans in the Crucible of Combat* (Lawrence: University Press of Kansas, 2015).

16 Robert Blake (ed.), *The Private Papers of Douglas Haig: 1914–1919* (London: Eyre and Spottiswoode, 1952), p. 325.

17 27th Division Historical Files, 'Report of 27th Division, File 11.4, and 30th Division Historical Files, Operations of the Thirtieth Division', *Old Hickory*, File 11.4, Entry 1241, Records of the American Expeditionary Forces (Record Group 120), and National Archives and Records Administration.

18 War Department, *Operations of the 2nd American Corps* (Washington: War Plans Division, 1926), pp. 36–39.

19 Albert Palazzo, *Seeking Victory on the Western Front: The British Army and Chemical Warfare in World War I* (London: University of Nebraska Press, 2000), p. 185.

20 Major General Sir Archibald Montgomery, *The Story of the Fourth Army in the Battles of The Hundred Days, August 8th to November 11th, 1918* (London: Hodder and Stoughton, 1920), p. 157.

21 Dennis Showalter, 'Coalition War: The Anglo-American Experience', in John Bourne, Peter Liddle, and Ian Whitehead, *The Great World War, 1914–1945: 1. Lightning Strikes Twice* (London: Harper Collins, 2002), p. 466.

22 War Department, *Field Orders of II Corps during the Somme Operation* (Washington: War Department, 1920), #17.

23 118th Infantry Regiment, 'Report of Operations of the 118th Infantry Regiment', 27 November 1918, Entry 1241, RG 120, NA.

24 The Papers of General Henry Lord Rawlinson, RWLN *1/11*, Diary entry for 28 September 1918. Churchill Archives Centre, Cambridge University (Hereafter cited as Rawlinson Papers).

25 Australian War Diaries, Entry 322, Record Group 165, NA.

26 Major General John F. O'Ryan, 'Operations Report, 27th Division, A.E.F., France, 1918', RG 120, Entry 267, NA.

27 Henry Berry, *Make the Kaiser Dance: Living Memories of the Doughboy* (New York: Arbor House, 1978), p. 217.

28 Office of the Chief of Staff, Second American Corps, 'Memorandum for G-5, GHQ, AEF', 24 October 1918, Secret Correspondence, Entry 7, RG 120, NA.

29 James M. Andrews, 'Operations–27th Div., Sept. 25–29, 1918', 27 November 1918, 27th Division, 105th Infantry Regiment, Entry 21, Records of the American Battle Monuments Commission (Record Group 117), NA.

30 Stephen L. Harris, *Duty, Honor, Privilege: New York's Silk Stocking Regiment and the Breaking of the Hindenburg Line* (Washington: Brassey's Inc., 2001), pp. 294–5, 329.

31 Rawlinson Papers, Diary entry for 29 September 1918.

32 The breakdown of casualties is as follows: 27th Division, 1,829 battle deaths and died of wounds, 6,505 wounded; 30th Division, 1,641 battle deaths and died of wounds, 6,774 wounded. *American Armies and Battlefields in Europe* (Washington: American Battle Monuments Commission, 1938), pp. 515–17.

33 Raised in remote Pall Mall Tennessee, York refused induction into the army for religious reasons. York's conscientious objector status was rejected and he reluctantly entered service with the regiment. In France the 328th Infantry saw action in the St Mihiel offensive.

34 Mark Ethan Grotelueschen, *The AEF Way of War: The American Army and Combat in World War I* (New York: Cambridge University Press, 2007), inside flyleaf.

Chapter 6

1 Ottokar Czernin, *Im Weltkriege* (Berlin: Ullstein, 1919), p. 243.

2 Glenn Torrey (ed.), *General Henri Berthelot and Romania: Memoires et Correspondance* (Boulder: East European Monographs, 1987), p. 124 (2 Dec. 1917); Michael Kettle, *The Road to Intervention: March to November 1918* (London: Routledge, 1988), p. 12.

3 The number of German divisions in the East declined from 85 to 47 between the October Revolution and the peace of Brest-Litovsk; a further 13 were sent West until May; see Giordan Fong, 'The Movement of German Divisions to the Western Fronts, Winter 1917–1918', *War in History* 7 (2000), pp. 225–35. The official German history, Oberkommando des Heeres, *Der Weltkrieg 1914–1918*, vol. 13 (Berlin: Mittler & Söhne, 1942), p. 397, has 40 divisions stationed in the East on 21 March, 31 (plus three cavalry divisions) at the end of the war.

4 John Hussey, 'The Movement of German Divisions to the Western Front, Winter 1917–1918', *War in History* 4 (1997), pp. 213–20, here: p. 219.

5 Maximilian Polatschek, *Österreichisch-ungarische Truppen an der Westfront 1914–1918* (unpublished PhD Thesis, Vienna, 1974), pp. 42, 54–7.

6 Lothar Höbelt, 'The Austro-Polish Solution: Mitteleuropa's Siamese Twin', in Jean-Paul Bled and Jean-Pierre Deschodt (eds), *Le crise de Juillet 1914 et l'Europe* (Paris: Editions SPM, 2016), pp. 125–36.

7 Winfried Baumgart, *Deutsche Ostpolitik 1918 – von Brest-Litowsk bis zum Ende des Ersten Weltkrieges* (Vienna: Oldenbourg, 1966), pp. 156, 168; Paul Halpern, *The Naval War in the Mediterranean 1914–1918* (London: Allen & Unwin, 1987), pp. 546–53; Kettle, *Road to Intervention*, p. 209.

8 See the chapters on 'Die Ukraine in den internationalen Beziehungen', in Wolfram Dornik et al., *Die Ukraine zwischen Selbstbestimmung und*

Fremdherrschaft 1917–1922 (Graz: Leykam, 2011), pp. 345–464, in particular the essays by Bogdan Musial on Poland and the Soviet Union.

9   Stephen M. Horak, *The First Treaty of World War I: Ukraine's Treaty with the Central Powers of February 9, 1918* (East European Monographs 236: Boulder, 1988); Olek Fedyshyn, *Germany's Drive to the East and the Ukrainian Revolution, 1917–1918* (New Brunswick: Rutgers University Press, 1971), p.59; Clifford F. Wargelin, 'A Huge Price of Bread: The Treaty of Brest-Litovsk and the Break-up of Austria-Hungary, 1917–1918', *International History Review 19* (1997), pp. 757–88; Wolfdieter Bihl, *Österreich-Ungarn und die Friedensschlüsse von Brest-Litovsk* (Vienna: Böhlau, 1970), pp. 77–121; Lothar Höbelt, *'Stehen oder Fallen?' Österreichische Politik im Ersten Weltkrieg* (Vienna: Böhlau, 2015), pp. 206–21.

10   Robert Service, *Lenin: A Biography* (London: Macmillan, 2004), pp. 338–42, 359; OHL, *Der Weltkrieg*, vol. 13, p. 365; Baumgart, *Ostpolitik*, p. 27.

11   Wolfgang Steglich (ed.), *Die Friedensversuche der kriegführenden Mächte im Sommer und Herbst 1917: Quellenkritische Untersuchungen, Akten und Vernehmungsprotokolle* (Stuttgart: Steiner, 1984), pp. 304, 366; see also the comment by Alexander Watson, *Ring of Steel: Germany and Austria-Hungary in World War I* (London: Penguin, 2015), p. 494: 'The bulk of the wealth lost by the Russian Empire was in Poland and Ukraine, lands to which Russia's rulers, regardless of ideological persuasion, had no moral claim.'

12   John E. O. Screen, *Mannerheim: The Finnish Years* (London: Hurst, 2000), pp. 2, 12–35; Wolfram Dornik and Peter Lieb, 'Die militärischen Operationen', in Dornik et al. (eds), *Ukraine*, pp. 203–48; Fritz Fischer, *Griff nach der Weltmacht: Die Kriegszielpolitik des kaiserlichen Deutschland* (Düsseldorf: Droste, 1961), pp. 611–13, 676–83, 811–22; *Der Weltkrieg*, vol. 13, p. 371.

13   Hannes Leidinger and Verena Moritz, *Gefangenschaft: Revolution, Heimkehr. Die Bedeutung der Kriegsgefangenenproblematik für die Geschichte des Kommunismus in Mittel- und Osteuropa 1917–1920* (Vienna: Böhlau, 2003); Reinhard Nachtigal, *Russland und seine österreichisch-ungarischen Kriegsgefangenen 1914–1918* (Remshalden: Greiner, 2003).

14   Josef Kalvoda, *The Genesis of Czechoslovakia* (East European Monographs 209: Boulder, 1986), pp. 172, 200, 310; Betty Miller Unterberger, *The US, Revolutionary Russia and the Rise of Czechoslovakia* (Chapel Hill: University of North Carolina Press, 1989), pp. 62, 136

15   Michael Kettle, *The Allies and the Russian Collapse, March 1917 to March 1918* (London: Routledge, 1981), pp. 222–8, 268; W. Bruce Lincoln, *Red Victory: A History of the Russian Civil War* (New York: Simon & Schuster, 1989), pp. 168, 187; Michael J. Carley, 'The Origins of the French Intervention in the Russian Civil War, Jan. – May 1918: A Reappraisal,' *Journal of Modern History* 48 (1976), pp. 413–39.

16 Lincoln, *Red Victory*, p. 187; Kettle, *Road to Intervention*, pp. 93, 112, 133, 152, 172.

17 See the brilliant synthesis by Ewan Mawdsley, *The Russian Civil War* (Edinburgh: Birlinn, 2nd ed. 2008), pp. 64, 75, 90–3; Karel Pichlik, *Boumir Klipa & Jitka Zabloudilova, Ceskoslovensti legionari (1914–1920)* (Prague: Mlada Fronta, 1996), pp. 170–92; Leidinger and Moritz, *Gefangenschaft*, pp. 365, 374; *Der Weltkrieg*, vol. 13, pp. 390–3.

18 Baumgart, *Ostpolitik*, pp. 127, 187, 291 (20 August 1918), 319 (9 September 1918); Kettle, *Road to Intervention*, p. 126; Manfred Nebelin, *Ludendorff* (Munich: Siedler, 2010), pp. 390 f.; Mawdsley, *Russian Civil War*, pp. 23, 28, 120–35.

19 Edward J. Erickson, *Ordered to Die: A History of the Ottoman Army in the First World War* (Westport: Greenwood, 2001), pp. 182–91; Wolfdieter Bihl, *Die Kaukasus-Politik der Mittelmächte, Teil II: Die Zeit der versuchten kaukasischen Staatlichkeit (1917–1918)* (Vienna: Böhlau, 1992), pp. 106 f., 123, 161 f., 204; Sir George Franckenstein, *Facts and Features of My Life: The Austrian Minister to the Court of St. James, 1920–1938* (London: Cassell, 1939), pp. 192–209; Kettle, *Road to Intervention*, pp. 205, 297, 311, 370 f.

20 The classic account is: James W. Morley, *The Japanese Thrust into Siberia* (New York: Columbia University Press, 1954); Paul E. Dunscomb, *Japan's Siberian Intervention, 1918–1922* (Lanham: Lexington Books, 2011) adds a bit on the domestic background; Eugene Trani, 'Woodrow Wilson and the Decision to Intervene in Russia: A Reconsideration', *Journal of Modern History* 48 (1976), pp. 440–61; Kettle, *Road to Intervention*, pp. 10, 78, 233, 247, 287 f., 323, 356.

21 Martin Müller, *Vernichtungsgedanke und Koalitionskriegführung: Das Deutsche Reich und Österreich-Ungarn in der Offensive 1917/1918* (Graz: Stocker, 2003).

22 See the volume of statistics by Helmut Rumpler and Anatol Schmid-Kowarzik (eds), *Weltkriegsstatistik Österreich-Ungarns 1914–1918: Bevölkerungsbewegung, Kriegstote, Kriegswirtschaft* (Die Habsburgermonarchie 1848–1918, vol. XI/2, Vienna: Akademie der Wissenschaften, 2014), p. 165. The Austro-Hungarian Army officially counted 66 infantry divisions in mid-1918. Dismounted cavalry divisions and independent brigades brought the fighting total to something between 75 and 80. Seven infantry divisions and six cavalry divisions had been withdrawn from the East and sent to the Italian front.

23 Haus-, Hof- und Staatsarchiv Wien (HHStA), Friedrich von Wieser diary, 15 June 1918.

24 John Gooch, *The Italian Army and the First World War* (Cambridge: Cambridge University Press, 2014), pp. 261, 280–8; Mark Thompson, *The White War: Life and Death on the Italian Front 1915–1919* (London: Faber

& Faber 2008), pp. 344–7; Peter Fiala, *Die letzte Offensive Österreich-Ungarns. Führungsprobleme und Führerverantwortlichkeit bei der öst.-ung. Offensive in Venetien, Juni 1918* (Boppard: Boldt, 1967); Fortunato Minniti, *Il Piave* (Bologna: Mulino, 2000); Kriegsarchiv (ed.), *Österreich-Ungarns letzter Krieg*, vol. VII (Vienna: Verlag der Militärwissenschaftlichen Mitteilungen, 1937), p. 359; Polatschek, *Truppen an der Westfront*, pp. 49 f.

25 HHStA, Berchtold Papers 5, diary 10 Sept. 1918; Polatschek, *Truppen an der Westfront*, pp. 66, 72, 91, 101 f.; Nebelin, *Ludendorff*, pp. 429–31.

26 David Dutton, *The Politics of Diplomacy: Britain and France in the Balkans in the First World War* (London: Tauris, 1998), p 187.

27 Glenn Torrey, *The Romanian Battlefront in World War I* (Lawrence: University Press of Kansas, 2011), pp. 263–92; Elke Bornemann, *Der Frieden von Bukarest* (Frankfurt/M.: Lang, 1978); Lisa Mayerhofer, *Zwischen Freund und Feind. Deutsche Besatzung in Rumänien 1916–1918* (Munich: Meidenbauer, 2010).

28 Gerard Fassy, *Le Commandement français en Orient (octobre 1915–novembre 1918)* (Paris: Economica, 2003), pp. 354–408.

29 Gooch, *Italian Army*, p. 263; Thompson, *White War*, p. 355.

30 Gooch, *Italian Army*, p. 247, pp. 288–97; Thompson, *White War*, p. 358; Bruno Wagner, *Der Waffenstillstand von Villa Giusti 3. November 1918* (unpublished PhD Thesis, Vienna, 1970), pp. 136, 152, 227, 235 f.

31 Kalvoda, *Genesis of Czechoslovakia*, p. 505; Daina Bleiere et al., *History of Latvia: The 20th Century* (Riga: Jumava 2006), pp. 130–6; Screen, *Mannerheim*, pp. 60–2; Mawdsley, *Russian Civil War*, pp. 160, 176 f., 197, 230 f. The Red Army expanded from less than 200,000 men in the spring of 1918 to 700,000 at the end of the year and three million at the end of 1919 (ibid., pp. 39, 86, 250).

Chapter 7

1 *Hansard*, 5th series [1917], vol. C., col. 2211.

2 Both sources cited in Malcolm Brown, *Tommy Goes to War* (London: J.M. Dent & Sons, 1978), p. 256.

3 Archibald Wavell, *Allenby: A Study in Greatness* (London: George G. Harrap, 1940), p. 186; John Grigg, *Lloyd George: War Leader* (London: Allen Lane, 2002), p. 150.

4 Basil Liddell Hart, *Strategy* (London: Faber & Faber Ltd., 1954), p. 179.

5 Hew Strachan, *The First World War in Africa* (Oxford: Oxford University Press, 2004).

6 Brigadier General J. H. V. Crowe, *General Smuts' Campaign in East Africa* (London: John Murray, 1918).

7   Edward Paice, *Tip and Run: The Untold Tragedy of the Great War in Africa* (London: Phoenix, 2008).

8   The logistical cost and commitment in shipping was the largest burden on the British. See Geoffrey Hodges, *The Carrier Corps: Military Labour in the East African Campaign, 1914–1918* (London: Greenwood Press, 1986).

9   S. A. Cohen, *British Policy in Mesopotamia, 1903–1914* (London: Ithaca, 1976; republished 2008), p. 308.

10 Robert Johnson, *Spying for Empire: The Great Game in Central and South Asia, 1757–1947* (London: Greenhill, 2006), pp. 218–22; Keith Neilson, '"For Diplomatic, Economic, Strategic and Telegraphic Reasons": British Imperial Defence, the Middle East and India, 1914–1918', in G. Kennedy and K. Nielson (eds), *Far Flung Lines: Essays on Imperial Defence in Honour of Donald Mackenzie Schurman* (London: Routledge, 1996), pp. 103–23.

11 C. E. Callwell, *Field Marshal Sir Henry Wilson: His Life and Diaries*, vol. II (London: Cassell, 1927), pp. 147–8.

12 Kaushik Roy, 'The Army in India in Mesopotamia from 1916 to 1918: Tactics, Technology and Logistics Reconsidered', in I. W. F. Beckett, *1917: Beyond the Western Front* (Leiden and Boston: Brill, 2009), pp. 131–58.

13 This is also the verdict of E. A. Cohen and J. Gooch, *Military Misfortunes: The Anatomy of Failure in War* (London: Macmillan, 1990), pp. 156–63.

14 George Barrow, *The Life of General Sir Charles Carmichael Monro* (London: Hutchinson, 1931), p. 132.

15 F. J. Moberly, *The Campaign in Mesopotamia*, vol. III (London: HMSO, 1924–7), pp. 79, 86–90; William Robertson, *Soldiers and Statesmen, 1914–1918*, vol. II (London: Cassell, 1926), pp. 79, 227; Paul Guinn, *British Strategy and Politics, 1914–1918* (Oxford: Clarendon Press, 1965), p. 219.

16 Guinn, *British Strategy and Politics*, pp. 113–14.

17 Moberly, *Campaign in Mesopotamia*, vol. III, pp. 204–11.

18 Guinn, *British Strategy and Politics*, p. 157; Robertson, *Soldiers and Statesmen*, vol. II, p. 74.

19 Moberly, *Campaign in Mesopotamia*, vol. III, pp. 125–6, 159, 199; Robertson, *Soldiers and Statesmen*, vol. II, p.77; Guinn, *British Strategy and Politics*, p. 200.

20 Eugene Rogan, *Fall of the Ottomans* (New York: Basic Books, 2015), p. 323.

21 Rob Johnson, *The Great War and the Middle East* (Oxford: Oxford University Press, 2016), pp. 253–4; James Barr, *A Line in the Sand: Britain, France and the Struggle that Shaped the Middle East* (London: Simon and Schuster, 2011), pp. 70–3, 89–92.

22 Major General Dunsterville, the inspiration for Kipling's 'Stalky and Co', was tasked to secure northern Persia and Baku on the Caspian with a brigade known as 'Dunsterforce'. L. C. Dunsterville, *The Adventures of Dunsterforce* (London: E. Arnold, 1920).

23 In general terms, for every battle death, there were just over two deaths through disease, with a higher proportion on the Ottoman side. An estimated 800,000 Allied troops were listed sick at some point in the campaign, although the majority returned to duty. It is thought that almost 90,000 died. Ottoman losses are unknown precisely but estimates are some 60,000 deaths from combat and 325,000 casualties overall.

24 Lieutenant General Sir George McMunn and Captain Cyril Falls, *Military Operations, Egypt and Palestine*, vol. I (London: HMSO, 1927–9), pp. 355, 356.

25 Ibid., p. 357.

26 Matthew Hughes (ed.), *Allenby in Palestine* (Stroud: Sutton, 2004), p. 8.

27 Robertson to Allenby, 1 August 1917, 8/1/67, Robertson Papers, Liddell Hart Centre for Military Archives, London.

28 Cyril Falls and A. F. Becke, *Military Operations, Egypt and Palestine*, vol. II (London: HMSO, 1930), p. 50.

29 Ibid., p. 56.

30 Ibid., p. 59.

31 Ibid., pp. 66–9.

32 Ibid., p. 64.

33 Ibid., pp. 95–101.

34 Sir William Robertson, *Future Operations in Palestine*, 26 December 1917, CAB/24/37/12, The National Archives.

35 Cited in Grigg, *Lloyd George*, p. 344.

36 Otto Liman von Sanders, *Five Years in Turkey* (Annapolis: US Naval Institute Press, 1927), p. 211.

37 Falls and Becke, *Military Operations, Egypt and Palestine*, vol. II, p. 337.

38 Ibid., p. 346.

39 T. E. Lawrence, XXXVIII, 'The Destruction of the Fourth Army', *Arab Bulletin* No. 106, 22 October 1918, available at http://www.telstudies.org/writings/works/articles_essays/1918_destruction_of_the_fourth_army.shtml (Accessed 18 July 2017).

40 T. E. Lawrence, XXXVIII, 'The Destruction of Fourth Army', dated 22 October 1918, originally in T. E. Lawrence, *Secret Despatches from Arabia* [compiled by his brother] (London: Golden Cockrell, 1939) and reproduced in Malcolm Brown (ed.), *T. E. Lawrence in War and Peace* (London: Greenhill, 2005), pp. 171–2. This source does not contain the whole document (unlike the source in footnote 38), but it provides some useful additional context.

41 Wilson to Allenby, 7 December 1918, Wilson Papers, Imperial War Museum, HHW2/33B/1.

42 This refers to Général de Division Franchet D'Esperay, the French commander in the Balkans.

Chapter 8

1 Address by Admiral Sir David Beatty on board HMS *Lion*, 24 November 1918, cited in B. McL. Ranft (ed.), *The Beatty Papers. Selections from the Private and Official Correspondence of Admiral of the Fleet Earl Beatty*, vol. I, *1902–1918* (Aldershot: Scholar Press, 1989), p. 570.

2 Beatty memo on 'The Situation in the North Sea', 29 December 1917, cited in Paul Halpern, *A Naval History of World War I* (London: UCL Press, 1994), p. 404.

3 See the Admiralty memos of 29 March 1918 and 5 April 1918, in Gerhard Granier (ed.), *Die deutsche Seekriegsleitung im Ersten Weltkrieg*, vol. 2 (Koblenz: Bundesarchiv, 2000), pp. 158–9, 162–4.

4 Cited in Halpern, *Naval History*, p. 418.

5 All figures from: Joachim Schröder, *Die U-Boote des Kaisers: Die Geschichte des deutschen U-Boot-Krieges gegen Großbritannien im Ersten Weltkrieg* (Lauf an der Pegnitz: Europaforum-Verlag, 2000), p. 430.

6 Ibid., p. 429.

7 Arthur J. Marder, *From the Dreadnought to Scapa Flow*, vol. V, *1918–1919: Victory and Aftermath* (New York, Toronto: Oxford University Press, 1970), pp. 12–13, 23–30.

8 Cited in Halpern, *Naval History*, p. 449.

Chapter 9

1 An example of one of these artillery direction code sheets from 1917 is found in the Latvian National Military Museum archives.

2 The new artillery methods of 1917–18 are described in Nick Lloyd, *Hundred Days: The End of the Great War* (London: Penguin, 2016), pp. 34–6. For a very detailed explanation of the typical 1918 fire plans and methods see David Zabecki, *Steel Wind: Colonel Georg Bruchmüller and the Birth of Modern Artillery* (Westport: Praeger, 1994).

3 Gen der Kavallerie Ernst von Hoeppner, *Deutschlands Krieg in der Luft* (Leipzig: Koehler and Amelang, 1921) provides a good overview of the German Air Service on all fronts. On German air photography see p. 108.

4 The operational planning maps for the September 1917 German attack still exist and the maps show every Russian position on the Riga front carefully mapped by the German Air Service. Latvian National Military Museum. Files: 2-174-DK_p; 2-175-DK_p; 2-174-DK_p2-179-DK_p; 2-177-

DK_p; 2-184-DK_p; 2-189-DK_p; 2-241-DK_p. On the German fire plan, which included assignments for the air squadrons, see Georg Bruchmüller, *Die Artillerie beim Angriff in Stellungskrieg* (Berlin: Verlag Offene Worte, 1926) pp. 54–71.

5 Zabecki, *Steel Wind*, pp. 63–6.

6 A good example of the operational doctrine is: Kommandierende General der Luftstreitkräfte, *Weisungen für den Einsatz und die Verwendung von Fliegerverbänden innerhalb einer Armee* (Instructions on the Mission and Utilization of Flying Units Within an Army), May 1917. For translated text see James Corum and Richard Muller, *The Luftwaffe's Way of War* (Baltimore: Nautical and Aviation Press, 1998) pp. 48–65.

7 John Buckeley, *Air Power in the Age of Total War* (Bloomington: Indiana University Press, 1999), pp. 63–4.

8 A translation of this manual is found in H. A. Jones, *The War in the Air*, vol. IV (Oxford: Clarendon Press, 1934), Appendix: Chief of Staff, German Field Army, 'Employment of Battle Flights' (20 February 1917).

9 Ibid. para. 2.

10 Commanding General Armies of the North and Northeast, *Instruction sur l'action offensive des grandes unités dans la bataille* (31 October 1917).

11 *Ausbildungsplan der Infanteriekommandos* (January 1918), in Bundesarchiv/ Militärarchiv BA/MA PH 17/98.

12 See Kommandierender General der Luftstreitkräfte, *Hinweise für die Führung einer Fliegerabteilung in der Angriffschlacht und im Bewegungkrieg* (10 February 1918). This pamphlet gives advice on how to organize the fighter and ground attack groups for close air support during different phases of the ground battle.

13 Richard Hallion, *Strike from the Sky* (Washington: Smithsonian Institution Press, 1989), p. 20.

14 Chief of Staff, German Field Army, 1917 'Employment of Battle Flights', para. 27.

15 Charles Christienne and Pierre Lissarague, *A History of French Military Aviation* (Washington: Smithsonian, 1986), pp. 125–30.

16 Kenneth Munson, *Aircraft of World War I* (Garden City: Arco Publishing,1977), pp. 93–4 and Richard Hallion, *Rise of the Fighter Aircraft 1914–1918* (Annapolis: Nautical and Aviation Press, 1984), p. 117. Brigadier General William Mitchell, *Memoirs of World War I* (New York: Random House, 1960 reprint of 1926 ed.), p. 306.

17 John Morrow, *The Great War in the Air* (Washington: Smithsonian, 1993) pp. 298–9.

18 Morrow, *Great War in the Air*, p. 371.

19 Ibid.

20 Christienne and Lissarague, *French Military Aviation*, p. 157.

21 For a good overview of the German aircraft industry see Terry Treadwell and Aslan Wood, *German Fighter Aces of World War I* (Gloucestershire: Tempus, 2003).

22 From 1 August to 1 November the RAF lost 2,692 planes at the front, and received 2,692 planes from industry. See Morrow, *The Great War in the Air*, p. 312.

23 Zabecki, *Steel Wind*, pp. 116–18.

24 Ibid.

25 Reichsarchiv, Abt. B., Ref., *Luftstreitkräfte Study of 1918 Air War* (2 April 1926), in BA/MA 2/2195, p. 5.

26 Ibid.

27 P. J. Daybell, 'The Marne Retreat of 1918: The Last Battle of the Royal Flying Corps', *Air Power Review* 1:1 (1998), pp. 86–101.

28 Brereton Greenhous, 'Evolution of a Close-Ground Support Role for Aircraft in World War I', in *Military Affairs* (February 1975), pp. 26–7.

29 Reichsarchiv Study of April 1926, in Bundesarchiv/Militärarchiv BA/MA RH 2/2195, pp. 12–14.

30 H. A. Jones, *The War in the Air*, vol. V (Oxford: Clarendon Press, 1935), pp. 424–7.

31 Christienne and Lissarague, *French Military Aviation*, pp. 290–1.

32 See James S. Corum, 'Starting from Scratch: The Luftstreitkräfte Builds a Bomber Doctrine, 1914–1918', *Air Power Review* 6:1 (Spring 2003), pp. 61–78 and William Fischer, *The Development of Military Night Aviation to 1919* (Maxwell AFB: Air University Press, 1998), pp. 73–7, 84.

33 Ibid.

34 Morrow, *Great War in the Air*, p. 310.

35 *Revue De L'Aeronautique Militaire*, July/August (1925).

36 Alistair McCluskey, *Amiens 1918: The Black Day of the German Army* (Oxford: Osprey, 2008), p. 18.

37 For a good overview of the RAF at Amiens see Alfred Price, 'The Battle of Amiens 8–11 August 1918', *Air Power Review* 4:4 (Winter 2001), pp. 118–34.

38 Oberstleutnant Baron von Loewenstern, 'Die Luftstreitkräfte in der Abwehrschlacht zwischen Somme and Oise vom 8 bis 12 August 1918', in *Militär-Wochenblatt*, No. 6, 1938.

39 Price, 'The Battle of Amiens', p. 131.

40 John Terraine, *White Heat* (London: Sidgwick and Jackson, 1982), p. 305.

41 James S. Corum, *The Luftwaffe: Creating the Operational Air War 1918–1940* (Lawrence: University Press of Kansas, 1997), pp. 42–3.

42 Ibid., p. 91.

43 David Bonk, *St. Mihiel 1918* (Oxford: Osprey, 2011), p. 90.

44 Robert Ferrell, *America's Deadliest Battle: Meuse–Argonne, 1918* (Lawrence: University Press of Kansas, 2007), p. 44.

45 Ibid., pp. 45–6, 69, 122–24.

46 Luftstreitkräfte Staff, 'Tätigkeit der Amerikanischen Fliegerverbände in Zusammenhang mit den Operationen bei St. Mihiel September 1918', Bundesarchiv/Militärarchiv BA/MA PH 17/I-55.

47 Morrow, *Great War in the Air*, p. 302.

48 Ibid., p. 303.

49 Ibid., pp. 316–17.

Chapter 10

1 See, for example, Peter Hart, *1918: A Very British Victory* (London: Weidenfeld & Nicolson, 2008) and David Stevenson, *With our Backs to the Wall: Victory and Defeat in 1918* (London: Allen Lane, 2011). Gary Sheffield's *Forgotten Victory: The First World War Myths and Realities* (London: Headline, 2001), although wider in scope, devotes a weighty chapter to '1918 Victory on the Western Front'. Both Hart and Sheffield focus predominantly on the achievements of the BEF; those of the French and the US Armies receive far less attention. Surprisingly, such eminent British military historians accord scant importance to the US-led Meuse–Argonne offensive (26 September–11 November 1918).

2 For reasons of limited space, in this chapter examples are only given from the British, French, and German armies.

3 Lieutenant General the Earl of Cavan commanded the first British deployment to Italy (XIV Corps, comprising the 23rd and 41st divisions), which was quickly followed by XI Corps (5th, 7th, and 48th divisions) under Lieutenant General Sir Richard Haking. With the deployment of the latter corps, General Sir Herbert Plumer departed the Western Front on 10 November 1917 to assume overall command of British forces in Italy. His Second Army in Flanders was renamed Fourth Army on 20 December 1917, commanded by General Sir Herbert Rawlinson.

4 Plumer and his staff returned to the Western Front on 10 March 1918. Headquarters Second Army was reactivated on 13 March 1918 under Plumer's command.

5 See Lieutenant Colonel Paolo Capanni, 'Italy', in Colonel John Wilson (ed.), *The First World War Battlefield Guide*, vol. 2, *The Forgotten Fronts*, 1st ed. (Andover: [British] Army Headquarters, November 2016), pp. 60–4. The two British divisions returned were the 41st and the 5th, which completed their moves back in France on 13 and 27 March 1918, respectively. The 41st, placed in GHQ reserve prior to 21 March, was subsequently committed to IV Corps of Byng's Third Army.

6 Developed from Brigadier General Sir James E. Edmonds, *History of the Great War: Military Operations France and Belgium, 1918*, vol. II, *March–April: Continuation of the German Offensives* (London: Macmillan, 1937), p. 470.

7 Ibid.

8 Ibid.

9 Described by Mungo Melvin, *Sevastopol's Wars: Crimea from Potemkin to Putin* (Oxford: Osprey, 2017), pp. 367–8.

10 General Erich Ludendorff, *My War Memories 1914–1918* (London: Hutchinson, 1919), p. 622.

11 For details of this largely unknown Crimean campaign, see Melvin, *Sevastopol's Wars*, pp. 369–77.

12 Ludendorff, *War Memories*, p. 625.

13 Brigadier General Sir James E. Edmonds, *History of the Great War: Military Operations France and Belgium, 1918*, vol. I, *The German March Offensive and its Preliminaries* (London: Macmillan, 1935), p. 337.

14 Ibid., p.549 and Edmonds, *History of the Great War*, vol. II, p. 486.

15 B. H. Liddell Hart, *Foch: The Man of Orleans* (London: Eyre and Spottiswoode, 1931), p. 280.

16 The battle for Villers-Bretonneux on 4 April 1918 involved the Second Army's 9th Bavarian Reserve Division, operating on the right (northern) flank of Eighteenth Army. A second battle, which took place on 24–27 April, a supporting attack to Operation *Georgette*, was also a Second Army action. This battle involved the first tank vs. tank engagement.

17 Elizabeth Greenhalgh, *Foch in Command: The Forging of a First World War General* (Cambridge: Cambridge University Press, 2011), pp. 300–7.

18 General Sir Hubert Gough, *The Fifth Army* (London: Hodder and Stoughton, 1931), p. 283.

19 Colonel T. Bentley Mott (trans.), *The Memoirs of Marshal Foch* (London: William Heinemann, 1931), p. 305.

20 Jonathan Bailey, 'The First World War: A Revolution in Military Affairs (RMA) and the Birth of the Modern Style of Warfare', in Major General Mungo Melvin (ed.), *The First World War Battlefield Guide*, vol. 1, *The Western Front*, 2nd ed. (Andover: [British] Army Headquarters, June 2015), p. 187.

21 Gary Sheffield and Peter Gray (eds), *Changing War: The British Army, the Hundred Days Campaign and the Birth of the Royal Air Force, 1918* (London: Bloomsbury, 2013).

22 Captain Wilfred Miles, *History of the Great War. Military Operations France and Belgium 1917, The Battle of Cambrai* (London: HMSO, 1948), p. 14.

23 Ibid.

24 J. B. A. Bailey, *Field Artillery and Firepower* (Oxford: The Military Press, 1989), p. 142, f. 35.

25 *G.H.Q. Memorandum on Defensive Measures* issued with O.A.D. 291/29 dated 14 December 1917. Reprinted as Appendix 6 of Edmonds, *History of the Great War* (1935), p. 22.

26 Ibid., p. 23.

27 SS 135 (January 1918) contained less than two pages (7–8) on defensive operations. It warned presciently, however, that 'attackers will seek ... to demoralize defenders' by 'overwhelming artillery fire, trench mortars, gas'; and by 'a surprise attack', probably consisting of 'a short bombardment, followed up by masses of troops pushed forward regardless of loss'.

28 The final paragraph of GHQ's *Memorandum* of 14 December 1917 drew particular attention to official British translations (SS 561 and SS 621) of two German documents: *The Principles of Command in the Defensive Battle in Position Warfare* dated 1 March 1917, which had absorbed the German learning from the battles of Verdun and the Somme the previous year; and *General Principles of the Construction of Field Positions*, 3rd ed., dated 15 August 1917. GHQ advised that 'the principles laid down by [the enemy] are thoroughly sound and should be carefully studied'.

29 Williamson Murray, 'Armored Warfare: The British, French, and German Experiences', in Williamson Murray and Allan R. Millett, *Military Intervention in the Interwar Period* (Cambridge: Cambridge University Press, 1996), p. 20. Significantly, Murray fails to mention the evolution of the British Field Service Regulations during the period 1920–35.

30 For an extreme version of this view, see John Laffin, *British Butchers and Bunglers of World War One* (Stroud: Sutton Publishing, 1988).

31 See, for example, Paddy Griffith, *Battle Tactics of the Western Front: The British Army's Art of Attack 1916–18* (New Haven & London: Yale University Press, 1994), Chapter 10, 'Doctrine and Training'.

32 Gary Sheffield and John Bourne (eds), *Douglas Haig. War Diaries and Letters 1914–1918* (London: Weidenfeld & Nicolson, 2005), p. 390.

33 Strictly speaking this represented Mangin's *third* chance as he had also been sacked as a divisional commander in 1916 for refusing to undertake an attack ordered by his corps commander, declaring 'it was for the gallery'.

34 John Terraine, *The Smoke and the Fire: Myths and Anti-Myths of War 1861–1945* (London: Sidgwick & Jackson, 1980), p. 184, compares Mangin favourably to Pétain: 'he was [his] exact opposite ... always aggressive, eager to attack. He was also highly professional, and in 1918 the combination of these qualities made the Tenth Army the most effective of the French Order of Battle'.

35 Significantly, Hubert Essame devotes an entire chapter of his *The Battle for Europe 1918* (New York: Charles Scribner's Sons, 1972) to Mangin, and a following one to the 'Eighteenth of July' – the counter-stroke at the Marne

(Chapters 6 and 7, respectively). Furthermore, the British Ministry of Defence deemed the French counterstroke at the Marne as worthy of detailed examination in the early 1980s. It was one of a number of historical studies undertaken to assist the development of the defensive battle then being planned by 1st (British) Corps of NATO's Northern Army Group (NORTHAG). See Correlli Barnett, 'A Successful Counter-Stroke: 18 July 1918', in Anthony Trythall (ed.), *Old Battles and New Defences: Can We Learn from Military History?* (London: Brassey's, 1986), p. 33.

36 *Les Armées Françaises dans La Grande Guerre* (Paris: Service Historique de l'État Major de l'Armée, 1923), Tome VII, vol. 1, Annexe 9, p. 16.

37 I am grateful to Dr Tim Gale for providing me with a detailed description of Pétain's Directive No. 5, together with permission to quote from his translated excerpts and advice on other matters.

38 From data given by Barnett ('A Successful Counter-Stroke', p. 43), Tenth Army comprised 16 infantry divisions (including two US), three cavalry divisions, 1,500 hundred guns, and 346 tanks, supported by 581 aircraft. Sixth Army contained eight infantry divisions (two US), nearly 600 guns, and 147 tanks, with 562 aircraft. Each of the four US divisions involved was double the size of their French and German counterparts. This impressive Allied grouping faced ten German divisions in the line and a further six in support, but no tanks.

39 In his memoirs (*Memoirs of Marshal Foch*, trans. Bentley Mott, p. 412), Foch noted tactfully of Pétain: 'Although he shared my confidence, the Commander-in-Chief of the French Armies, in more direct contact with the events on the battlefield, was especially preoccupied by the German advance south of the Marne in the direction of Epernay, and to cope with it, he contemplated drawing on the troops designated for the counter-attack and thereby postponing its preparation.'

40 Barnett, 'A Successful Counter-Stroke', p. 48.

41 Ludendorff, *War Memories*, p. 677. Ludendorff contradicted himself here for on the previous page (p. 676), he observed that the 'six American divisions that had taken part in the battle had suffered particularly severely without achieving any success'.

42 'The Advance to Victory' is the sub-title to Volume V of Brigadier General Sir James E. Edmonds' *History of the Great War*.

43 Dwight D. Eisenhower, *Crusade in Europe* (London: William Heinemann, 1948), p. 489. Chapter 23, 'Operation "Study"', is well worth reading today.

44 By way of contrast, Montgomery's 21st Army Group of 1944–45 was about a third of the size of the BEF of 1917–18. Yet there was an important difference between the two wars: the Royal Air Force of World War II was greatly stronger in both size and effect. There was simply not enough manpower and equipment available to furnish Montgomery with

the additional 12 divisions he would have required to fight the campaign in North-west Europe in a manner he desired.

45 The Kirke Report, PRO WO33/1297, *Report of the Committee on the Lessons of the Great War* (London: War Office, October 1932), reproduced in Colonel (Ret'd) Mike Crawshaw OBE (ed.), *The British Army Review*, Special Edition (April 2001), p. 37.

46 Robert Allan Doughty, *The Seeds of Disaster: The Development of French Army Doctrine, 1919–1939* (Hamden: Archon Books, 1985), p. 90.

SELECT BIBLIOGRAPHY

Chapter 1

Boff, Jonathan, *Winning and Losing on the Western Front: The British Third Army and the Defeat of Germany in 1918* (Cambridge: Cambridge University Press, 2012)

Chickering, Roger and Stig Förster (eds), *Great War, Total War: Combat and Mobilization on the Western Front, 1914–1918* (Cambridge: Cambridge University Press, 2000)

Duppler, Jörg and Gerhard P. Groß (eds), *Kriegsende 1918: Ereignis, Wirkung, Nachwirkung* (Munich: Oldenbourg, 1999)

Gerwarth, Robert, *The Vanquished: Why the First World War Failed to End, 1917–1923* (London: Allan Lane, 2016)

Herwig, Holger, *The First World War: Germany and Austria-Hungary 1914–1918* (London: Bloomsbury, second edition 2014)

Horne, John (ed.), *A Companion to World War I* (Oxford: Blackwell, 2012)

Ludendorff, Erich, *My War Memories 1914–1918*, vol. II (London: Hutchinson, 1920)

Kitchen, Martin, *The German Offensives of 1918* (Stroud: Tempus, 2001)

Melvin, Mungo (ed.), *The First World War Battlefield Guide*, vol. I, *The Western Front* (Andover: [British] Army Headquarters, second edition 2015)

Reichsarchiv, *Der Weltkrieg 1914–18*, vol. XIV, *Die Kriegführung an der Westfront im Jahre 1918* (Berlin: Mittler und Sohn, 1944)

Stevenson, David, *With our Backs to the Wall: Victory and Defeat in 1918* (London: Penguin, 2012)

Weber, Thomas, *Hitler: The Making of a Nazi* (New York: Basic Books, 2017)

Chapter 2

Barnett, Correlli, *The Swordbearers: Studies in Supreme Command in the First World War* (London: Eyre & Spottiswoode, 1963)

285

Boff, Jonathan, *Crown Prince Rupprecht and Germany's War on the Western Front* (Oxford: Oxford University Press, 2018)

Görlitz, Walter, *History of the German General Staff, 1657–1945* (New York: Praeger, 1953)

Great Britain, War Office General Staff, *Handbook of the German Army in the War, April 1918* (London: Arms & Armour Press, reprint 1977)

Groß, Gerhard, *The Myth and Reality of German Warfare: Operational Thinking from Moltke the Elder to Heusinger* (Lexington: University Press of Kentucky, 2016)

Gudmundsson, Bruce I., *Stormtroop Tactics: Innovation in the German Army, 1914–1918* (New York: Praeger, 1989)

Ludendorff, General Erich, *My War Memories, 1914–1918*, 2 vols (London: Hutchinson, 1920)

Ludendorff, General Erich, *Urkunden der Obersten Heeresleitung über ihre Tätigkeit 1916/18* (Berlin: Mittler und Sohn, 1921)

Millotat, Christian O. E., *Understanding the Prussian-German General Staff System* (Carlisle, PA: Army War College, 1992)

Oberkommando des Heeres, *Der Weltkrieg 1914 bis 1918*, vol. 12, *Die Kriegsführung im Frühjahr 1917* (Berlin: Mittler und Sohn, 1939)

Oberkommando des Heeres, *Der Weltkrieg 1914 bis 1918*, vol. 13, *Die Kriegsführung im Sommer und Herbst 1917* (Berlin: Mittler und Sohn, 1942)

Oberkommando des Heeres, *Der Weltkrieg 1914 bis 1918*, vol. 14, *Die Kriegsführung an der Westfront im Jahre 1918* (Berlin: Mittler und Sohn, 1944)

Rupprecht, Kronprinz von Bayern, *In Treue Fest: Mein Kriegstagebuch*, 3 vols (Munich: Deutscher National Verlag, 1929)

Showalter, Dennis, *Instrument of War: The German Army 1914–18* (Oxford: Osprey Publishing, 2016)

Wilhelm II, *The Kaiser's Memoirs 1888–1918* (London: Harper Brothers, 1922)

Zabecki, David T., *Steel Wind: Colonel Georg Bruchmüller and the Birth of Modern Artillery* (Wesport: Praeger, 1994)

Zabecki, David T., *The German 1918 Offensives: A Case Study in the Operational Level of War* (London: Routledge, 2006)

Zabecki, David T., *Chief of Staff: The Principal Officers Behind History's Great Commanders*, vol. I, *Napoleonic Wars to World War I* (Annapolis: US Naval Institute Press, 2008)

Zabecki, David T. and Dieter Biedekarken (eds and trans.), *Lossberg's War: The Memoirs of a World War I German Chief of Staff* (Lexington: University Press of Kentucky, 2017)

Chapter 3

The main archives for the records of the French Army during the war are held at the Service Historique de la Défense at Château de Vincennes near Paris. In the early 1920s, the French General Staff began publishing an official history of the war. This series would eventually number over 100 volumes in eight tomes. These official history volumes included copies of original documents and maps. These volumes are an invaluable resource for anyone researching the activities of the French Army during the war. Imprimerie Nationale, *Les Armées Françaises dans la Grande Guerre* (Paris, 1922–39).

Becker, Jean-Jacques, *The Great War and the French People* (Oxford: Berg, 1985)

Clayton, Anthony, *Paths of Glory: the French Army 1914–18* (London: Cassell, 2003)

Doughty, Robert, *Pyrrhic Victory: French Strategy and Operations in the Great War* (Harvard: Harvard University Press, 2005)

French General Staff, *French Trench Warfare 1917–1918: A Reference Manual* (English translation, Imperial War Museum, 2009)

Greenhalgh, Elizabeth, *Foch in Command: The Forging of a First World War General* (Cambridge: Cambridge University Press, 2011)

Greenhalgh, Elizabeth, *The French Army and the First World War* (Cambridge: Cambridge University Press, 2014)

McPhail, Helen, *The Long Silence: the Tragedy of Occupied France in World War 1* (London: I.B. Tauris, 2014)

Murphy, David, *Breaking Point of the French Army: the Nivelle Offensive of 1917* (Barnsley: Pen & Sword, 2015)

Pierrefeu, Jean de, *French Headquarters, 1915–1918* (Paris, n.d.[1923?], General Books reprint, London)

Porch, Douglas, *The French Secret Services: a History of French Intelligence From the Dreyfus Affair to the Gulf War* (New York: Farrar, Straus & Giroux, 1995)

Sumner, Ian, *French Poilu 1914–18* (Oxford: Osprey, 2009)

Sumner, Ian, *They Shall Not Pass: the French Army on the Western Front, 1914–1918* (Barnsley: Pen & Sword, 2012)

Williams, Charles, *Pétain* (London: Little, Brown, 2005)

Zaloga, Steven J., *French Tanks of World War I* (Oxford: Osprey, 2010)

Chapter 4

Beach, Jim, *Haig's Intelligence: GHQ and the German Army, 1916–18* (Cambridge: Cambridge University Press, 2013)

Beckett, Ian, Timothy Bowman and Mark Connelly, *The British Army and the First World War* (Cambridge: Cambridge University Press, 2017)

Boff, Jonathan, *Winning and Losing on the Western Front: The British Third Army and the Defeat of Germany in 1918* (Cambridge: Cambridge University Press, 2012)

Boff, Jonathan, *Haig's Enemy: Crown Prince Rupprecht and Germany's War on the Western Front* (Oxford: Oxford University Press, 2018)

Fox, Aimée, *Learning to Fight: Military Innovation and Change in the British Army, 1914–1918* (Cambridge: Cambridge University Press, 2017)

Griffith, Paddy, *Battle Tactics of the Western Front: The British Army's Art of Attack 1916–18* (New Haven: Yale University Press, 1994)

Griffith, Paddy (ed.), *British Fighting Methods in the Great War* (London: Frank Cass, 1996)

Harris, J. P., *Sir Douglas Haig and the First World War* (Cambridge: Cambridge University Press, 2008)

Harris, J. P. with Niall Barr, *Amiens to the Armistice: The BEF in the Hundred Days Campaign, 8 August–11 November 1918* (London: Brassey's, 1998)

Lloyd, Nick, *Hundred Days: The End of the Great War* (London: Viking, 2013)

Philpott, William, *Bloody Victory: The Sacrifice on the Somme and the Making of the Twentieth Century* (London: Little, Brown, 2009)

Prior, Robin and Trevor Wilson, *Command on the Western Front: The Military Career of Sir Henry Rawlinson* (Barnsley: Pen & Sword 2004 [1992])

Robbins, Simon, *British Generalship on the Western Front 1914–18: Defeat into Victory* (London: Frank Cass, 2005)

Samuels, Martin, *Command or Control? Command, Training and Tactics in the British and German Armies, 1888–1918* (London: Frank Cass, 1995)

Sheffield, Gary, *Forgotten Victory: The First World War: Myths and Realities* (London: Headline, 2001)

Sheffield, Gary, *The Chief: Douglas Haig and the British Army* (London: Aurum, 2011)

Simkins, Peter, *From the Somme to Victory: The British Army's Experience on the Western Front 1916–1918* (Barnsley: Pen & Sword, 2014)

Simpson, Andy, *Directing Operations: British Corps Command on the Western Front 1914–18* (Stroud: Spellmount, 2006)

Stevenson, David, *With Our Backs to the Wall: Victory and Defeat in 1918* (London: Allen Lane, 2011)

Travers, Tim, *How the War Was Won: Command and Technology in the British Army on the Western Front, 1917–1918* (London: Routledge, 1992)

Chapter 5

Coffman, Edward M., *The War to End All Wars: The American Experience in World War I* (New York: Oxford University Press, 1968)

Davenport, Matthew, *First Over There: The Attack On Cantigny, America's First Battle of World War I* (New York: Thomas Dunne Books, 2015)

Finnegan, Terrence J., *Delicate Affair on the Western Front: America Learns How to Fight a Modern War in the Woëvre Trenches* (Stroud: The History Press, 2015)

Grotelueschen, Mark Ethan, *The AEF Way of War: The American Army and Combat in World War I* (New York: Cambridge University Press, 2007)

Lengel, Edward G., *Thunder and Flames: Americans in the Crucible of Combat* (Lawrence: University Press of Kansas, 2015)

Palmer, Frederick, *John J. Pershing, General of the Armies: A Biography* (Harrisburg: Military Service Publishing Company, 1948)

Pederson, Peter, *Hamel: Battleground Europe* (Barnsley: Pen and Sword, 2003)

Pershing, John J., *My Experiences in the World War* (New York: Frederick A. Stokes Company, 1937)

Yockelson, Mitchell, *Borrowed Soldiers: Americans under British Command, 1918* (Oklahoma: University of Oklahoma Press, 2008)

Yockelson, Mitchell, *Forty-Seven Days: How Pershing's Warriors Came of Age to Defeat the German Army in World War I* (New York: New American Library, 2016)

Chapter 6

Baumgart, Winfried, *Deutsche Ostpolitik 1918 – von Brest-Litowsk bis zum Ende des Ersten Weltkrieges* (Vienna: Oldenbourg, 1966)

Fassy, Gerard, *Le Commandement français en Orient (octobre 1915–novembre 1918)* (Paris: Economica, 2003)

Gooch, John, *The Italian Army in the First World War* (Cambridge: Cambridge University Press, 2014)

Kalvoda, Josef, *The Genesis of Czechoslovakia* (East European Monographs 209: Boulder, 1986)

Kettle, Michael, *The Allies and the Russian Collapse, March 1917 to March 1918* (London: Routledge, 1981)

Kettle, Michael, *The Road to Intervention: March to November 1918* (London: Routledge, 1988)

Mawdsley, Ewan, *The Russian Civil War* (Edinburgh: Birlinn, 2nd ed. 2008)

Minniti, Fortunato, *Il Piave* (Bologna: Mulino, 2000)

Torrey, Glenn, *The Romanian Battlefront in World War I* (Lawrence: University of Kansas, 2011)

Chapter 7

Brown, Malcolm (ed.), *T.E. Lawrence in War and Peace* (London: Greenhill, 2005)

Falls, Cyril, and A. F. Becke, *Military Operations, Egypt and Palestine*, vol. II (London: HMSO, 1930)

Gingeras, Ryan, *Fall of the Sultanate: The Great War and the End of the Ottoman Empire, 1908–1922* (Oxford: Oxford University Press, 2016)

Grigg, John, *Lloyd George: War Leader* (London: Allen Lane, 2002)

Hughes, Matthew (ed.), *Allenby in Palestine* (Stroud: Sutton, 2004)

Johnson, Robert, *The Great War and the Middle East* (Oxford: Oxford University Press, 2016)

Kitchen, James, *Other Combatants, Other Fronts: Competing Histories of the First World War*, edited with Alisa Miller and Laura Rowe (Newcastle: Cambridge Scholars Publishing, 2011)

Liman von Sanders, Otto, *Five Years in Turkey* (Annapolis: US Naval Institute Press, 1927)

McMeekin, Sean, *The Ottoman Endgame: War, Revolution and the Making of the Modern Middle East, 1908–1923* (London: Allen Lane, 2015)

McMunn, Lieutenant General Sir George, and Captain Cyril Falls, *Military Operations, Egypt and Palestine*, vol. I (London: HMSO, 1927–9)

Rogan, Eugene, *The Fall of the Ottomans: The Great War in the Middle East, 1914–1920* (London: Allen Lane, 2015)

Travers, Tim, *How The War Was Won* (London: Routledge, 1994)

Woodward, D. R., *Field Marshal Sir William Robertson* (Westport: Praeger, 1998)

Chapter 8

Epkenhans, Michael, *'Mein lieber Schatz!': Briefe von Admiral Reinhard Scheer an seine Ehefrau, August bis November 1918* (Bochum: Winkler, 2006)

Epkenhans, Michael, *Tirpitz: Architect of the German High Seas Fleet* (New York: Potomac Books, 2008)

Granier, Gerhard (ed.), *Die deutsche Seekriegsleitung im Ersten Weltkrieg* (Koblenz: Bundesarchiv, 2000)

Groß, Gerhard P., *Die Seekriegführung der Kaiserlichen Marine im Jahre 1918* (Frankfurt/ Main: Peter Lang, 1989)

Halpern, Paul, *A Naval History of World War I* (London: UCL Press, 1994)

Marder, Arthur J., *From the Dreadnought to Scapa Flow*, vol. V, *1918–1919: Victory and Aftermath* (New York, Toronto: Oxford University Press, 1970)

Ranft, B. McL. (ed.), *The Beatty Papers. Selections from the Private and Official Correspondence of Admiral of the Fleet Earl Beatty*, vol. I, *1902–1918* (Aldershot: Scholar, 1989)

Schröder, Joachim, *Die U-Boote des Kaisers: Die Geschichte des deutschen U-Boot-Krieges gegen Großbritannien im Ersten Weltkrieg* (Lauf an der Pegnitz: Europaforum-Verlag, 2000)

Sondhaus, Lawrence, *The Great War at Sea: A Naval History of the First World War* (Cambridge: Cambridge University Press, 2014)

Chapter 9

Christienne, Charles and Pierre Lissarague, *A History of French Military Aviation* (Washington: Smithsonian, 1986)

Corum, James S., *The Luftwaffe: Creating the Operational Air War 1918–1940* (Lawrence: University Press of Kansas, 1997)

Duroselle, Jean Baptiste, *La Grand Guerre des Français 1914–1918* (Paris: Perrin, 1994)

Hallion, Richard, *Rise of the Fighter Aircraft 1914–1918* (Annapolis: Nautical and Aviation Press, 1984)

Hamilton-Paterson, James, *Marked for Death: The First War in the Air* (London: Head of Zeus, 2015)

Hudson, James J., *Hostile Skies: A Combat History of the American Air Service in World War I* (Syracuse: Syracuse University Press, 1997)

Jones, H. A., *The War in the Air*, vol. V (Oxford: Clarendon Press, 1935)

Morrow, John, *The Great War in the Air* (Washington: Smithsonian, 1993)

Price, Alfred, 'The Battle of Amiens 8–11 August 1918', *Air Power Review* 4:4 (Winter 2001), pp. 118–34.

Treadwell, Terry and Aslan Wood, *German Fighter Aces of World War I* (Stroud: Tempus, 2003)

Chapter 10

Barnett, Correlli, 'A Successful Counter-Stroke: 18 July 1918', in Anthony Trythall (ed.), *Old Battles and New Defences: Can We Learn from Military History?* (London: Brassey's, 1986)

Bentley Mott, Colonel T. (trans.), *The Memoirs of Marshal Foch* (London: William Heinemann, 1931)

Doughty, Robert Allan, *The Seeds of Disaster: The Development of French Army Doctrine, 1919–1939* (Hamden: Archon Books, 1985)

Edmonds, Brigadier General Sir James E., *History of the Great War: Military Operations France and Belgium, 1918*, vol. I, *The German March Offensive and its Preliminaries* (London: Macmillan, 1935)

Edmonds, Brigadier General Sir James E., *History of the Great War: Military Operations France and Belgium, 1918*, vol. II, *March–April: Continuation of the German Offensives* (London: Macmillan, 1937)

Eisenhower, Dwight D., *Crusade in Europe* (London: William Heinemann, 1948)

Gough, General Sir Hubert, *The Fifth Army* (London: Hodder and Stoughton, 1931)

Greenhalgh, Elizabeth, *Foch in Command: The Forging of a First World War General* (Cambridge: Cambridge University Press, 2011)

Griffith, Paddy, *Battle Tactics of the Western Front: The British Army's Art of Attack 1916–18* (New Haven & London: Yale University Press, 1994)

Hart, Peter, *1918: A Very British Victory* (London: Weidenfeld & Nicolson, 2008)

The Kirke Report. PRO WO33/1297, *Report of the Committee on the Lessons of the Great War* (London: War Office, October 1932), reproduced in Colonel (ret'd) Mike Crawshaw OBE (ed.), *The British Army Review*, Special Edition (April 2001)

Laffin, John, *British Butchers and Bunglers of World War One* (Stroud: Sutton Publishing, 1988)

Ludendorff, General Erich, *My War Memories 1914–1918* (London: Hutchinson, 1919)

Melvin, Mungo, *Sevastopol's Wars: Crimea from Potemkin to Putin* (Oxford: Osprey, 2017)

Murray, Williamson, 'Armored Warfare. The British, French, and German Experiences', in Williamson Murray and Allan R. Millett, *Military Intervention in the Interwar Period* (Cambridge: Cambridge University Press, 1996)

Sheffield, Gary, *Forgotten Victory: The First World War Myths and Realities* (London: Headline, 2001)

Sheffield, Gary and Peter Gray (eds), *Changing War: The British Army, the Hundred Days Campaign and the Birth of the Royal Air Force, 1918* (London: Bloomsbury, 2013)

Stevenson, David, *With our Backs to the Wall: Victory and Defeat in 1918* (London: Allen Lane, 2011)

Strohn, Matthias, *The German Army and the Defence of the Reich: Military Doctrine and the Conduct of the Defensive Battle 1918–1939* (Cambridge: Cambridge University Press, 2010)

Terraine, John, *The Smoke and the Fire: Myths and Anti-Myths of War 1861–1945* (London: Sidgwick & Jackson, 1980)

GLOSSARY AND ABBREVIATIONS

Allgemeines Kriegsamt	General War Office
AEF	American Expeditionary Forces
Aéronautique Militaire	the French air service
AOK	Armeeoberkommando (Army Command)
BEF	British Expeditionary Force
Chef des Großen Generalstabes	Chief of the Great General Staff
Conseil superieur de la guerre	Supreme War Council
DCM	Distinguished Conduct Medal
DSO	Distinguished Service Order
EEF	Egyptian Expeditionary Force
Erster Generalquartiermeister	First Quartermaster General
GHQ	British General Headquarters
GOC	General Officer Commanding
GQG	Grand Quartier Général (French General Headquarters)
Großer Generalstab	Great General Staff
Heeresgruppe	Army Group
Jagdgeschwader	fighter wing
Kriegsministerium	War Ministry
Luftstreitkräfte	the German air service, after October 1916

MC	Military Cross
Oberste Kriegsleitung	Supreme War Command
OHL	Oberste Heeresleitung (Supreme Headquarters of the Field Army)
POW	prisoner of war
RAF	Royal Air Force
RFC	Royal Flying Corps
Seekriegsleitung	Naval Command
Vollmacht	mandate or proxy

Ranks

British Empire	France	German Empire
Field Marshal	Maréchal de France	Generalfeldmarschall
General		Generaloberst
Lieutenant General	Général de Division	General der Infanterie, General der Kavallerie General der Artillerie
Major General		Generalleutnant
Brigadier General	Général de Brigade	Generalmajor
Colonel	Colonel	Oberst
Lieutenant Colonel	Lieutenant-Colonel	Oberstleutnant
Major	Commandant	Major
Captain	Capitaine	Hauptmann
Lieutenant	Lieutenant	Oberleutnant
Second Lieutenant	Sous-Lieutenant	Leutnant

INDEX